THE INDUSTRIAL DECLINE IN INDIA

Owing to the antiquity and rarity of this book, certain pages are regrettably absent, and readability is compromised due to the blurring of the original text. If you possess any insights regarding the availability of these missing sections, kindly inform us. Your assistance is crucial in ensuring the completion of this significant work for the benefit of future generations.

THE INDUSTRIAL DECLINE IN INDIA

BALKRISHNA

GYAN

Published by

Gyan Publishing House
5, Ansari Road
Daryaganj, New Delhi-110002
Phone: 011-47034999, 9811692060
E-mail: books@gyanbooks.com

Distribution Network
gyanbooks.com
India, USA, Canada, UK, Australia

ISBN: 978-93-6433-016-9 (PB)

First Published, 1917

2nd Impression 2024

Printed at: Gyan Press, Delhi.

THE INDUSTRIAL DECLINE IN INDIA
Author: BALKRISHNA

THE

INDUSTRIAL DECLINE IN INDIA.

BY

BALKRISHNA, M. A.,

FELLOW OF

The Royal Statistical Society, London ; The Royal Economic Society, London ; The American Economic Association, Cambridge ; The American Statistical Association, Boston; and Professor of Economics, Gurukula University Haradwar.

PRINTED AND PUBLISHED

BY

K. C. BHALLA, AT THE STAR PRESS,

ALLAHABAD

1917

DEDICATED

TO

The Motherland

AND

The British Democracy

सत्यमेव जयति नानृतं

Magna est veritas, et prevalebit.

Truth is mighty, & will prevail.

CONTENTS.

RURALIZATION

AND

Industrial Decline in India

The people of India have come to the parting of the roads. A decision must be made which will affect the destiny of India and determine its status amongst the nations for centuries to come. To the people of India, it may be truly said.

"Speak now or for ever hold your peace."

A few months hence the die will be cast, the decision made, and the consequence of that decision must run its course for weal or woe. Such is the momentous character of the times and the question to be decided is : Are the people of India to remain in servitude to an alien bureaucracy, or shall they be placed on an equal footing with the other free nations of the empire ?

—*Mr. Sutcliffe, Sholapur.*

CHAPTER I.

THE COMING CRISIS.

THE DISILLUSIONMENT OF ENGLAND.

The War has abruptly disillusioned England of the long-cherished notion of her inherent naval strength and economic supremacy. It has thoroughly revealed the economic weaknesses of India and England. The cry of self-sufficiency and Imperial Federation, of the capturing and crippling of German commerce and of the expansion of Imperial trade and industry is heard from every corner of the vast British Empire.* Statesmen, economists, traders, merchants, manufacturers and agriculturists have fully recognized that the most vital problem of the day is the problem of Inter-Imperial relations. The distant ideal of a closer-knit, indivisible, self-sustaining and self-contained Empire, so long cherished by the Tariff Reformer and the Imperialist but flouted by the English public all along, now seems to lie within the range of practical politics.

---

cf. Mr. A. D. Hall's remark in his 'Agriculture After the War'. P.1. '*Some of the consequences of that dependence are only just being brought home to us by the course of the present European war.* The possibility of starvation or of such grave interruption to the ordinary course of our trade as to enforce our submission to our enemies has for the present been averted ; but enough has been *seen of the unanticipated development of* modern warfare and of the financial situation that it creates, to call for a review of our national policy with regard to food supply and the consideration of our agricultural position from a standpoint that has hitherto been neglected.'

Various committees of experts have been appointed to investigate the manifold issues involved in securing the self-sufficiency of the Empire as a whole. The post-bellum political reconstruction has given way to the more prominent problem of the post-war economic re-adjustment of the different parts of the vast Empire.

BALFOUR COMMITTEE AND INDIA.

In July, 1916 the Balfour of Burleigh Committee was appointed to consider the commercial and industrial policy to be adopted after the war, with special reference to the conclusions reached at the Economic Conference of the Allies and to the following questions:—

(*a*) What industries are essential to the future safety of the nation; and what steps should be taken to maintain and establish them.

(*b*) What steps should be taken to recover home and foreign trade lost during the war and to secure new markets.

(*c*) To what extent and by what means the sources of the Empire should and can be developed.

(*d*) To what extent and by what means the sources of supply within the Empire can be prevented from falling under foreign control.

It hastened to issue as a White Paper (Cd. 8482) on February 20, 1917 the following resolutions on the subject of Imperial Preference to be put before the forthcoming Imperial War Conference:—

"1. In the light of experience gained during the War, we consider that special steps must be taken to stimulate the production of foodstuffs, raw materials and manufactured articles within the Empire wherever the expansion of production is possible and economically desirable for the safety and welfare of the Empire as a whole.

2. We, therefore, recommend that H. M. Government should now declare their adherence to the principle *that preference should be accorded to the products and manufactures of the British Overseas Dominions* in respect of any Customs Duties now or hereafter to be imposed on imports into the United Kingdom.

3. Further, it will in our opinion be necessary to take into early consideration, as one of the methods of achieving the above objects, the desirability of establishing a wider range of Customs Duties which would be remitted or reduced on the products and manufactures of the Empire, and which would form the basis of Commercial treaties with Allied and Neutral Powers.'

The preceding resolutions were briefly explained in a covering letter addressed to the Prime Minister. It is full of interesting details and completely foreshadows the abject position which the Indian people will be called upon to occupy under the new scheme of the post-bellum reconstruction. We will reproduce those passages alone which relate to the Autonomous and Dependent parts of the Empire.

---

* The Italics are ours.

"We *think it necessary* that for the sake of the unity of the Empire a serious attempt should now be made to meet the *declared wishes of the Dominions and Colonies for the development of* their economic relations with the United Kingdom and that any abstract opinions we may hold should not, under the circumstances in which we are placed and with the experience gained during the war, stand in the way of any measures which are seen to be important, having regard to the general interests of the Empire.

It will be recalled that at the Colonial Conference of 1902 the Prime Ministers of the Self-Governing Colonies unanimously urged the expediency of granting in the United Kingdom preferential treatment to the products and manufactures of the Colonies either by exemption from or reduction of duties then existing or thereafter to be imposed and that a Resolution in the same terms was passed at the Conference of 1907.

Whatever controversies may have arisen in the past, we think that, regard being had in particular to the sacrifices made and the services rendered by our fellow-subjects overseas for a common purpose during the present war the time has now arrived at which this request should be granted to the fullest extent which if now or may hereafter become practicable.

We do not overlook the practical difficulties involed, but we desire to emphasize the fact that for the purpose of recovering trade lost during the war, of securing new markets, and *of consolidating the resources of the British Empire the development throughout the Empire of system of mutual tariff preference is a subject which cannot in our opinion, any longer be neglected.*

The special *position of India, as well as of Egypt and the Sudan, will require consideration* and account must be taken both of our commercial treaty obligations and of the bearing of the proposed policy upon the interests of those countries, our trade relations with which are of special importance.

MEMORANDUM BY FREDERICK H. SMITH.

While I am in general sympathy with the resolutions passed by the Committee, I feel very strongly that, in view particularly of the present international situation, the moment is inopportune to bring forward recommendation on the subject of Imperial Preference, which may involve an alteration in our fiscal policy towards our Allies. In my opinion, it would be desirable that, before arriving at any conclusion on the subject, we should meet the representatives of the Dominions for a confidential discussion, at which the question of our commercial relations with our Allies and other practical difficulties could be fully and freely discussed.

FREDERICK H. SMITH."

The whole tenor of the resolutions and of the letter of the Balfour Committee reveals an undue anxiety for winning the good will of the self-governing Dominions and Colonies; however, *the poor Dependency of India with its teeming millions has received but scant notice. The special position of India will, we are told, require consideration* but will the Government and the people of India be satisfied with one-sided considerations and shadowy concessions ? Has not the solution of the Indian fiscal problem proved a *Pons osinorum* up to this time and can it be satisfactorily solved without *free* discussion and deliberation in the Indian press and on the platform ? Would it be justice that any fiscal decree be issued to India without fully hearing her case through her freely chosen representatives ? The Memorandum of Mr. Frederick H. Smith is full of evil bodings for India, because according to the opinion of that representative of international peace and inter-colonial good relations, it is desirable to assemble the representatives of the Dominions (but not of India) for a *confidential discussion* of the subject. What ! Is India with 315 million inhabitants who amount to one-fifth of the human race, to be excluded from that committee of confidential enquiry ? If she is not to be represented on it, it is high time that the voice of her people should be raised in defence of her rights, that a strong demand should be made for *Indian representation freely decided upon by the chosen representatives of the people* and not by the Indian Government, that the responsible public of India and England should be enlightened on the real economic conditions of this vast dependency, so that the Indian ideal of full fiscal autonomy may be realized.

THE IMPERIAL WAR CONFERENCE,

The Imperial War Conference and the Imperial War Cabinet have unanimously accepted the principle and policy of Imperial Preference for the British Empire and the so-called Indian representatives, his Highness the Maharaja of Bikanir and Sir S. P. Sinha are reported to have approved of the proposals of imperial preference and of the appointment of trade commissioners. Is India to be bound by the opinions of these so-called representatives? Is she to adopt the preferential policy at the mandate of England or by her own free will? If by the latter, why has she not been given an opportunity of presenting the Indian case from the Indian point of view by any one of her elected and responsible representatives? It is passing strange that India should not get even this scant justice of real representation in the future councils of the Empire even after so much suffering and sacrifice and especially during the ministry of Mr. Austen Chamberlain than whom, it is said, no stauncher champion of Indian interests has held office in the Whitehall. Is it all lip sympathy? Yes, such is the impression produced by the proposals of the War Conference as well as of the Dominions' Royal Commission, as put forth in their Final Report issued in March last.

DOMINIONS' ROYAL COMMISSION.

This Commission, an outcome of a resolution of the 1911 Imperial Conference was appointed in 1912 with the express object of devising ways and means for the development of the Empire's resources and the furtherance of the inter-Imperial trade It has now strongly recommended the creation of an Imperial Development Board to be composed of twelve representatives in the following proportions: United Kingdom, India, Crown Colonies, and Protectorates, seven; Canada, Australia, New Zealand, South Africa and New Foundland, one each.

Here again, the representation of the United Kingdom and its dependencies has been lumped together, while the separate representation of each of the self-governing colonies including even New Foundland with a population of about 3 million inhabitants has been definitely specified. India is, therefore, sure to occupy a secondary position in the '*constellation of free nations*' which would constitute the Imperial Commonwealth. But the worst of it is that *Dependent India* is to be made a plantation for the supply of food stuffs, raw materials, and other commodities essential for the industrial development of this world-wide *Commonwealth of Free Nations.* The London correspondent of the *Tribune* has timely struck a note of warning in these words :

"Indian interests will want careful watching in connection with these proposals. It may be that the resources of India have only been discovered by the

Tribune of Lahore, May 2.

Commissioners in order to be exploited by other people. More than one reference in their report gives colour to this suggestion. They put in the forefront of their proposals the taking of immediate steps by the Imperial and Dominion Governments to stimulate and control supplies on certain indicated lines, such as bounties on output; Government purchases at a minimum price; restitution of foreign control; and restriction of Government purchases to articles produced from Empire materials."

THE INDUSTRIAL DEVELOPMENT BOARD.

The thoughtful people can also fully divine the position of India in the self-contained Empire by pondering over the following main functions of the Board which is

(*a*) to continue, to complete, and thereafter keep up-to-date the survey begun by the Commission of the relation between the production and requirements of the Empire in the matter of food supplies, raw materials and all other commodities essential to its well-being;

(*b*) to watch and report upon the changing requirements of the Empire in respect of such materials and commodities, and to mature plan for promoting and improving their production within the Empire;

(*c*) to investigate in collaboration with existing institutions and committees for scientific research—

(1) the possibilities of production within the Empire of such of these essential materials and commodities as now are, or may in the future be found to be, mainly produced and controlled outside

its limits, as well as the possibilities of new supply generally;

(2) the best means of promoting efficiency and preventing waste in existing methods of production;

(3) the possibilities of the utilisation of substitutes for essential commodities which are not found to be available within the Empire;

(*d*) to consider and devise means for the direction of Empire capital towards the development of Empire resources.

There is a great apprehension that the most important duty of the Development Board would be to consider and make suggestions regarding the lines on which Indian industrial development should be pursued in the interests of the Empire as a whole. Consequently it is of paramount importance to reveal the mighty economic changes that have passed and are passing over the Indian Empire, changes so extensive and intensive that the whole economic fabric is being transformed unnoticed by the enlightened few even. We should be on our guard lest a dependent India be exploited by England and her colonies in the name of Empire.

McLEOD COMMISSION AND INDIAN INDUSTRIAL COMMISSION.

Again, great things are expected even in their limited scopes from the McLeod Commission in London and the Indian Industrial Commission which has abruptly finished its labours of examining various problems of vital importance for the expansion and development of Indian industries and manufactures. The personnel of the Indian Commission with Sir T. H. Holland as President and Mr. A. Chatterton, Sir F. C. Ebrahim, Sir D. J. Tata, P. Madan Mohan Malaviya and other public men of high reputation, wide experience and deep sympathies for the industrial regeneration of this country, as members, is all that could be desired.

But it is regrettable that the most vital problem of Protection or Free Trade or Fiscal Autonomy for India was specifically left out of consideration. Sir William Clark most frankly admitted that such a momentous decision could not be independently arrived at by the Government of India. 'Their policy is, and must be, the policy of His Majesty's Government.' 'The same considerations apply with even greater force to any proposals involving the imposition of duties for the specific purpose of protecting Indian industries, a policy which would very directly affect the relations of India with the outside world.'

But these reasons of the Hon'ble Member for excluding the fiscal policy from the scope of the Commission's enquiries appeared quite inadequate even to the *Englishman* of Calcutta that has pertinently and felicitously remarked that it is acting the play of Hamlet without the Prince of Denmark. Now that the tariff question is to be settled after the war by the English

Parliament and the Imperial Economic Conference that is to hold its sessions after the declaration of peace, it is of supreme importance that "India should have her own real representatives and not the mere dummy representative of the India office*." But this timely warning of even Sir Roper Lethbridge, K. C. I. E., has not been heard and the late Imperial War Conference has only accepted the *representation of the Indian Government* on the future Conferences. India is already unrepresented in the British Parliament and she has been granted no *real* representation in the future Imperial Conferences. Then her people have no controlling power in the Executive or Legislative Councils of the land. Thus the impression is gaining strength in the Indian mind that their sacred, inalienable and unassailable rights have everywhere been ignored, nay, positively trampled underfoot.

THE GREAT BETRAYAL

The recent utterances of liberal, enlightened and responsible statesmen of England and of the Self-Governing Dominions have given a knock-down blow to Indian aspirations. Is it not highly to be deprecated that there should be no prospects of the abandonment of the abominable policy of exploiting India and sacrificing her vital economic interests for the sake of England? The following statements

---

* Prospects of Industry and Commerce after the War, *Indian Review* for December, 1916.

which have appeared in the *Times of India Imperial Trade Supplement* form the greatest tragedy in the calculations of the Indian educated public. They are, indeed, the worst betrayal of the deep-rooted principles of English Democracy, Liberty and Equality and of the true interests of India. It is known to all that coming events cast their shadows before, so these statements have been made by the arbiters of Indian destiny to put down those wild (?) aspirations for Economic or Fiscal Autonomy which have found expression in these days.

The right Hon. Joseph Austen Chamberlian, M, P., Secretary of State for India:—

India rightly desires to develop her own manufacturing industries; but there is plenty of room for *all the enterprise; on the part of British merchants and manufacturers in ultilising her raw materials and in supplying her with the goods that even under the most favourable circumstances she cannot hope to provide for himself. It must be the hope of all of* us that the cessation of the considerable share in her trade taken before the war by Germany and Austria may henceforth enure to the benefit of the Empire.

INDIA—THE GREATEST COMMERCIAL ASSET OF THE BRITISH EMPIRE.

Lord Hardinge of Penshurst, the ex-Viceroy of India:-

India is one of the greatest commercial assets of the British Empire, the importance of which cannot be overestimated as a factor in consolidating and strenghtening the bonds by which the mother country and the Family of the nations composing the British Empire are so happily united in mutual understanding and reliance.

The surplus of India's immense resources in produce and raw material should find a ready demand within the Empire, while her population of over 315 million souls forms a vast potential market for the British manufacturers. A closer study of Indian conditions with the view of supplying India's exact requirements would repay the outlay a hundredfold.

INDIA TO REMAIN THE PRODUCER OF RAW MATERIAL.

Lord Curzon, the ex-Viceroy of India:—

"I see no reason why the British Empire should not supply to India nearly the whole of the manufactured articles of which she stands in need, while, reciprocally, India produces an ever increasing amount as staple necessities for which the Empire constitutes the best market. In this Exchange not only will there be found great commercial advantage for both parties, but fresh links will be forged in the chain that binds Great Britain to the foremost of the overseas possessions of the crown."

INDIA—A BEST FIELD FOR BRITISH ENTERPRISE.

The Right Hon. Sir George Houston Reid, M. P., ex-Prime Minister of Australia:—

We are all talking of the great things we will attempt in the way of trade "after the war." Is there any field for British enterprise more likely to yield good results than India ?

EXPANSION OF BRITISH IMPORTS INTO INDIA.

Sir Albert Stanley, President of the Board of Trade :—

The aim of all of us must be to make the Empire after the war so far as possible Self-Supporting, and though the United Kingdom already holds the lion's share in India's import trade, there is still room for expansion, especially in those trades where German competition had begun to encroach upon our commerce.

CAPTURE OF GERMAN TRADE.

Earl Gray, G. C. B., G. C. M. C., G. C. V. O., President, Royal Colonial Institute and late Governor-General of Canada :—

United Kingdom exports to India could be greatly increased if it were possible for United Kingdom manufacturers to see and to handle duplicates of the articles of foreign make which find a ready sale in India. Our home manufacturers by ascertaining the requirements of India and how to meet them would be able to win back the large part of that £11,000,000 trade which before the War had been captured by Germany and other enemy countries through superior organisation.

A PLEA FOR ENQUIRY.

It must have now become abundantly clear that Indian interests have not been adequalely protected in the various councils of the Empire, nor are they ever likely to be safeguarded in these busy years of political and economic reconstruction. It is to be mightily feared that without any voice of her responsible representatives for the protection, advocacy and furtherance of her vital interests either in the British Parliament or the Economic Conference or even in the Indian Councils, India will severely suffer from the one-sided decree of her competitors. It is more than strange that amidst profuse declarations of liberty, equality and democracy, the liberal and responsible statesmen and far sighted-politicians should ignore the just claims of India for a full fiscal autonomy or even for a complete representation of her case. Mr. J. S. Mill with prophetic insight into the future developments of democracy laid down the memorable principle which has since been guiding civilized nations :—

> 'It is a great discouragement to an individual and a still greater one to a class, to be left out of the constitution ; to be reduced to plead from outside the door to the arbiters of their destiny, not taken into consultation within.'

Even just recently Mr. E. S. Montague most frankly expressed that 'our task, it seems to me, *is to set ourselves so to perfect the institution for the expression of their ideals so as give them the opportunities* which, with our help, they have won and are winning, and which they demand now from us as fellow-fighters in the struggle for our existence and for the overthrow of our common enemy'.

Mr. Balfour was even more emphatic in his utterance:—

We are convinced that there is only one form of government, whatever it may be called, namely, where the ultimate control is in the hands of the people.

Then, Mr. Chamberlain nobly declared at a recent Parliamentary luncheon party that 'Nowhere were we confronted by greater problems than in India, and it was for us to help to our full measure the realisation of India's natural aspirations to play a full part in the life of the Empire', and then before the British Empire Producers' Organization that 'India will not remain and ought not to remain content to be a hewer of wood and a drawer of water for the rest of the Empire." But the resolutions of the Imperial War Conference and the recent utterances of responsible statesmen have doomed to bitter disappointment all the legitimate hopes and aspirations of India for becoming an autnomous political portion of the Imperial Com monwealth. They have, however, awakened a general feeling of discontent, alarm and anxiety, and are likely to provoke considerable controversy as regards the fiscal relations of India to the rest of the Empire. Economic questions as brought to light by the Conference are sure to deeply agitate the minds of the Indian people. We are certain that a united and decisive expression of Indian opinion shall be carried to the English people who are the ultimate arbiters of Indian destinies.

Political autonomy is even now a question of the dim and distant future, and hence we have been reminded by His Excellency Lord Chelmsford that 'all thoughts of the early grant of Self-Government should be put *entirely* out of mind', but *Economic* Autonomy ought to be secured now or never. Now there is a golden opportunity, but we can never have it again in near future. If we lose it, we shall have to wait again for more than half a century. One swing of the pendulum has taken full seventy years, the returned swing cannot be very much quicker in a conservative country like England.

> There is a tide in the affairs of men
> Which taken at the flood, leads on to fortune ;
> Omitted, all the voyage of their life
> Is bound in shallows and miseries.

Never, indeed, have questions of such momentous importance been surpassed in the history of British India. Shall they pass us by like the idle wind ? No, at least, they ought not. The policy of Imperial Preference would mightily transform the economic condition of India, it would be attended with far-reaching and momentous consequences; in fact, it is a grave menace to the future industrial development of India.

Now that the vital interests of India are at stake, now that our destinies seem to be in the melting pot, now that the Tory War Cabinet is endeavouring to rush through this scheme of Imperial Preference without confering fiscal freedom on India, now that all dreams of economic autonomy even appear to vanish before our very eyes, it is high time that a comprehensive and impartial study of the past and present economic conditions be made, that the vast and stupendous change that has been passing over the land be outlined in its various shapes and stages and that an effective appeal be made to get recognition of the just claims of India for a separate fiscal treatment and to secure full fiscal freedom for India on lines which regulate the fiscal policy of the self-Governing Dominions of the Empire. When the schemes of Imperial reconstruction and Imperial preference are being sedulously developed by the Milner-Curzon school and when the whole Conservative press is backing them up, we cannot but be sure that India's real and vital interests are in danger of being sacrificed even at this critical hour of her destiny. The issues raised by these policies are many, complex, and critical. They affect the interests of every class in India. Agriculturists, manufacturers, craftsmen, merchants, workmen, consumers and producers, Indians and Englishmen, statesmen, economists, professors, public functionaries, members of the aristocracy, beaurocracy and royalty, one and all should, at the present moment, endeavour honestly to grapple with this problem of the greatest possible importance. The matter should be pressed home at this time when England—the apostle of world's freedom is ready to lend a sympathetic ear to Indian demands, when India has proved herself worthy of obtaining substantial reforms and concessions by her unflinching loyalty to the British flag in this hour of pressing need and by her munificent sacrifices of men, money and materials.

The present work is a contribution towards the solution of the most pressing problem of the day. The writer has, in the first volume of this book, exhaustively dealt with the fatal consequences of the Free Trade policy on Indian industry and agriculture on the basis of a wide array of facts and figures since 1870; in the second volume he has surveyed the manifold tendencies and consequences of the various fiscal policies adopted in relation to India by England since the beginnings of British Rule in India: in the third volume he has drawn a statistical picture of the attempts at industrial reconstruction in India; while in the fourth he has analysed the future economic effects of the triumph of this Tory scheme of Imperial preference. In the fifth and the last volume he has given the views of representative Indians and Englishmen on the need of protection for India. No one can regret more than the author himself that his analysis should have entailed the presentation of some unpleasant facts, but truth, however bitter, ought to be expressed and frankly listened to, when vital problems such as the future industrial development or decadence, improvement or impoverishment, prosperity or poverty of a once great and rich nation are to be decided by the arbiters of its destinies. The progress of this country, the welfare of its people and the prosperity of the coming generations depend upon the right solution of this burning question of the day. The war, the Russian Revolution, the recrudescence of monarchy and the re-establishment of republic in China, the grant of Home Rule to the Irish, the notable utterances of prominent statesmen and leading exponents of democracy have aroused and intensified a host of expectations and aspirations which cannot now be satisfied by eloquent words and mere shadows. Any sudden and unexpected collapse of these would consequently give a tremendous shock to the awakened national consciousness of the people and raise a storm of opposition which it would be impossible to quell in the dawn of the post-war new era of liberty, democracy, free press and platform. Hence the writer cannot but hope and trust that responsible British and Colonial Statesmen and administrators in every portion of the Imperial Commonwealth would in the light of facts, figures and quotations presented in this work, approach this momentous question with an open mind, with a magnanimous soul and with an eye solely to the present and future prosperity of 315 millions of men, women, and children of this vast section of the planet, would secure for these the same fiscal autonomy which they themselves have long been enjoying in their own countries, would win an immortal gratitude of these politically voiceless people whom Providence has placed under their charge, and would ultimately ask this important question with the benevolent Cowper,

> Is India free? And does she wear her plum'd.
> And jewell'd turban with a smile of peace?
> Or do we grind her still?

Stagnation and dependence, depression and poverty—these are written in broad characters on the face of the land and its people. To these must be added the economical drain of wealth and talents, which Foreign subjection has entailed on the country.

The late *Mr. Justice M. G. Ranade.* Essays on Indian Economics, p. 24.

CHAPTER II.

PROGRESSIVE RURALIZATION IN INDIA.

It is a common belief that the lot of Indians as a whole has been vastly and constantly improving under British Rule, that signs of a wonderful development are visible in that restless activity which meets us incarnated in our big towns that the 'unweildy wealth and cumbrous pomp,' peace and plenty, profusion and prosperity, opulence and splendour of busy seaports are incontrovertible evidences of the amelioration of the condition of the people. But it is forgotten that

PAUCITY OF INDIAN INDUSTRY

(a) Only 18·5 per cent. of the Indian people are engaged in trade, commerce and industry, while England employs more than 75 per cent. of her population in these very occupations.

INSIGNIFICANT INDIAN URBANIZATION.

(b) Optimistic observers consciously or unconciously also ignore the fact that there are only seventy-five towns having 50,000 inhabitauts or more with an aggregate population not exceeding 8, 656,938 in this vast Empire of India including Burma and Baluchistan. In other words,

the population of towns with 50,000 or more inhabitants is only 3·6 per cent. of total population. Of these 75 towns, thirty only have a population above 100,000 and of these again 10 only have above 200,000 [1]. But in England and Wales with a population of 36 millions, *i. e.* $\frac{1}{9}$ of India, there were 98 towns, with an aggregate population of 17,303,812 or 48 per cent of the whole, (including London with a population of 4,522,961 souls as one town) which had in 1911 a population exceeding 50,000. Of these, 44 had a population above one lakh and of these again 16 had above 200,000.

There is still another startling fact that in England and Wales the proportion of persons living in towns in 1911 was 78·1 per cent., while the remaining 22 per cent. alone lived in rural districts. Possibly the English percentage is becoming too high but there can be little doubt that the Indian percentage of 9.12 istoo low for healthy and pro gressive life on modern lines. India is predominently an agricultural and rural country, but the pity of it is that ever since its political contact with England it is becoming more and more rural and agricultural and less and less urban and industrial.

STATEMENT OF THE PROBLEM.

'In a country devoted to mere raw agriculture, dullness of mind, awkwardness of body, obstinate adherence to old notions, customs, methods, and pro-

(a), Statistics of British India, 1912 Part V, Pp. 3,26.
(b) Statistical Abstract for British India, 1913-14 Vol. IV.

cesses, want of culture, of prospertiy, and of liberty, prevail. The spirit of striving for a steady increase in mental and bodily acquirements, of emulation, and of liberty, characterise, on the contrary, a State devoted to manufactures and commerce,' *Friedrich List.*

In such words of pregnant truth the defects of an exclusive pursuit of agriculture and the merits of manufactures have been pointed out by one of the greatest economists of Germany. Our study of the Census Reports of India and its various parts has forced upon us some important conclusions such as these :

(I) That this land of sturdy Aryas and lusty Muslams is becoming more and more agricultural under the British administration,

(ii) That the indigenous industries are being constantly killed by the stress of unrestricted foreign competition,

(iii) That low paid workers and tribes of menials are increasing by hundreds and thousands,

(iv) That we are becoming a nation of petty shop-keepers in the sense of distributers of foreign articles alone,

(v) That in short, during the last one hundred and sixty years, we have been more and more subjected to the dangers pointed out by List. Instead of progressing we are being crippled, our arm of manufacture is being cut from us and we are thus on the way to become a purely agricultural state instead of the agricultural-manufacturing state in the pre-British period.

It is very strange, indeed, that such a change should have taken place under the most civilized, efficient and industrially supreme government that has ever been known to India during the last thousand years. But we have been forced to arrive at these results by the stern logic of incontrovertible facts and figures enshrined in official publications—the blue-books of the Government of India and the various Parliamentary Reports.

CONCETRATION OF WEALTH IN FEW TOWNS.

The country blooms—a garden and a grave.

If the reader should take a walk in any one of the big cities like Bombay, Karachi, Calcutta, Delhi and Lahore, he would see wonderful things if he has eyes to see and a heart to feel. From one end of the Anarkali and Upper Mall of Lahore to the other end he would see shops of various kinds. Tailors, milliners, dress-makers, darners, embroiders of linen, hair-dressers and wig-makers with their gaudy show cases, attractive sign-boards, and hundred and one devices to catch the fancy of the passers-by would meet his eye. A few steps more and he comes upon some highly embellished curio shops. His heart leaps up with joy at their splendid sight and he thanks his stars for having seen without payment the curiosities of this wide wide world. Scarcely he comes out of a shop, when the dealer in the opposite row winks his eyes at him and invites him to see his beautiful goods—hats, umbrellas, socks, perfumes, carpets, curtains, fans, toys, paper-flowers, etc. Let him go onward still and he would see enamellers, guilders, imitation jewellery sellers sitting in highly decorated shops whose showy and profuse ornamentation enslaves his heart and be he a European or an Indian—at the sight of that dazzling brilliance he readily jumps up to the conclusion that India has made wonderful progress, that India is fast growing rich. This erroneous idea is strengthened at the sight of dozens of booksellers, publishers, stationers, photographers, watch-makers, dealers of pictures, optical, surgical or musical instruments. The idea becomes a conviction at the sight of banks, insurance companies, hotels, liquor and aerated water-shops !

OUR REAL ECONOMIC POSITION.

Reader, this is what you see at the surface and therefore have your heart so much captivated that it beats high with joy at the prospects of progressive India. *But stop and think for a moment whether you saw any article, among those hundreds of thousands of articles, of Indian make?* That dazzling brilliance, that captivating ornamentation and embellishment, that profusion of decoration, that exuberance of adornment and beautification, that fairy enchantment so lovely to see, that graceful charm of tawdry, handsome, comely or showy curiosities' is not Indian but Western !!

It will thus be seen that we are only distributers of commodities received from the West. Our towns have become centres of distribution and all the display of Western wealth, civilization and culture is highly concentrated at a point in them. When these few cities are the standard of the measurement of our wealth, it is but necessary that extravagant calculations should ever be made of the wealth of India. But a Westerner does not know that our hand industries have been so much stifled, and killed by him outright, that our villageman unlike olden days cannot get even ordinary things of Indian make in his own village and he has therefore to go to towns for shopping.

POLICY OF LAISSEZ FAIRE AND THE DECLINE OF INDIAN INDUSTRIES.

The Globe trotters and other travellers in India, as well as the Anglo-Indian community here move in these cities and hence they carry away exaggerated and really false ideas of the wealth and progress of this country. They forget that all this concentrated wealth has been received from the West in exchange for the raw material which the Western manufacturer is impatiently anxious to get from this land, that the sons of the soil have taken no share in manufacturing it, that their handicrafts and industries are being fast killed by Western giants, that people are being forcibly pushed to unremunerative, primitive, wasteful and unadvancing agriculture where no machinery, no new-manures, no new seeds for plants and no new and cheaper methods are employed; in short, they do not grasp the most important fact that we are fast becoming a nation of agriculturists and petty shop-keepers on account of the open-door or Free Trade policy of our Rulers. Unless this stern, solid and irrefutable fact is comprehended in all its bearings, no impartial and correct estimate of the economic situation of this country can ever be made. Unless it is fully grasped that only on account of the Free-trade policy of England every decennium has thrown out hundreds of thousands of men and women from their hereditary professions to die of starvation or seek employment anywhere as best they can, unless it is honestly recognized that by reason of the absence of capital, captains of industry, efficient labour, organizing skill, mobility of labour, free cumpulsory education, technical, mechanical, electrical, commercial, industrial, in one word, practical education—Indians cannot adopt the new methods of production, India would ever suffer the consequences of a huge misunderstanding. Indians as well as Europeans should clearly comprehend the situation—the trend of past events and the tendency of the future in trade, industry and agriculture. Those of us who have the welfare of our mother country at heart and especially the Government of this Great Empire, will do well to ponder over the real situation in India in the light of succeeding facts and figures and adopt means for the betterment of this economically backward country.

SITUATION SUMMED UP.

It must be distinctly said that the absence of a strong tariff wall and of an active state aid have led to the gradual extinction of our handicrafts and the snail-like progress of our mechanical industries, beeause the one from senility and the other from infantile frailty could never compete with the giant and long established industries of the West.

ECONOMIC RETROGRESSION IN INDIA DURING 1891—1901.

It would be a veritable revelation to many to know at the very threshold of our inquiry that in the decade 1891-1901, although the **population of India increased by** 6,856,157 **souls, the total increase in the agricultural population was** 20,293,385.

That is, while the total population increased at the rate of 2 per cent. the agricultural population multiplied at the rate of 12 per cent., during the same period.

Thus it is clear as daylight that men of non-agricultural occupations must have been forced into the ranks of low paid agricultural labour.

TABLE 1.

The following figures of the population of India classified according to occupation should be carefully observed :—

Occupation	1891	1901	Aggregate increase and decrease
Government service and professions.	12,576,601	10,662,669	—1,913,932
Domestic occupations	11,219,951	10,717,294	—502,657
Commerce ...	8,638,485	7,725,737	—912,748
Industrial occupations ...	47,594,251	45,719,645	—1,874,606
Labourers ...*	25,467,971	17,953,230	—7,514,741
Total decrease ...	...	...	12,818,684
Agriculture ...	175,373,460	195,666,843	+20,293,385

* Statistics of British India, 1912, Part V, page 22.

Thus it is more than evident that as many as 12,818,684 persons were obliged to give up the highly paid and socially better services such as Government employment, professions, trade, commerce, industry, domestic and somewhat skilled occupations; while more than twenty millions of persons just amounting to half the population of Great Britain, were somehow or other forced into the ranks of low paid and starving agriculturists

In fact, the state of things can be briefly represented as follows:—

Pushed out of higher services (leaving out indefinite and independent occupations) = 12,818,684 persons

Addition to total population = 6,856,157

Rough estimate of the **population available for agriculture** = 19,674,841

Actual addition to agriculture ... ... = 20,293,385

INCREASE OF LANDLESS LABOURERS—AN ECONOMIC DANGER.

There is yet another heart-breaking phase of this downward evolution which the Government of the country has fully recognized. "*The number of agricultural labourers nearly doubled.* The increase is largely due to changes in classification; but a *considerable landless class is developing which involves economic danger* because the increase has been most marked in districts where the rural population is already congested or in provinces in which there is special liability to periodic famines. Even in normal seasons the ordinary agricultural labourers in some tracts earn a poor and precarious livelihood.' *Ind. Emp., Vol. III, p. 2.*

AN UNTENABLE EXPLANATION.

*Messsrs. Risley and Gait, writers of the Census Report 1901, have tried their utmost to explain away the large increases that have taken place in agrestic pursuits and conclude after a brief discussion that "it is of value as showing that no deduction can be made from the comparative results of the two enumerations in support of the contention that the people of India are becoming more and more dependent on the soil as a means of livelihood."

It is passing strange that the two statisticians should reach this conclusion and should ignore the deficits that have occured in the various occupations named above. Where could millions of people go after abandoning the various industrial occupations but to agriculture ? They ought to have shown that there have been no decreases in the various pursuits. In comparing the figures of 1901 with 1891, orders have been rearranged by them and even then, the results go against their conclusions. We wish that there should have been no migration to land, but this is a pious wish alone ; people are deserting their ancient occupations, hand-industries are fast declining and their places are not being taken by Mill-industries in India, but by agriculture alone.

*C. R. 1901, pp. 238—241

RURALIZATION DURING 1901—1911.

The next decade from 1901 to 1911, presents the same sorry tale of this progressively disastrous ruralization. The facts in respect to this subject are still more despiriting, because although the total increase of population was 20,795,340 souls during this decade,

Agriculture claimed 2,81,90,863 persons more in its fold, so that there must have been a vast migration and shifting of population from non-agricultural, from skilled and economically as well as socially better to unskilled and hence economically as well as socially inferior occupations. Or, if these mighty changes have been accomplished without any dire necessity on the part of skilled artisans to part with their hereditary occupations, then the new generation must have gone more and more to agricultural pursuits than to the industrial ones. But the latter alternative is less probable because Indians are fast bound by customs, conservatism and love of their hereditary professions ; because land is most difficult to be obtained ; because the ignorant masses are the most immobile creatures on earth and lastly because the additions to agriculture have been more by 7,738,165 persons than those to total population. Consequently, we can in no case escape the conclusion that people of higher grades were forced to eke out their livelihood from pursuits connected with agriculture. Prof. Nicholson speaking on the criteria of the progress of a nation says,

"One of the decisive marks of economic progress is found in the increase of the numbers of the classes with higher earnings relatively to those with lower incomes."

But in India an enormous decline in the numbers of the classes with higher incomes has been happening ever since the contact of India with the West, and yet no real efforts have been made to stem the tide.

The following table gives the actual figures for the shifting of the different strata of the society in the first decade of the twentieth century :—

TABLE 2.

Variation in Occupational Distribution in India during 1901 and 1911.

Occupation.	1901.	1911.	Actual Increase+or Decrease—.	Percentage Increase or Decrease.
Population of India ...	285,398,117	304,233,535	+18,835,418	+6·6
Public administration and Liberal Arts ...	10,418,526	10,352,888	—65,638	—·6
Miscellaneous ...	26,944,205	16,847,958	—10,096,247	—37·5
Trade ...	17,824,823	17,230,329	—594,494	—3·3
Industrial occupations ..	34,296,318	34,245,957	—50,359	—·7
Transport ...	3,769,307	4,877,958	+1,108,651	+29 4
Total Decrease in Non-Agricultural Occupations.	...	...	9,698,087	
Production of Raw Materials ...	192,144,940	220,678,445	28,533,505	+14·8

DEGRADATION OF 28½ MILLION PERSONS.

From the preceding statements it would have been observed that with the exception of 'transport' which shows a marked increase of 29·4 % on account of the ever-swelling foreign trade of the country and the growth of railways, all the non-agricultural classes of occupations exhibit decreases ranging from ·6 to 37½ per cent. Deducting the increase affected in the sub-class of Transport, we find that the net loss of numbers supported, by all the thousand and one occupations of the non-agricultural classes amounts to 9,698,087 persons. *It means that about ten million souls had lost their employment at the day of the Census enumeration inspite of the large increase of 18,835, 418 persons in the total population*, so for as the adjusted figures of the two census enumerations are concerned, otherwise the actual variation of the Indian population during these ten years was more than twenty millions.

It will have become positively clear now that about ten million persons bidding farewell to their hereditary professions, migrated to land to swell the ranks of the poverty-stricken agricultural community. But that was not all. We have not found any place for the 18,835,418 persons added to our national population. These could find no occupations in the heirarchy of their home industry and had consequently to adopt the already crowded agricultural pursuits. That this was the real state of things is remarkably well proved by the statistics of the preceding table. Therein we have shown that

The increase in total population	= 18,835,418
Industrial Exodus	= 9,698,087
Total available Migration	= 28,533,505
Addition to Agriculture	= 28,533,505

WHAT THAT DEGRADATION MEANS.

It is clear as noonday light that persons amounting to the aggregate populations of the Republic of Argentina (8,700,000) and New Zealand (1,071,000) were forced out of the industrial and commercial, that is, socially, intellectually, artistically and economically better occupations to the primitive agrestic pursuits. Nay, a further migration of the Indian population amounting to the total population of Spain (19,944,000) or equal to the inhabitants of Australia (4,733,000) Canada (7,467,000) and Belgium took place—a migration to land such as is unprecedented in the annals of India!

That this influx is real and not apparent has been very well acknowledged by the distinguished writer of the Census Report, Mr. E. A. Gait whose remarks on the decennial variations of the principal occupations deserve to be widely read by every student interested in the economic growth or decay of Indian industries:—

PASTURE AND AGRICULTURE.

As compared with 1901, the number of landlords and cultivators combined has risen from 155 to 175 millions. *The rate*

India Census R., 1911, P. 413.

of increase is thus 13 *per cent., or double that of the general population.* This result is due partly to changes in the method of classification.

At the same time there seems to be no doubt that the number of persons who live by cultivation is increasing at a relatively rapid rate.

On the one hand, the rise in price of food grains has made agriculture more profitable, while, on the other, the profits of various artisan classes have been diminished, owing to the growing competition of machine-made goods, both *locally manufactured and imported, with the results that these classes show a growing tendency to abandon their traditional occupation in favour of cultivation.*

The number of farm servants and field labourers has risen from 34 to 41 millions. The increase may also be due partly to the fact that at the time when the census of 1901 was taken agriculture was depressed, owing to the famine of previous year, whereas the census of 1911 came at a time of more than average agricultural prosperity. On the former occasion, the demand for agricultural labour was below, while on the latter it was above, the normal.

Pp. 413-14.

Textiles :—

As compared with 1901 there has been a decrease of 6·1 per cent. in the number of persons supported by textile industries. This is due mainly *to the almost complete extinction of cotton spinning by hand. Weaving by hand has also suffered severely from the competition of goods made by machinery in Europe and this country.* There has been a large increase in the number of Indian cotton mills, but as the output per head in factories is far greater than that from hand looms, the addition of a given number of factory hands involves the displacement of a far larger number of hand workers. Where land is available, the rise in the price of agricultural produce tends to make the weaver, like other artisans, take to the plough as principal means of subsistance. P. 148.

Hides, skins etc :—

The local cobbler, on the other hand, having to pay more for his raw material and feeling the increasing competition of machine-made goods has been tempted to abandon his hereditary craft for some other means of livelihood, such as agriculture or work in factories of various kinds. P. 419.

Metals :—

The total number of persons dependent on metal industries shows a decline of 6·6 per cent. as compared with 1901. The decrease in number of metal workers and the concomitant increase in that of metal dealers is probably genuine, and is due largely to substitution, for the indigenous brass and copper utensils of enamelled ware and aluminium articles imported from Europe. P. 420.

Chemical products :—

There has been a slight decrease in the course of the decade in the number of persons supported by these industries, owing to the extended use of mechanical power for oil pressing. P. 421.

Food industries :—

The number of persons supported by these industries has fallen somewhat since 1901, owing chiefly to the introduction of flour-grinding and rice husking machinery. The number of grain parchers has declined considerably, though it is hard to say why. *Ibid.*

Relative progress of Industry and Trade:—

On the other hand, the trading head has gained at the expense of the industrial one in the case of textiles, hides, and metals. The reason here is that the articles manufactured at home by the village artisan are being displaced by machine-made goods. Most of these are still imported from Europe, but even when made in India, as is largely the case with cotton goods, the substitution of machinery for the hand loom means the employment of much less labour for a given quantity of finished articles, while they are produced at a limited number of centres, numerous middlemen are needed for their distribution, for whom there was no place in the days when the village weaver made all the clothing of his fellow villagers. P. 424.

TABLE 3.

The following table of the decline of a few important industries in the whole of India between the years 1901 and 1911 would be highly instructive as it visualizes what has been said in the remarks of Mr. Gait.

SPECIMENS OF DECLINING INDUSTRIES.

		Decrease in Nos.	Decrease.
Paper	...	43,280	55 per cent.
Chemical products	...	71,704	5·6 ,,
Toys and curiosities	...	24,663	35 ,,
Bangles, necklaces sacred threads	...	37,910	6 ,,
Textiles	...	520,545	6.1 ,,
Cotton	...	1,118,650	13 ,,
Hides, skins, etc.	...	330,402	33·9 ,,
Wool and fur	...	193,853	3·3 ,,
Food industries	...	98,664	2.6 ,,
Metals & precious stones	...	127,041	6·1 ,,

MR. DUTTA ON THE CAUSE OF THIS DECLINE.

Mr. Dutta has also frankly drawn attention to the main cause of the decline of these industries:—

"This (a large increase in the export of raw hides and skins) coupled with an increasing import of European-made shoes and other leather articles, has evidently led to a *large decline in the leather industry in India*. There is also a decrease in the number of rice grinders and huskers and *workers in metals and chemicals* in consequence of the introduction of rice mills worked by machinery and the importation of larger quantities of metal manufactures and chemicals from foreign countries.

Prices Enquiry. Vol. I, p. 153.

UNIVERSAL TENDENCY OF PROGRESSIVE RURALIZATION.

This deplorable tendency is visible throughout the length and breadth of India. No province and no native state has escaped this terrible fate of more and more ruralization. Bengal, Bombay and Madras which seem to have easily adopted the western methods of production and which are veritable centres of modern industrialism in India—even these three presidencies have not been able to ward off this fate. This may sound startling, but it is a fact that the so-called Industrial Bombay is the greatest sufferer in this respect amongst the three presidencies. These statements would be amply borne out from our detailed examination of the ruralization of each province, but the following table which has been prepared from the 1st. volumes of the Census Reports of India 1901, P. 242 and 1911. P. 432 would throw a flood of light on the economic transformation of India in the last two censual decades.

TABLE 4.

AGRICULTURISTS PER 1000 OF POPULATION.

PROGRESSIVE RURALIZATION.

Territory	...	*1891*	*1901*	*1911*
India	...	*645*	*675*	*716*
Assam	...	863	855	861
Bengal	...	707	736	762
Berar	...	694	744	787
C. P.	...	674	706	
Bombay	...	616	607	673
Burma	...	635	671	703
Coorg	...	747	824	825
Madras & Cochin	...	600	691	701
Punjab & N.W.P.	...	603	591*	601
U. Provinces	...	690	691	733
Baroda	...	600	529	654
Central India	...	481	530	634
Hyderabad	...	478	516	619
Kashmir	...	681	765	796
Mysore	...	673	693	730
Rajputana	...	540	601	647

* See Chapter VII

But table No. 5 prepared from the Census Reports of India, 1911, Vol. I, pp. 334–5 and 1901, Vol. I, pp. 224—5, presents details regarding all the principal occupations of the people. The figures relating to agricultural proportion differ from those of the preceding table; because the partly agriculturists have been excluded from it. It will be evident from these figures that in all the main provinces amd states except the two insignificant native states of Coorg and Cochin, the agricultural population has enormously increased. Madras alone shows a little decrease from 690 to 687 per thouand in her agricultural population, otherwise the transformation of this vast continent abounding in unlimited resources of each and every description is proceeding apace for the worse.

TABLE 5.

Number per 1,000 of total population in 1911 and 1901.

	Agriculture 1911	Agriculture 1901	Industry 1911	Industry 1901	Commerce 1911	Commerce 1901	Professions 1911	Professions 1901
India	698	652	114	155	13	14	17	17
Ajmere-Merwara ...	538	534	170	179	154	15	38	25
Assam ...	854	842	32	78	45	8	13	14
Bengal ...	754	715	77	123	70	8	18	17
Bihar and Orissa ...	783		77		52		10	
Bombay ...	643	586	127	182	92	20	21	19
Burma ...	691	661	68	186	133	22	21	25
C. P. and Berar ...	755	700 732 }	102	162 129	51	8+16	15	(19+15)
Coorg ...	816	818	66	95	58	2	12	10
Madras ...	687	690	134	175	80	8	16	16
N. W. F. P. ...	667	569 }	115 }	194	86 }	28	24	21 }
Punjab ...	580		205 }		94 }		25	
U. Provinces ...	716	655	122	149	54	8	11	13
Baroda ...	633	520	123	142	72	31	37	27
C. India ...	607	503	123	171	60	21	15	13
Cochin ...	504	508	209	324	136	9	33	32
Hyderabad ...	571	461	141	173	92	38	16	13
Kashmir ...	785	752	89	113	48	19	17	17
Mysore ...	725	660	86	107	46	19	14	16
Rajputana ...	625	564	148	182	89	25	37	21
Travancore ...	531	472	172	259	99	26	29	25

INDIAN RUSTICATION.

Having briefly surveyed the occupational changes which have occurred during the two last Censual periods, we ought to enquire whether these tendencies are temporary or permanent. It is highly regrettable that although the Chapter on the Occupations of the People in the Census Report of 1881 extends to 120 pages, yet it is exceedingly poor in comparative statements. We can, therefore, offer no conclusions on the variations of the preceding decade. But even a comparison of the figures of 1881 with those of the succeeding decennium is no more easy. The principles of collecting statistics have been changing in each succeeding census. The figures of 1881 were collected and classified on lines widely different from those of 1871, but these new principles were adopted only to be abandoned in the next Censual enumeration. With such mighty modifications in the first principles of statistics-collection, tabulation and classification, it is impossible for us to furnish comparative results for the period of 19 years from 1872 to 1891.

However a few stray facts concerning the vocational distribution of the three censual years 1871, 1881 and 1891 are given below :—

TABLE 6.

PRINCIPAL CLASSES OF OCCUPATIONS OF ADULT MALES OF 20 YEARS AND UPWARDS.

In 1871.

Occupation.	No. in thousands.	Per cent.
Professional, including Govt. service ...	2,232	3·6
Domestic ...	3,844	6·2
Agricultural ...	34,844	56·2
Commercial ...	3,224	5·2
Industrial ...	8,122	13·1
Labourers ...	7,626	12·3
Independent and Non-productive	2,108	3·4
	62,000	100

(India Census Report, 1871, p. 32.)

TABLE 7.

MAIN OCCUPATIONS OF MALES (ALL INDIA)

In 1881.

	Numbers.	Per cent.
1. Government ...	1,816,219	1·3
2. Pasture and agriculture	52,029,098	40·04
3. Textile, fabrics and dress ...	5,080,389	3·9
4. No stated occupation...	48,794,195	37·5
Total Males ...	129,942,051	

TABLE 8.

PERCENTAGE STRENGTH OF OCCUPATIONS IN 1891 FOR INDIA.

Government	...	...	2·36
Pasture and agriculture	...	...	61·06
Personal service	...	...	3·91
Preparation and supply of material substances	...	...	15·43
Commerce and Transport	...	...	2·91
Professions	...	...	2·02
Indefinite and indescribable	...	...	1·66

Pp. 99–100, India Census Report, 1891, Vol. I.)

TABLE 9.

The **Textile Industry** supported the following persons in each group in 1891 :—

Wool and fur	...	...	587,70
Silk	...	...	319,397
Cotton	...	...	8,820,466
Jute and hemp	...	...	461,193
Dress, etc.	...	...	2,422,510
(P. 104.)		TOTAL	12,611,267

This was 4·39 % of the whole population. (Page 99).

TABLE 10.

The strength of some other occupations was:—

			per cent.
Metals	...	3,821,433	1·33
Glass and earthenware	...	2,360,623	·82
Wood, cane and matting	...	4,293,012	1·50
Drugs, gums and dyes	...	391,575	·14
Leather	...	3,285,307	1·14
Agriculture	...	171,735,390	61·06
Pasture	...	3,645,849	

(P. 100, India C. Report, 1891)

TABLE 11.

In the following statement the percentages borne by the few principal orders to the total population of all India and eleven other Provinces including Hydrabad are depicted for easy comparison :—

	Assam	Bengal	Bombay	Berar	Burma	C. P	Coorg	Punjab	Madras	Hydrabad	Mysore	All India
Administration	·67	·98	3·25	2·98	1·36	1·82	2·20	1·79	2·45	4·69	4·32	1·95
Pasture ...	·128	·64	1·37	1·21	·69	2·47	·72	1·29	2·01	2·46	·47	1·27
Agriculture ...	76·91	63·19	58·24	68·55	63·44	64·04	72·00	55·65	58·81	44·88	66·61	59·79
Textile & Dress	1·37	2·60	5·42	3·87	4·93	6·74	1·15	7·59	4·71	6·28	2·94	4·39
Metals ...	·75	1·13	1.51	1·32	·91	1·51	1·59	1·64	1·38	1·49	1·49	1·33
Dyes, Gums and Drugs	·04	·17	·12	·13	·15	·11	·01	·21	·12	·17	·06	·14
Leather ...	·11	·48	1·28	·82	·26	1·37	·22	2·74	1·38	1·37	·49	1·14
Commerce ...	·82	1·58	2·12	1·82	1·73	1·04	·37	1·76	·97	1·53	3·26	1·63

Hydrabad Census Report of 1891, P. 282, India Census Report, 1891, Pp. 119-120.

SUMMARY STATISTICS.

These preceding statements are most valuable as a basis for future comparisons. Inspite of 9·7 percent. increase in the total population of India there is noticeable a general decline in industrial workers during the twenty years succeeding 1891. There have been considerable reductions in the actual numbers and in percentage proportions of persons supported by our main industries. A few telling instances would clear up the situation ;—

TABLE 12.

	Actual Nos.		% of total Pop.	
	1891	*1911*	*1891*	*1911*
Textiles...	12,611,267	8,045,040	4·39	2·6
Metals ...	3,821,433	1,794,763	1·33	·59
Wood ...	4,293,012	3,668,800	1·50	1·21

MR. JUSTICE RANADE ON INDIAN RURALIZATION.

This ruralyzing tendency was fully realized by *Mr. Justice Ranade* who made a strong protest in his several speeches. Here we will quote two passages from his "Essays on Indian Economics" for exposing the real economic situation of India up to 1891.

'This Dependency has come to be regarded as a Plantation, growing raw produce to be shipped by *British Agents* in *British Ships*, to be worked into Fabrics by *British* skill and capital, and to be re-exported to the Dependency by *British merchants* to their corresponding *British Firms* in India and elsewhere. The development of steam power and mechanical skill, joined with increased facilities of communication, have lent strength to this tendency of the times, and, as one **result of the change, the gardual ruralization of this great Dependency, and the rapid decadence of Native Manufacture and Trade become distinctly marked.**

"EVEN NOW THE DANGER IS NOT OVER."

"They have aggravated the situation by making us more than ever dependent upon a single and precarious resource. P. (106. Natesan's Second Edition.)

The Industry and Commerce of the Country, such as it was, is passing out of our hands, and, except in the large Presidency Towns, the country is fed, clothed, warmed, washed, lighted, helped, and comforted generally, by a thousand *Arts and Industries in the manipulation of which its sons have every day a decreasing share. Foreign competition*, not because it is foreign, but because it is the competition of Nature's powers against man's labour, —it is the competition of organized Skill and Science against Ignorance and Idleness,—is transferring the monopoly not only of wealth, but what is more important, of skill, talent, and activity to others.

Pp. 196, 197.

SUMMARY.

TABLE 13.

Now the results of our study of the last two Inter-censual periods can be summarized in the tabular form as below :—

	Percentage Variation Decade ending 1901	Decade ending 1911
Increase in Total Population ...	2	6·6
„ Agri. Population ...	12	14·8
Decrease in Personal Services ...	−4	... *
„ in the preparation and supply of material substances ...	— 6	−·7
„ Commerce, transport ...	—11	... *
„ Professions ...	—13	−·6

But mere percentages may as much conceal as reveal the real magnitude of the changes that are occurring in the Occupational Distribution of the Indian people. Hence, a comparative statement of the actual increases in the total and agricultural populations is given below :—

TABLE 13.

	Actual strength (in millions) 1891	1901	Per Centage.
Total population ...	287·22	294·19	2
Agricultural „	175·38	195·67	12
	1901	1911	
Total „ ...	285·39	304·23	6·6
Agricultural „ ...	195·14	220·67	14·8

* Census Report of India, Vol. I, 1901, P. 238,
Census Report of India „ 1911, P. 439,

* Identical orders not found.

The figures of this table differ a little from those of the Table No. 1 and even show a little internal disparity. But the discrepancy is due to the reason that the figures of 1901 have been brought on the lines of 1911 and those of 1891 on the lines of 1901 for reducing them to a common basis.

RURALIZATION MORE INTENSIVE AND RAPID IN BRITISH PROVINCES THAN IN THE NATIVE STATES.

The Confession of the British Government.

The Indian Empire, published under the authority of His Majesty's Secretary of State for India in Council, informs us that "the census returns show that in British Provinces the proportion of the total population *directly engaged in agriculture* was 62 per cent. in 1891 and 68 per cent. in 1901, the corresponding figures for Native States in those years being 57 and 60 per cent." Vol. III, P. 1.

That the next decade has seen very rapid dislocation of industry in this country is borne out by the figures quoted from the Indian Government Reports. The rates of Ruralization and Industrial decadence have not been surpassed before. In 1911 the proportion of the agricultural population in the British Provinces rose to 73·5 and in the States to 67·8.

INDUSTRIAL VOCATIONS LEFT FOR AGRICULTURE.

"Taking India as a whole, although there has been an increase in industrial prosperity and development in the period between the censuses of 1901 and 1911, competition with imported articles and the products of factories organised on the latest methods and worked by machinery, *have ruined many of the handicrafts, especially the handloom industry and compelled people to leave their ancestral vocations for other means of livelihood, notably agriculture. It is not therefore*, surprising that there should be an actual decrease in the number of men depending upon industrial employment." Inquiry Into The Rise of Prices In India.

Vol. I., P. 154.

11½ PER CENT. INCREASE IN THE PERCENTAGE STRENGTH OF THE AGRICULTURAL POPULATION.

Thus it will have been noticed that an enormous displacement has taken place in the vocational strength of the people, that the Native states were not so much ruralized as British India, but during the last decade they have felt the effects of the ruralizing forces in a greater degree than the British Provinces. These disheartening results can be summarized as below :—

TABLE 14,

Percentage of Agricultural Population.

	British India	*Native States.*
1891 ...	62	57
1901 ...	68	60
1911 ...	73-5	68
1891—1911 ...	11·5	11

In other words, the agricultral community strengthened its percentage in the British Provinces by 11½ per cent. and in the Native States by 11 per cent. during the twenty years from 1891 to 1911. However, it is eminently gratifying to find that the States are even now 5½ per cent. less ruralized than the British Provinces.

THE FIRST THING TO BE REMEMBERED.

The general reader might have lost his way through the intricacies of dry statistics and hence it is essential to focus his attention on the vital point of ruralization. He will do well to remember that during the decade 1891—1901, 20,293,385 persons and during the next ten years 28,533,505 persons, in all, 48,826,890 souls were thrown out of non-agricultural occupations from 1891 to 1911 and were pushed to the land to live, starve or die as best as they could. And this was due directly or indirectly to the ruinous policy of Free Trade which has for a century and a half been thrust upon the voiceless millions of India against their vital interests.

The Second Significant Fact To Notice Is

That India Is In The Throes of A Mighty Economic Transition.

A sure barometer of the Economic storms that have passed over India during the forty years from 1871 to 1911 is to be seen in the occupational variations that have occurred during the period named. The succeeding figures would conspicuously depict the dismal changes that have been coming upon the Indian society—changes that were fraught with struggle and suffering of a magnitude unknown in the annals of any time and clime.

THE RESULT OF FORTY YEARS' RURALIZATION.

Proportion of Agricultural to Total Population in 1871 and 1911.

Province	1871	1911	Rise in per cent. strength
N. W. Provinces...	56	$73\frac{3}{10}$ (N. W. Provinces and Oudh together)	20
Oudh ...	50		
Punjab ...	55	60	5
Central Provinces...	$37\frac{1}{2}$	$78\frac{7}{10}$ (Central Provinces and Berar together)	41
Berar ...	61		17
Mysore ...	20	73	53
Coorg ...	$12\frac{1}{2}$	$82\frac{1}{2}$	70
British Burma ...	27	70	43
Bombay ...	26	67	41

(* India Census Report, Vol. I, P. 432.)

Here the matter lies in a nutshell. It is now superfluous to comment upon this self-explanatory statement. This forty years' period has enormously altered the whole aspect of our home industry, has shaken the industrial fabric of our society to its very foundations, and has terribly transformed the face of this country. All the outlets of capital, skill, talent and activity to the thousand and one industries are barred!

And barred, to the sons of the soil !!

The figures for 1871 are based on the following statistics :—

IN THOUSANDS

Provinces	Total Population	Agricultural Population	% of II to I
N. W. Provinces ..	30,781	17,376	56
Oudh ...	11,220	6,542	50
Punjab ...	17,611	9,683	55
Central Provinces...	8,201	3,058	37½
Berar ...	2,231	1,369	61
Mysore ...	5,055	1,034	20
Coorg ...	168	21	12½
British Burma ...	2,747	736	27
Bombay ...	16,349	4,188	26

(India Census Report 1871, P. 65)

Industrial Coorg, Mysore, Burma, Bombay and Central Provinces have become *predominently Agricultural* and so have the United Provinces of Oudh and Agra. During these fatal years the once happy and rich *industrial classes* have been changed as if by a magician's wand, into the poor, miserable, hopeless, helpless, homeless, starving and *labouring masses.* These millions amounting to more than the inhabitants of the United Kingdom, have been reduced to such a misery and penury as are unknown in any country or clime.

The third thing to bear in mind is the number of half-starved wretches, stupid and stunted specimens, or poor, puny, prostrate pieces of imperfect humanity whom we call

INDIA'S HELOTS.

50 MILLOIN LABOURERS IN INIDA.

Nothing can illustrate the poverty and penury of India more decisively than the number of the millions who are born for service, serfdom and struggles, starvation, suffering and sorrow. The number of farm servants and field *labourers rose from 34 to 41 millions.* But we read the same consoling clause that 'this is largely a matter of classification.' (See p. 31), because persons enumerated under the head of 'insufficiently described occupations' fell from 17,776,874 in 1901 to 9,045,804 in 1911. However the increase in the Agricultural Labourers is also due partly to the fact that the demand for agricultural labour in 1901 was below, for the industry was then depressed, owing to the famine of the previous year, while in 1911 it was above the normal, because at the time of the census there was more than average agricultural prosperity.*

Thus the Submerged Labouring Humanity in India Amounts to Fifty Million souls. Out of every hundred men, women and children in India sixteen are Landless Labourers, the adult alone earning three pence a day.

Some Charles Booth is required to lay bare the hellish degradation, depression and depravement of these walking mummies of living humanity. Yet Edward Carpenter's stirring words would be a fitting conclusion to this chapter.

'Think for a moment of the vast floating, fluctuating, tramping, toiling population that does the manual work' of India to-day. There was a time when a landless, houseless family was almost unknown. 'What material for reflection lies in these words! Think of the vast patient toiling population of to-day, homeless, tramping from place to place, thrice blessed when it can get into some squalid corner of workshop or factory and be *allowed* to grind at one eternal and monotonous operation for nine hours a day. Think of the insults and mockery, of kicks supplemented by patronage and good advice.'

---

* P. 414, Census R., 1911.

NOTE I TO CHAPTER II, Pp. 26—27.

Sir M. Bhownagree's Views on *The Economic Slavery of India.*

WHAT DO THE PEOPLE USE EVERY DAY?

"What do these poorer classes use every day? Take *the humblest household first.* You will find there metal pots and pans for cooking purposes, kerosine or mineral oil and matches for light, cotton, bone or metal buttons, pins, hooks and eyes, needles and thread, which enter into the preparation of the family garments of rough native-made fabrics. Then there are tacks and nails, twine and string, a hammer and other tools in many houses. *All these articles, every one of them, are of foreign make.*

"Peering into *another household*, a stage or two upraised in the social scale, you find nearly all the articles *common to the daily use of a European* working man, most of the culinary utensils, lamps, candle, soap, paper, ink, pen, pencil, *not a single one of which is made in India.* This house is painted with colour or washes of foreign composition, the wood-work of it is varnished with foreign varnish, *the occupant's clothes are of European manufacture.* One degree higher again, and four-fifths of the articles in the domicile of a peon, a petty schoolmaster or a clerk, and on his own person and his wife's and children's persons, *are of foreign make.* Then come the household of the middle class, of the successful and comfortable tradesman, the merchant and the professional man. There, and, in a still greater degree, in the mansions of millionaires and the palaces of princes *the predominating proportion of articles are all of foreign manufacture. I try hard to recall to my mind what particular article I should find of Indian workmanship in places like these last, and I do not see any of that description, from the kitchen and stable to the drawiag-room and the hall,* Some critics, who do not fall in with my views, might point to the furniture. That would make a somewhat important exception if I viewed this considerable part of a household as a superficial observer would; but then he does not remember that, save in the simplest and crudest class of furniture, a good proportion of what is known as local furniture is not native-made at all. *The spring of* a coach or chair, the lining, the buttons, the threads, the hinges of a cupboard, or box, the screws, the nails, the locks, the very tools with which these are put together and formed into shape are all made abroad. So that what remains is the wood and the labour. That even these contribute their due proportion of profit to the Native worker, I doubt.

English firms and European employers in very many instances control the production of the raw material and the labor, and very appropriately take the profit of it, the Native's gain being the bare living wages of his daily toil.''

NOTE II ON RELIGION AND VAGRANCY.

A survey of the occupational distribution of the Indian people would be imperfect if we failed to take account of the numerous class of men who live by administering to the religious want of the people or who live by beggary, vagrancy and prostitution. In this vast continent of India every thing is starling.

29½ Million Persons are supported by religion and vagrancy. That is 9·4 persons out of every hundred of the national population are either sadhus or beggars, economically unproductive people, adding nothing directly to the wealth of the country, but consuming what others have produced. But the services of *real* sadhus, Maulavies and missionaries are invaluable for comforting and consoling the comfortless and toiling masses, although they are bought at a price which poor India can hardly spare.

CHAPTER III.

GROWTH OF POPULATION.

AND

DECLINE OF URBANIZATION.

SUMMARISED GROWTH OF THE INDIAN POPULATION.

The Census of 1911 showed a total population of 315 million, of whom 244 million lived in British Territory and 71 million in the Native States. *The Census of 1901 gave a population of 294 million, that of 1891, 287 million, that of 1881, 254 million and that of 1872, 206 million.* In other words, the gross increase in the population of each census over the preceding one was respectively 21, 7, 33, and 48 million in round numbers, or *the total difference between the populations of 1911 and 1872 amounts to 108,994,036.*

But this growth does not represent the natural increase, *i.e.*, it is not all due to an excess of births over deaths or of immigrants over emigrants. Fresh territories have from time to time been added to the old ones and an appreciable increase has resulted from the greater accuracy of the later enumerations. A statement representing additions due to these causes and a percentage rate of real increase is as follows :—

TABLE 1.

Period	Increase due to — Inclusion of new areas Millions.	Improvement of method Millions.	Real increase of population Millions.	Total Increase Millions	Rate per cent of real increase.
1872-81	33·0	12·0	3·0	48·0	1·5
1881-91	5·7	3·5	24·3	33·5	9·6
1891-01	2·7	·2	4·1	7·0	1·4
1901-11	1·8	...	18·7	20·5	6·4
Total	43·2	15·7	50·1	109	19·0

REAL INCREASE IN POPULATION.

It is obvious therefore that the increase in population during the period of 39 years from 1872 to 1911, is not 109 millions, but only 50 millions, that is, 19 per cent. On the basis of these figures, the annual rate of increase amounts to a little less than ½ per cent. alone. It is simply insignificant when compared with the similar growth of England and Wales. Here are the figures of the

TABLE 2.

GROWTH OF POPULATION IN

	The United Kingdom Millions	Increase per cent.	England and Wales. Increase per cent.
1871	31·48		
1881	34·8	10.8	14·36
1891	37·73	8·2	11·65
1901	41.45	9·2	12·17
1911	45·21	9·1	10·91

(The Industrial History of Modern England, C. H. Perris P. 550)

This table shows that the increase in the populations of the two Kingdoms has been 43·6 and 58·8 per cent. during the forty years under review. In other words the annual percentage increase has been respectively 1·09 and 1·47 per cent. against ·5 per cent. in India.

COMPARATIVE STATEMENT 3.

For comparative purposes the following statement will prove of great value.

Percentage in 1872 when the population of 1911 = 100

United States	...	...	43·28
Germany	...	...	63·54
United Kingdom	...	...	70·77
India	...	Apparent	69·00
		Real	80·4

No part of the increase in Germany and the United Kingdom is due to the inclusion of new territories or the greater accuracy of census enumeration, but a part of the increase of the United States population is certainly due to new territories. In the above table the fallacious increase due only to the improvement in the methods of census enumerations in India has been added to the numbers returned in 1872 and the result is most satisfactory, but if increases mentioned in columns II and III of Table 1 be deducted, the percentage figure for 1872 rises to 80·4· That is, there was a rise of 19·6 per cent in the population of India during those 39 years. It is needless to comment that this increase is insignificantly small and highly discouraging when compared with the three progressive countries.

TOWN AND COUNTRY PEOPLE.

9 In Every 100 Live In Towns.

India is predominently a rural country. In 1911, she contained *2,153 towns* with 29,748,228 inhabitants as against *720,342* villages with 285,408, 168 inhabitants. While at the preceding census the number of towns and villages was *2148* and *7,282,605* respectively and the distribution of the country's population in urban and rural areas was 29,240,000 against 265,110,000.

URBAN DECLINE.

A comparison of these two censuses shows an *increasing predominence of the Rural* as compared with the Urban element, because in 1901, *9·9 per cent. of the population were dwellers in towns, but the proportion fell to 9·12 in 1911. Thus, there has been a discouraging decrease in Urbanization.*

TABLE 4.

Year	Percentage of Urban Population.
1901	9·9
1911	9·12

REMARKABLE REVELATION.

The table below furnishes the most remarkable instance of the Decline of Urban Population as compared with the total or Rural Increase :—

TABLE 5.

RESULTS OF THE CENSUS OF 1911.

Rate of the Increase of Urban Pop.	...	1·7
,, Total Pop.	...	6·6
,, Rural Pop.	...	7·6
,, Agricultural Pop.	...	14·8

TABLE 6.

CHANGES IN URBANIZATION DURING 20 YEARS.

Inhabitants	1891	1901	1911	Resulting Increase or Decrease	
				In 20 years	In 10 years
Above 50,000 ...	76	78	75	—1	—3
From 20,000 to 50,000 ...	166	164	178	+12	+14
„ 10,000 to 20,000 ...	515	499	485	—30	—108
„ 5,000 to 10,000 ...	1,501	1,507	1,615	+114	+108
Total villages and towns ...	711,474	731,016	722,268	10,794	—8,748

A remarkable feature of these figures is the decline in towns of more than 50,000 inhabitants and of towns having persons between 10,000 and 20,000. The same decline is visible in the number of villages and towns *that have decreased within one decade to the extent of 8,748.* But the census figures were notable for the startling evidence they gave of

URBAN DEPOPULATION.

There have been large decreases in urban population. Out of the 78 towns named in Table No. 10,* 37 show depressing and discouraging decreases. Sharp changes have occurred in the population of the following towns:

TABLE 7.

POPULATION IN THOUSANDS.

	1901	1911		1901	1911
Bellary	58	35	Nagpur	128	101
Salem	72	59	Alwar	57	41
Sholapur	75	61	Baroda	104	99
Surat	119	115	Bharatpur	44	34
Cawnpur *	202	178	Bhopal	77	56
Benares	213	203	Indore	87	45
Gaya	71	50	Patiala	54	47
Mandalay	184	138	Lashkar	89	47

Another side of the picture is presented by the fact that the population in *toto* of the 78 towns of that Table was 10,036,414 in 1901 but in 1911 it

* P. 32 of Statistical Ab. for B. India, Vol. IV, 1913-14.

rose to be 10,281,030, that is, the increase was only 2·43, while the *total population* of India increased by 6·6 percent.

TABLE 8.

SUMMARY OF TEN YEARS FOR TOWNS OF 50,000 OR MORE.

Province.	*Towns.*			*Result.*
Bengal ...	4	Increase		
Madras ...	8	,,	+ 3	Decrease
Bombay ...	4	,,	+ 2	,,
Sind ...	2	,,	+ 0	,,
Agra ...	2	,,	+ 13	,,
Oudh ...	2	,,	+ 0	,,
Bihar and Orissa ...	1	,,	+ 4	,,
Punjab ...	7	,,	+ 2	,,
Burma ...	1	,,	+ 2	,,
C. Provinces ...	1	,,	+ 1	,,
N. W. F. P. ...	1	,,		
Ajmere-Merwara ...	1	,,		
N. States ...	7	,,	+ 9	,,
1891	1901		1911	
78 towns	76		69	

Thus, during the two intercensual periods nine towns which had a population of 50,000 or more in 1891, fell out of that category. There is then a *galloping decline in the Urban population* of the British Provinces of Agra, Bihar and Orissa and of nine Native States. Does such a sharp decline augur an economic progress and prosperity for India? or does it call for a most serious consideration of the problem? We are sure that an impartial examination of the foregoing pages undoubtedly shows that there is.

Something Rotten in the State of Denmark.

So many decaying towns, cities and villages once famous for their flourishing arts and crafts cannot but be lamentable monuments of the industrial decline of the people and most gloomy evidences of our unexampled national degradation and general distress.

TABLE 9.

URBAN POPULATION IN 1881.

Ranked according to the percentage on the total population of the Urban section the Provinces stood thus:—

Per cent. of Urban to Total Population.

Ajmere ...	20	Madras	9·7
Baroda ...	18·6	Hydrabad	9·0
Bombay, B. T. ...	17·8	C. India	8·6
Bengal B. T. ...	12·9	Mysore	8·3
Bombay, F. S. ...	12·8	C. Provinces, B. T.	6·8
North & West, F. S.	12·4	Bengal	5·3
Berar ...	11·6	Travancore	5·2
Burma ...	11·4	Coorg	4·7
Punjab, F. S. ...	11·2	C. P., F. S.	1·5
Rajputana ...	10·8	Assam	1·4
North-West, B. T...	9·7		

(P. 273, Census Report, 1881.)

In India out of every 1,000 persons 91 resided in towns and 909 in villages in 1881.

The decline of the next decade will best be described in the words of the writer of the Census Report.

Urban growth from 1881-1891.

"The statement, taken with the above qualification and explanation shows that the Urban population has increased on the whole at a rate less by 1½ % than that of the population at large, whilst that of females instead of being higher, is lower than that of males to a considerable extent."

The following table gives the figures of Urban growth in the different Provinces and States as compared with that of the whole population thereof :—

TABLE 10.

INCREASE PER CENT. OF POPULATION.

		Urban Pop.	Total Pop.
Madras	...	10·75	15·58
Bombay and Sindh	...	10·29	14·51
Bengal	...	7·37	6·89
N. W. Provinces	...	2·32	4·55
Oudh	...	6·18	11·09
Punjab	...	7·93	10·74
Lower Burma	...	17·86	24·67
C. P.	...	7·11	9·61
Assam	...	10·37	11·30
Berar	...	8·49	8·41
Ajmer	...	22·44	7·72
Coorg	...	7·36	2·94

States			
Hydrabad	...	11·09	17·18
Baroda	...	7·02	10·54
Mysore	...	13·55	18·09
Rajputana	...	12·22	20·22
C. India	...	7·27	9·92
Bombay States	...	12·67	16·35
Madras States	...	·85	·63
C. P. States	...	12·09	26·36
Bengal States	...	8·85	18·30
N. W. P. States	...	2·01	6·84
Punjab States	...	6·77	10·42

P. 80, India Census Report of 1891.

The above table is the most eloquent testimony of the almost universal urban decline in India. Leaving the large province of Bengal and the two insignificant parts of Ajmere and the Madras States, throughout the length and breadth of India, urban growth lagged behind that of the total population during the decade of 1881—1891.

Thus a review of the thirty years from 1881 to 1911 shows that a marked tendency of urban depopulation, industrial decline, and of migration to exhausted and overcrowded land is observable throughout the vast continent of India. But this state of things is quite dissimilar, as will be seen, to that distinctly visible in most European countries.

COMPARATIVE PROGRESS OF URBANIZATION.

How the English Are Becoming A Race of Townspeople.

The urban increase in England and Wales has been simply remarkable. While the population in towns exceeding 5,000 inhabitants was 26 per cent of the whole in 1801, it was 44·7 per cent. in 1851 and 68 forty years after. The actual growth and distribution of the population during these 90 years have been as below :—

TALE 11.

GROWTH AND DISTRIBUTION OF THE POPULATION IN ENGLAND AND WALES.

	1801	1851	1891
Population in towns exceeding 5,000 inhabitants	2,314,515	8,028,011	19,763,264
Population in towns having less than 5,000 inhabitants and in the country ...	6,578,021	4,899,598	9,239,261
	8,892,536	17,927,609	29,002,525

URBAN PROGRESS FROM 1851 TO 1911.

The following statement summarizes the comparative relation of the two populations in a very distinct manner :—

TABLE 12.

Year	Urban	Rural
1851	50·08	49·92
1871	61·80	38·20
1881	67·9	32·1
1891	72·05	27·95
1901	77·00	23·00
1911	78·1	19 9

It is more than obvious now that in England and Wales there has been the most rapid and remarkable development of urbanization.

The percentage of urban population has risen from 61·8 per cent. to 78·1 per cent during the 40 years from 1871 to 1911, but in India it has positively declined. Such are the opposite tendencies of the two countries!

INDIAN AND ENGLISH CITIES COMPARED.

The Table No. 13 presents a comparative view of the large *cities* in England and Wales and India at the last census enumeration of 1911.

TABLE 13.

Towns of	India	England and Wales
50,000 or more	75	98
100,000 ,,	30	44
200,000 ,,	10	16
Aggregate Urban population	8.7	17·3 millions
	—	—
Total population	315	361 ,,

Thus England and Wales are approximately eighteen times as urbanized as India.

ANOTHER REMARKABLE DIFFERENCE.

In 1871 *British* India contained 44 great cities * having a population above 50,000. Their population was not much more than five and-a-half millions, or 2·90 per cent. of the total population. But there were 34 towns of the same description

* India Census Report, 1871. P. 12.

in England and Wales whose residents exceeded 7¼ millions, or were 32 per cent. of the total population.

Forty years pass by, then England and Wales contain 98 towns having an aggregate population of 78 per cent. to the total, but the whole of India in spite of all the new territories and states that it has added to itself during the period, contained 75 towns with a population of 8·7 millions which is 2·80 per cent. of the whole.

Thus India is either stationary or retrogressive, while England has been wildly galloping in the race for industrial and urban advancement Such are the striking differences between the economic conditions of the two countries!

Although Germany is not so highly urbanized as England and Wales, yet its urban growth is most satisfactory.

TABLE 14.

PER CENT. URBAN IN THE GERMAN EMPIRE.

Year	% of Total Pop.	Year	% of Total Pop.
1871	36	1900	54
1880	41	1905	57
1890	47		

In 1871 Germany had only 8 cities of 100,000 souls with an aggregate population of 2 million inhabitants, but in 1911, she had 47 cities with 13·7 millions, i.e., 21 per cent. of the total population. Again, while in 1871 there were but

9 towns in Germany having a population of 75,000 souls, in 1905 there were 63. But the United States of America have shown an astounding tendency for a progressive urbanization. That the urban population is rapidly developing, is conclusively proved by the following two statements :—

TABLE 15.

PER CENT. URBAN IN U. S. A.

1880	1890	1800	1910
29.5	36·1	40·5	46·3

While the urban population in India from 1881 to 1911 has been either stationary or declining, the urban increase during 30 years has been 16·8 in the United States!

TABLE 16.

Cities Having 50,000 or More Inhabitants At Each Census, From 1850 To 1910.

Year	Cities	Year	Cities
1850	11	1890	60
1860	19	1900	83
1870	24	1910	115
1880	37		

Thus, while in the U. S. A. 78 new towns rose up, during the thirty years from 1880 to 1910, in India 3 cities alone entered into this category.

St. Ab. 1913, Pp. 41—43.

TABLE 17.

A. Statement regarding *France* would be no less interesting :—

	1846	1906
Rural Population ...	75·6	57·9
Urban „ ...	24·4	42·1

The first and foremost conclusion from these comparative returns is the lowest position of India in the heirarchy of progressive nations. While in these days of strenuous competition every nation is trying its level best in making rapid advances in urban and industrial expansion,

THE INDIANS ARE BECOMING A RACE OF VILLGERS.

India's position is growing worse in each succeeding year. In every civilized country rural life is yielding to urban and agricultural occupations to industrial and commercial. 'The process may be summed up in one word—the Town. The development of the town is the outstanding feature of industrialism.' It has been truely said that the same signs are visible in every Western country—namely a relative decline of agricultural occupation and rural population and an increasing aggregation of people in large towns. However these persistent tendencies have been reversed in India where the village population is increasing relatively more and more at the expense of the urban. In fact India has been passing through the severest depression of indigenous industries, through an unprecedented crisis in her arts and crafts as well as an abnormal and portentous growth of primitive agriculture.* The reciprocal relations of industry and agriculture have been abruptly upset and both of them have been jeopardised and paralysed. This paralysis has extended to all the limbs of industry. Agriculture, indeed, seems flushed up, but it is all an unhealthy growth. Moreover, the pity of it is that there are yet no signs of regeneration in this slumbering India. On the basis of the facts brought to light in the second chapter of this volume it can be safely predicted that the future is as dark and cloudy as was the past. Unless we soon remedy the evils that have led to the present depression and lesser urbanization we shall have soon to witness the final collapse of our remaining indigenous handicrafts.

The causes of this deplorable decline in urban growth, of this unprecedented decay of our once-flourishing towns and industries have been frankly and ably analysed by Mr. E. A. Gait in the following passage. :—

"Throughout India there are many former Capitals of defunct dynasties whose population is steadily dwindling. During the last ten years, Mandalay, the last Capital of the Kings of Ava, has lost a quarter of its population. There are other towns such as Baroda, which though still the capitals of Native Chiefs, are losing population because their rulers, more enlightened than their predecessors, no longer think it essential to their dignity to maintain in the vicinity of their palace a large rabble of useless parasites. Other towns again were important distributing centres in the days of river borne trade, but are decadent now that the railways have become the chief means of transport. Patna is a case in point; but it may confidently be anticipated that the selection of this ancient city as the Capital of Behar and Orissa will restore its waning prosperity, and that it will soon recover its lost ground, just as did Dacca during the brief period for which it was the Capital of the short-lived province of Eastern Bengal and Assam. While fostering the growth of some towns, the improvement of communications by rail often has a bad effect on others. It encourages the opening of shops in the smaller towns and villages, where people in the neighbourhood can get their supplies instead of, as formerly, having to make a journey to a more distant market, and it enables the residents in many of the large towns to make their home in the suburbs even further away."*

With due deference to the distinguished writer it may be boldly said that this analysis of the causes of urban depopulation is not true to the point. Almost all these causes have operated with greater force in Europe and America and yet we are met with an exceedingly rapid concentration and congestion of the population in towns. Being less intensive in their operation why should they then be subversive of the urban and industrial growth in India?

In our opinion the one supreme cause of the declining urbanization is the industrial decadence of this country. With the loss of political independence India witnessed the disappearance of independent Chiefs, Rajas, Zemindars, Talukedars, the dwindling away of the military, ruling and judicial classes of Pre-British India, the thinning

* Mr. Gait, Census of India, Vol. I, P. 41.

down of the upper and the middle classes of merchants and agriculturists in many provinces on account of the Ryotwari system and on account of the passing of the external trade of the country out of the hands of native inhabitants. India painfully observed the ever-increasing importation of cheap foreign goods, and the decreasing demand for her manufactured merchandise in home and foreign markets. These causes and many more allied to them have conspired to bring about urban depopulation. It is an undisputed fact that Hindu and Mohammedan rulers of India had an unbounded taste for architectural magnificence. There being a thousand and one independent states scattered throughout India, each state great or small, vied with others in adorning its capital cities and religious centres with public and private edifices of great strength and magnificence. Every ruler from the Great Moghul to the petty chief of a hill state attracted artisans and handicraftsmen to his capital city, gave them state protection and encouragement and thus served to promote the industrial advancement of this country. But the English have substituted one government for many in this vast continent, their sway has swept away all independent kingdoms, then their pronounced policy has been the constant discouragement of the arts and crafts, industry and commerce of the country, hence those towns and cities could not but decline in trade, commerce, industry and prosperity.

AUDI ALTERAM PARTEM.

CHAPTER IV.

FREE TRADE, THE MAIN CAUSE OF INDIAN RURALIZATION.

The foregoing tables are based on carefully compiled official statistics and they present a most ghastly picture of the all-round ruralization of a once industrially supreme India. Her handicrafts and industries have become extinct and her skilled sons are being forced to adopt poor, primitive and crowded agriculture. Thus it is to be greatly feared that almost the whole population of India would one day be transformed into stupid, stolid, oppressed over-taxed, *and poverty-stricken* agriculturists.

MAIN CAUSES OF RURALIZATION.

But why ? Because we have been foolishly inviting every giant competitor from all the points of the compass to sell his bounty-fed, highly subsidized or Cartell-produced, cheapest goods in India, while the state has all along refrained from aiding any industries only in deference to the impracticable, and exploded theories of Free-Trade and Laissez Faire. The state has religiously but blindly worshipped them as fetishes, and consequently brought a train of irrepairable evils both in England and India. While these policies have caused the decline and dacadence of Indian industries, they have ruined some of the important industries of England and have made that great country more and more dependent on foreign supplies for her food and hence, 'dependent absolutely on the mercy of those who envy its present prosperity.' (*J. Chamberlain*). That to these policies alone is due the ultimate collapse of indigenous industries has been established in the foregoing pages on the authority of officials and non-officials of very high standing. But we will yet bring to a focus the views of a few more distinguished officials, writers and statesmen that this vital point be fully brought home and settled once for all.

Mr. Gait, the distinguished writer of the India Census Report, 1911 has truly grasped the situation. "The extensive importation," writes he, "of cheap European piece-goods and utensils, and the establishment in India itself of numerous factories of the Western type, have more or less destroyed many village industries. The high prices of agricultural produce have also led many village artisans to abandon their hereditary craft in favour of agriculture. The extent which this disintegration of the old village organization is proceeding varies considerably in different parts." Vol. I. P. 409.

Mr. Dutta has frankly pointed out that foreign imports and factory products have ruined many Indian handicrafts and caused the desertion of ancestral vocations for agriculture.* On page 153 he has thus summed up his opinion. 'To sum up,

* Enquiry into the Rise of Prices, Vol. 1, P. 153.

both agriculturists and labourers, more especially the former, have increased more than the other classes, and this is not surprising, in view of the increased profits of agriculture and a large increase in the wages of agricultural labourers."

In other words, by reason of the keenest competition from abroad, industrial and commercial pursuits have been growing less and less remunerative than primitive agriculture and the people have consequently been swelling the ranks of the agricultural classes.

Sir Valentine Chirol on Indian Ruralization.

'It is at least equally important for India to save her home industries, and especially her hand-weaving industry, the wholesale destruction of which under the pressure of the Lancashire power loom has thrown so many poor people on to the already over-crowded land.' Indian Unrest, P. 266.

The Hon'ble Rai Sitanath Roy Bahadur on Present Industrial Condition.

"Gentlemen, industrially India is almost on her last legs. While other countries have been making rapid strides in industrial progress, India has practically stood still. In the meanwhile, the population of the country has been growing and

A continuously increasing proportion of the people has been thrown upon agriculture

for subsistence. In 1891, 62 per cent. of the people were returned as depending on agriculture, in 1901, 68 per cent., and in 1911, 71 per cent.

In England, of every hundred workers, 58 are engaged in industrial pursuits and only 8 in agriculture, whereas in India the industries give employment to only 12 per cent. of the population. This is, on the face of it

AN UNNATURAL STATE OF THINGS.

It is a well-known fact that the occupation of agriculture, being precarious, is not so remunerative as manufacture. The result is that we are to-day very poor compared with other nations."

Wealth of India, Jan. 1916, P. 11.

Dr. W. W. Hunter on the Destruction of Indian handicrafts.

THE PLOUGH FOR THE LOOM.

'In architecture, in fabrics of cotton and silk, in goldsmith's work and jewellery, the people of India were then unsurpassed. But while the east has stood still, as regards manufactures on a great scale, the west has advanced by gigantic strides without a parallel in the history of the human progress. On the one hand, the downfall of the native courts deprived the skilled workman of his chief market, while on the other, the English capitalist has enlisted in his service forces of nature against which the village artisans in vain try to compete.

The tide of circumstances has compelled the Indian weaver to exchange his loom for the plough, and has crushed many of the minor handicrafts.'

In other words, besides the weaver, the potter, the blacksmith, the brazier, the oilpresser, the leather-worker, the dyer and many more members of the industrial community have been compelled to exchange their various trades for agriculture. Indian Empire, P. 469.

Mr. S. Ranganath on Indian Poverty and Ruralization.

'At the very threshold of our inquiries it would be better to throw away all mistaken impressions about India. That India is poor and is growing poorer is admitted by all except those who visit our country in the winter, drive about in broughams sight-seeing, dine and loll and sleep in some Anglo-Indian Club and then go home to write a book on India, abusing us poor Indians and cursing us for our 'ingratitude.' We only know where the shoe pinches. What do *they* know of Indian conditions? Do they know that India has been visited by a dozen famines during the last 30 years? Do they know that 20 millions of poor, suffering humanity have been carried off the face of our land? Do they know that millions more are even on the brink of starvation?

The sources of our national wealth are agriculture and manufactures. India in the 18th century had both; to-day she has less of the former than before, and very little indeed of the latter, in proportion to her population and advancement.'

Hindustan Review of Jan. 1914, Pp. 49—50.

Mr. P. N. Bose, B. Sc. (Lond.), F.G.S., Author of the History of Hindu Civilization during British Rule.

EFFECTS OF THE EXTINCTION OF INDIGENOUS INDUSTRIES.

The all but utter extinction of our industries has ruined our artisan classes. Down to the commencement of the present century we used to make enough clothes, not only to meet our own demands, but also to export a good portion of them. Our export trade then consisted mainly of manufactured cotton; now it consists mainly of raw produce. In the beginning of the present century India exported to England piece-goods worth more than a million and-a-half pounds; in 1892 we imported over twenty eight million worth of manufactured cotton.

The profits of manufacture which a century ago remained in the country and enriched it, now swell the ever increasing drain to Europe. The greater majority of the artisan classes who once formed large flourishing communities have been driven to earn their subsistence as agriculturists or labourers.

INCREASED PRESSURE UPON LAND.

Large towns with urban populations have dwindled into inconsiderable villages.

It has been estimated that nearly ninety per cent. of our population is now dependent, directly or indirectly, upon agriculture. But, the extent of cultivable waste-land, in proportion to the population, is rather small. Consequently, as population has been increasing and becoming more and more largely agricultural, the pressure upon land has been gradually increasing. The time is not far distant when it will fail to meet the enhanced demand upon it, unless its food-growing capacity increases. That with improving methods this capacity will, to some extent, increase, there can be no doubt. But the present prospect is not very cheering.

Dr. Birdwood on Progressive Ruralization in his Industrial Arts of India.

Indigenous industries, such as weaving, salt-making, carrying by men or bullocks, have, in various instances, been ousted by superior European methods and products, and the classes concerned have no doubt suffered. The 19 or 20 millions' worth of cotton goods yearly imported must have displaced an appreciable amount of the native manufacture; while the altered and more peaceable condition of society has sent back into the civil community, and, practically, upon the land, thousands of men who formerly earned a living as soldiers of the state or retainers of the powerful chieftains.

Mr. Justice H. S. Cunningham on the condition of Indian Agriculturists.

On the whole, it may be said that the great mass of the occupants of the

Soil of India must be, from the smallness of their holdings and the members who have to be supported on

them, at the best of times hard pressed for the means of subsistence; that in the case of a very large number in Bengal and Upper India, the hardships of their position are enhanced by the presence of a class of more or less exacting landlords, whose eagerness for increased rental is favoured by the increased necessity of a growing population to find room on the soil; and that, as no considerable outlets, other than in agricultural employment, at present exist, the pressure on the soil and **the penury of the less thrifty and capable agriculturists, is likely, in the absence of some new form of relief, to become still severer than at present.**"

British India and Its Rulers, P. 30.

Mr. Romesh C. Dutt, C. I. E.

THE decline of Indian manufactures and indigenous industries within the last 150 years is one of the saddest episodes of British Rule in India, and presents one of the most difficult economic problems to Indian administrators at the dawn of a new century.

Our national industries, specially spinning and weaving, have declined within the last hundred years, firstly through the illiberal policy of the East Indian Company, and secondly by competition with the steam and machinery of Europe.

What has been said about the spinning and weaving industry of India applies to some extent to other old Indian industries. Dying and the manufactures of dyes, tanning and leather work, working in iron and other metals, the weaving of shawls and carpets, muslins and brocades, the manufacture of paper and stationery articles—all have declined.

Millions of the Indian population who made a livelihood from these industries are now compelled to agriculture as the one remaining source of their subsistence; and responsible statesmen in the present day, in the House of Commons and outside, are trying to think out how they can undo the mischief done in the past, and again diversify Indian industries. I have myself, during the many years of my service under the Indian Government, visited villages and towns which were once the homes of flourishing communities of weavers—those who produced that famous Indian muslin which was once the wonder of Europe. **Those villages are now deserted and desolate ; the great lakes excavated in the olden times are silted up; the temples and religious edifices are in decay ; the streets are covered with jungle ; and the old weaver families have migrated elsewhere to seek a scanty subsistence, and their old ancestral villages know them not.**

Speeches and Papers on Indian Qusstions, Pp. 106, 90, 81.

Mr. G. Subramania Iyer.

Formerly Editor of the 'Hindu' a leading daily of Madras.

Millions of workmen who pursued hereditary occupations, which called into exercise their intelligence and imaginations, and who therefore led a life of decent means and self-respect, have been reduced to a condition of abject poverty, having become agricultural labourers or day-labourers in towns. Agriculture has become the sole occupation of the great bulk of the nation, who, earning *much lower wages than their forefathers did*, degenerate in vitality and add to the annual mortality of the country, to the disease and suffering of the people, and to the burden of the earning classes by setting on the world at large ever-increasing numbers of weaklings, cripples, and men smitten with infirmity and disease. It is the hypocritic cry of the apologists of British rule in India that the investment of British capital furnishes means o employment to hundreds of thousands of labourers who would otherwise have remained a burden on the income of the villagers or competed with other coolies in towns. But it seldom occurs to them to ask themselves how such a state of things has to come to pass. It is nothing but the heartless industrial vandalism of Britain that has brought it about, and to-day we are called upon to admire the feeble palliation of its effects in the factories, mines, and plantations owned by the very authors of the evil. The industrial greatness of Britain was built on the ruin of India, and the classes that have been ruined have no hope, under existing political conditions, of the advent of better times.

Some Economic Aspects of British Rule in India, P. 249.

Mr. H. J. S. Cotton on Ruralization.

Not a year passes in which the commissioners and district officers do not bring to the notice of Government that the manufacturing classes from all parts of the country are becoming impoverished. ....Agriculture, is everywhere expadning at the expanse of manufacturing industry.

Quoted from the Hindu Civilization during British Rule.

Mr. E. B. Hewell on the Degeneration of Arts and Crafts.

This chapter cannot be better concluded than in the strong protest of a high English official of very long standing—Mr. E. B. Hewell, against depriving the Indian fellow-subjects of their magnificent heritage of artistic culture and draining the vitality of Indian craftsmanship by the cursed policy of *Laissez Faire* of the State.

'By the official boycott of the Indian master builder we also boycott not only all the higher handicrafts for which India has always been one of the greatest schools in the world—wood and stone carving and inlaying, metal-work, lacquer-work terra-cotta and tile-work—but the fine arts as well. It is chiefly through this official neglect of Indian architecture and contempt for Indian art that the Indian aristocracy now fill their palace with tenth-rate European pictures, instead of employing the Indian artists, descended from the court painters of Akbar, Jahangir and Shah Jahan, to decorate their *chitra-salas* or picture halls, with splendid fresco paintings, as they did in the days of the Great Mogul.

I will now turn to the economic, or industrial side of the question. Here, too, the official policy has been characterised by just the same ineptitude and lack of imagination as on the artistic side. While the governments of Europe have been vying with each other in their efforts to revive the old traditions of craftsmanship, and while India possesses in the inherited skill of her millions of artisans a source of enormous potential wealth, which is steadily deteriorating mainly from the want of technical knowledge and proper organisation, the only policy of the Anglo-Indian administration has been to encourage the propagation of the crude barbarities of the factory system from which Europe is now trying to emancipate herself.

While the *Government of India for fifty years has completely neglected the home industries*, which represent by far the largest proportion of India's industrial wealth, its efforts to develop export markets for Indian handicrafts have been wholly futile and unproductive; so much so that other countries in Europe are now keenly exploiting the field which the Indian handicraftsman ought to make entirely his own.

So while Austria, Holland, Germany and Italy are developing profitable handicrafts at India's expense, the Indian handicraftsmen are being driven to agriculture or into the factories of the capitalist, both from want of efficient instruction and organisation, and by the direct influence of our wholly unintelligent system of artistic administration.

Hindustan Rev., April, 1909.

CHAPTER V.

EFFECTS OF FREE TRADE ON AGRICULTURE IN ENGLAND AND INDIA.

There is now a universal conviction that the policies of Free-trade and non-interference of the State have well nigh strangled English Agriculture. The import of cheap foreign agricultural products has caused an irrepairable mischief in so far as it has ruined that most important industry. The extent of the evil has now been brought fully home when the unexpected has happened. The cry of 'back to the land' has been raised in all quarters. A vast amount of literature advocating the resurrection of agriculture is fast springing up.

(A.) 4,000,000 ACRES THROWN OUT OF THE PLOUGH.

Indeed, the dismal decline of English agriculture may be judged by the facts that four million acres of arable land have been thrown out of the plough during the last forty years.

(B) INCREASING DEPENDENCE ON THE FOREIGNERS.

Then there has been an increasing rural exodus in industrial towns, and England has been raising ever less and less of even the primary necessities of life. While in 1860, nearly three-quarters of wheat was grown at home, in 1915, England only produced one-fifth of it.

(C.) DECREASE OF LIVE STOCK.

The official records show that during the thirty years from 1884 to 1914, there has been a terrible decrease of 2,572, 067 acres in arable land, an increase of 2,031,929 acres under permanent grass, and a decline of 850,173 heads of live stock.

(D) MR. STEAD'S ESTIMATE.

Mr. Alfred Stead in a recent issue of the *Review of Reviews* thus justly complained of the blind neglect of agriculture by the responsible state :—

" While the area under wheat had been reduced in 1887 by fully 1,590,000 acres from 1853-60, the average crop of the years 1883-86 was below the average crop of 1853-60 by more than 40,000,000 bushels ; and this deficit alone represented the food of more than 7,000,000 *inhabitants*. In 1910 the total acreage under wheat was 1,809,000 acres, showing a further shrinkage of 693,000 acres from 1886. Thus we see that increased importation of wheat and other agricultural produce was not primarily a result of increase in population, but because land went out of cultivation at an astounding rate, no fewer than 2,000,000 acres ceasing to be productive."

(E) DECAY OF ENGLISH AGRICULTURE SUMMARIZED.

The following table summarizes (1) the agricultural position in 1872 and 1913 for England and Wales :—

	Total cultivated area 1,000 acres.	Arable Land 1,000 acres.	Wheat 1,000 acres.	Wheat per cent. of arable-land.	Total value of produce £ Millions.
1872	23,830	13,839	3,337	24·1	106·01
1913	24,375	10,362	1,663	16·1	98·08

It is clear that in spite of a little increase in the cultivated area, arable land under cereals and green crops has suffered a terrible decline of about 3½ million acres, but the loss sufferred by wheat land is no less appalling. *1,674,000 Acres of wheat land have gone out of cultivation* and nothing but grass grows where the valuable cereal crops used to be seen. Hence the total value of agricultural produce has declined from 106 millions pounds sterling to 98.

VALUE OF THE LOSS.

But Sir Inglis Palgrave estimates that the agricultural loss from 1874 to 1904 amounted to 1700 millions pounds sterling, that is, the loss was more than twice the national debt which

(1) Agriculture After the War.

stood at 794,498,100 £ in 1904. Ten years after the loss amounted to about three times the national debt.

FREE TRADE AND AGRICULTURAL DECAY.

The main cause of this continuous decline of British agriculture and the steady conversion of arable land into grass is the open-door policy of the state which permitted the import of cheap foreign wheat into the country. The position of wheat-exporting England under the regime of protection has been totally reversed under the Free-trade regime. British agriculture acutely 'suffers from the free competition of the wheat raised on the boundless plains of America.

Free Trade and landlessness have combined in destroying our rural industries."[1]

Mr. A. D. Hall speaking of the cause of the decline of British agriculture writes : "This process was undoubtedly brought about in the earlier part of the period by the great fall in prices which set in during the later 'seventies and 'eighties."[2]

GERMAN AGRICULTURE UNDER PROTECTION.

While loudest lamentations about the decay of British agriculture on account of the Free Trade policy of the state are, on the one hand, being continuously heard from all quarters, agricultural prosperity has, on the other, been enormously increasing

1. J. Ellis Barker in the Daily Mail Year Book, 1910, P. 40.
2. Agriculture after the War.

in Germany, only because the German state has all along vigilantly protected agrarian interests and guided and encouraged agriculturists in improving their industry by all means.

While decadence, depression and darkness are universally prevalent in the British agricultural world, progress, prosperity and profusion are generally visible in German agriculture.

Why? because the Germans fully realised that

'The German Empire will collapse without firing a shot when German agriculture collapses.'

While this assertion of the German military hero, Moltke, emphatically expresses the keynote of the attitude of the German state and people towards agriculture, the Gospel of German Agrarianism has been admirably epitomised by Von Rumker as follows:—

"Germany's armaments by land and sea and her industrial and commercial development are pointless and hopeless from the national standpoint except upon the basis of Germany's national ability to feed her own population."

All along for so many years the German ideal has been that Germany should feed and support her own people and be independent of foreign countries and foreign products of all kinds; hence she built up a strong tariff wall to defend her home market against foreign aggression. The customs duties on the chief agricultural products about the year 1911 were as follows:—

Wheat, 5s. 6d. per 100 kilos; rye, 5s.; oats, 5s.; malt barley, 4s. , fodder barley ; 1s. 4d.; maize, 3s. ; meal, 10s. 2d. Live stock pay from 8s. to 9s. per double hundredweight, slaughtered cattle (meat), 27s. 6d. per double hundredweight; butter, 20s., cheese, 15s., eggs 2s.

Protection has really given an unprecedented fillip to German agriculture. While the cultivated area was almost doubled in 40 years from 1856 to 1896, the extension of agriculture made prodigious progress in the next 16 years.

The area under principal crops in thousand hectares was.

	1896-7	*1913*
Wheat ...	1,927	4,935
Rye ...	5,982	16,035
Barley ...	1,653	4,134
Oats ...	3,979	11,095
Potatoes ...	3,053	8,530
Hay ...	5,909	14,808
Beat ...	435	1,369
Hops ...	41	68
	22,979	60,974

Thus the area under cultivation has increased by 261 per cent. during sixteen years alone, but as the output per hectare has also been rapidly increasing, the value and quantity of the total agricultural produce in the German Empire must have grown at a remarkable rate. It is protection alone that has enabled Germany not only to shut out the cheap agricultural products of foreign countries, and thus to save her agriculture from being crushed like England, but ultimately to see her agrarian industry as prosperous and progressive as her marvellously developing manufacturing industries. *(See Notes at the end of this chapter.)*

EFFECTS OF FREE-TRADE ON INDIAN AGRICULTURE

While English Agriculture has been strangled by the Free Trade policy of the State, Indian Agriculture has most severely suffered from the twofold policy of state indifference and exploitation. Some of the most revolting consequences have already been shown, while others remain to be revealed to the reader.

COMPARATIVE WHEAT YIELDS.

The present low condition of Indian agriculture can be best understood by comparing the *wheat yields per acre* of the thirty following countries :—

		Bushels per acre.			Bushels per acre.
1	Denmark	... 44·90	7	Sweden	... 30·63
2	Belgium	... 36·43	8	New Zealand	... 29·88
3	Holland	... 35·53	9	Egypt	... 26·32
4	Great Britain and Ireland	32·41	10	Norway	... 24·53
			11	France	... 22·22
5	Switzerland	... 31·81	12	Luxemburg	... 22·15
6	Germany	... 30·63	13	Asutria	... 19·92

		Bushels per acre.			Bushels per acre.
14	Japan	... 19·33	23	*India*	... *11·44*
15	Canada	... 19·03	24	Australia	... 10·30
16	Hungary	... 18·44	25	Argentina	... 10·26
17	Chile	... 17·55	26	Russia in Europe	... 9·81
18	Bulgaria	... 15·46	27	Algeria	... 9·52
19	United States	... 14·72	28	Russia in Asia	... 9·36
20	Italy	... 14·42	29	Uruguay	... 8·33
21	Serbia	... 12·94	30	Tunis	... 4·49
22	Spain	... 13·53			

COTTON, MAIZE AND BARLEY YIELDS.

	Barley	*Maize*	*Cotton.*
Belgium	51	...	...
Netherlands	47	...	...
Germany	34	19	...
U, Kingdom	33	...	...
France	23	30	...
Austria	23	18	...
Hungary	22	19	...
India	13	16	88
U. S. A.	...	25	233
Australia		23	

Thus Denmark has the heaviest wheat crops as compared with all other countries. The average yield of wheat is now almost four times that of India, while in 1890 it was but 37 bushels and in 1880, 31 bushels. Such a heavy yield can be explained by the use of improved methods, the latest and the best machinery and the enterprise and intelligence of the people.

A summary of the history of Danish agricultural progress cannot but be intensely interesting and instructive to every reader. It would serve to throw a searchlight on the lowest status of the agricultural industry of our own country.

DANISH AGRICULTURE.

"Denmark has already been mentioned as a country possessing an exceptionally high proportion of arable land, but Denmark is even more instructive as an example of how a country can regenerate its agriculture within a comparatively short space of time. After the disastrous war of 1864 a great national movement towards education took place; the results of that movement in the development of agriculture are seen in the following figures.

Year.	Cultivated area, 1,000 acres.	Corn and other crops.	Rotation and permanent grass.
1871	6,412	1,837	3,575
1912	7,289	4,522	2,767

The effect of the extension of the cultivated area and other improvements is most strikingly to be seen in the numbers of the live stock, as follows:—

Year.	Total cattle.	Milch cows.	Pigs.
1871	1,238,898	...	442,421
1881	1,470,078	898,790	527,417
1914	2,462,862	1,310,268	2,496,686

Nor has the improvement been confined to numbers and acreage ; from the following table it will be seen how the yield of cereals has been raised by selection of better varieties, more fertilizers and improved cultivation.

Denmark.				England.			
Years.	Wheat.	Barley.	Oats.	Years.	Wheat.	Barley.	Oats.
	Bushels per acre.				Bushels per acre.		
1888—92	34·6	29·9	32·2	1885—94	29·4	33·1	40·6
1908—12	42·0	36·5	41·3	1902—11	31·8	33·4	42·3

The average Danish yield has increased by 24 per cent. in twenty years and now overtops the English, which only increased in seveteen years by 4 per cent., a barely significant figure.

The average annual yield of butter per cow was estimated in 1864 as about 80 ℔, by 1887 it had risen to 116 ℔., by 1908 to 220 ℔., and 1914 to 229 ℔. In the competition between herds as to butter production, the tests and observations for which extend over two years, the average production of butter per cow in the four prize winning herds in 1897-9 was a trifle over 300 ℔. per annum ; in 1911-13 in the four prize winning herds it had reached the astonishing average of 445 ℔.

Naturally this progress in the industry has been attended by an increase in the numbers of people "living by agriculture," as follows:

Year	No. of Persons
1870	... 788,735
1911	... 969,227

Now all this remarkable advance within half a century has been achieved deliberately by the educative activity in its widest sense of the state, working it is true on a favourable soil—the temper of a people who were rousing themselves to shake off the effects of defeat.

In the face of these figures, which cover the period during which as the records show British farming was declining, will any one be found seriously to maintain that the stimulus of the state cannot be applied to agriculture and that our farmers know how to make the best use of the land when left to themsevles" Pp. 100-103. A. D. Hall's Agriculture After the War.

Such are the splendid achievements of the Danes in agriculture, but mainly on account of the active aid of the State and persistent assistance of an even-growing scientific knowledge. The Danish yield of wheat per acre is the heaviest in the world, it is four times that of India, but 'in his very valuable lecture at the Royal Institution the other day, Professor R. H. Biffen said that twice the Danish figure can be achieved now, and that no one may venture to name the further upward limit.

The New Statesman, May 12,1917,- P. 131).

But what do we find in India? The lowest yield in the world and the law of diminishing returns in full force!

PROGRESSIVE DECREASE IN AVERAGE YIELD.

Such has not been the heart-breaking condition of Indian agriculture in past times. The Hcn'ble Mr. Mirza Abdul Husain, K. B., has conclusively shown* from figures taken from the *Ayean-i-Akbrai* that, first, the Indian soil has deteriorated and, secondly, that there is something wrong with our system of agriculture. His figures can be summarized thus :—

AVERAGE YIELD PER ACRE.

	As told in Ayean-i-Akbari.	*To-day*	*Other countries.*
Rice	1,338 lbs.	800	2500 (Italy)
Wheat	1,155 ,,	660	1500
Cotton	223 ,,	52	400 (Egypt) 300 (America)

* Indian Review of June, 1911, P. 400.

The latest average yield per acre of various crops for the whole of India for the period of three years form 1912-13 to 1914-15 has been calculated by us as below:—

		lbs.
Rice	...	836
Wheat	...	702
Sugar, raw	...	2199
Tea	...	503
Cotton, ginned	..	83
Jute	...	257
Linseed	...	282
Sesamum	...	209
Rape	...	418
Groundnut	...	996
Indigo	...	19

Thus, there has been without doubt, a large deterioration in the productive power of the Indian soil. If further evidence be required, we cannot do better than quote the memorable words of the late illustrious patriot and statesman, Mr. G. K. Gokhale.

"The exhaustion of the soil is proceeding fast, the cropping is becoming more and more inferior, the crop-yield per acre, already the lowest in the world, is declining still further."

This view has been contradicted by Mr. Dutta in his Enquiry, Vol. 1, pp. 68—74. But the whole evidence resting upon facts, figures and quotations is full of very interesting contradictions and revelations. While he attempts to show that there has been no progressive exhaustion of the soil and the average outturns have not decreased, his witnesses often err into truth as shown in the following passages :—

'A poll of agriculturists would give a vast majority in favour of the view that fertility has decreased.' After detailing the reasons, he proceeds. 'Thus, it is probably true for the greater part of the provinces, that the land **is less productive now than it was at some particular period, or periods in the past."** *Director of Agriculture, U. P.*

'In the present day practically all good land has been taken up and regularly cultivated and much land that is really unfit for cultivation is also cultivated. This latter class of land produces very poor crops and, of necessity, *brings down the average outturn per acre.' Director of Agriculture, Bombay.*

'The supply of cattle-dung, practically the only manure used in the province, has been greatly reduced, and what there is of it, is reserved principally for that comparatively small area which is devoted to commercial crops like jute, sugar-cane, and tobacco, to the deprivation of the *rice lands which consequently are less productive than before.* Moreover, with the extension of cultivation, inferior descriptions of land which had been lying waste in former times were brought under the plough, *caused a still further depression in the average yield of land.* There can be no doubt that in the permanently cultivated parts of the country where the soil is under continuous cultivation from year to year and gets no benefit either from river silt or from long periodical rest, *the average outturn of land peracre* is less now than it used to be (say, 50 or 100 years ago.) *Mr. B. C. Bose of the Assam Agricultural Department.'*

Let us now refer to the conclusions of Mr. Dutta himself. "(A) With an increase in the pressure of population on the soil and increased demands for agricultural products from other countries, new lands had to be broken up. The produce of this inferor land cannot be so good as that of the richer soils, and consequently the addition of these poorer lands *has diminished, to some extent, the average yield per acre for India as a whole.*

(*B*) Non-food crops, such as jute and cotton, have in some areas displaced food crops or ousted them from the richer soils, and *also have affected the average yield of food grains per acre.*

(*C*) *Most of the Indian witnesses*, whom we examined, appeared to be under the belief that *there has been a decrease in the supply of agricultural products, owing to inefficient tillage of the land.*

(*D*) *The Indian soil has reached maximum impoverishment.* Thus, it seems to be a universal belief in India that the average yield of agricultural land has decreased, although it is another matter that it is not measurable in statistics or it is slow and insignificant. But it is a revelation to read that 'in India also the so called worn-out soils, having been under cultivation for a considerable period of years, *have long since reached a stage of more or less maximum impoverishment*, and that the average crop outturns in so far as they depend on the fertility of the soil have been in a more or less stationary condition for many years.'

Extract from the Report of the Deccan Riot's Commission, 1875.

STRIKING REVELATIONS.

Cultivation has reached its limits. The area of six cultivated acres per head of agricultural population must, considering the precariousness of the climate, be taken to mean that the produce of a good season of but three acres is available to each person of the cultivating class, half of the area of six acres being deducted on account of bad seasons, and the average yield being thus reduced to about half a *good* crop per annum. Comparing this with Guzerat, where the rainfall is rarely deficient, we find that each member of the ryot's family here has yearly the net produce of three acres of 8 annas assessment, while in Guzerat each person has the produce of two acres of Rs. 2-13-4 assessment, the former paying Rs. 3, the latter Rs. 5-11, to Government, the net produce being in the case of the latter both of much higher value and having the additional advantage of not being received all at once. It has been estimated that the yearly cost of food and necessaries to each member of a Kunbi's family is about Rs. 25. Admitting that the food consumed by his family does not cost the ryot the market value, it is nevertheless plain from the figures of estimated yield of land, that in a year of average rainfall his receipts from six acres—two of each kind of soil—will leave a very narrow margin for Government assessment and expenses amongst which the interest on the sowkar's loans in bad years must count as a current and unavoidable charge.

The deficit which frequently exists is made up by the produce of stock and of the diary and by the labour of the kunbi and that of his family and his cattle.

Industry and enterprise being discouraged by pressure of debt, production is not increased.

The normal effect of a pressure of population upon land is that; so soon as extended cultivation has reached the limit of profitableness, the cultivating class by improved agriculture and increased industry to obtain more from the soil.

This result is under the present conditions, not to be looked for here; on the contrary, there is a wide-spread belief that land is not so productive as it used to be. That their present state of indebtedness prevents the ryots from making efforts to improve the outturn of their land, there can be no doubt.

Productive-ness said to be di-minishing.

Whether the land itself now yields less than formerly it is impossible to determine with certainty. Possibly the belief generally held on this point is in some measure due to the fact, that as cultivation extended until it embraced the poorest and most unprofitable soils, *the general average of returns per acre diminished.* The estimate of the cultivator was formerly based on the return of the better lands; he has now to include much inferior soil, but has not proportionately reduced his expectations.

The following causes, however, *may have operated to decrease the actual out-turn of land in cultivation.* A consequence of the payment of assessment by registered holdings instead of by actual cultivation is the discouragement of fallows. The ryot who has nothing to pay for his wastes could well afford to let his land rest and cultivate portions in rotations. During the early period of administration, the lands of this region were largely devoted to grazing purposes, and there was no direct Government demand upon the wastes so used. The encouragement given to cultivation by the survey was accompained by a discouragement to grazing, through the right of pasture being made subject to purchase from Government. The supply of manure from flocks and herds, the demand for which should have increased with this increase in cultivation, diminished, and doubtless with it must have diminished the fertility of the soil.

Thus it will be seen that while increasing population demands more from the land than it yielded 40 years ago, the conditions of agriculture have not tended to increase its fertility, and indebtedness has taken away the natural motive for industry—the hope of gain—and thereby prevented relief from the increasing pressure being sought in improved cultivation.

Extracts from the Punjab Famine Commission Report, 1878-9, Vol I, pp 299—312 on the Deterioration of tho soil.

Mr J. B. Lyall, Settlement Commissioner, Multan and Derajat Divisions.

There is a popular belief in the Punjab generally that the yield has decreased; the people often say that the virtue or blessing has gone out of the lands, and attribute the fact to the want of faith, irreligion, and lying spirit of the age. They also, however, admit in argument that it may be partly due to the fact that the land gets less rest than formerly. This I think

The true expianation of the diminution of yield which has occurred.

In countries like the Manjha which formerly depended on the rain-fall and have since got canal water, it is commonly said that the rate of yield has fallen off.

Raja Sir Sahib Dyal, K.C.S.I., of Amritsar.

In the canal irrigated villages of Gurdaspur, the people say that the canal water has injured their soil. But the truth is that they have given up the old custom of the country, under which only one crop a year was taken from the soil; viz., a rabi crop from half the land, and a kharif crop from the other half. Instead of this they try to take two crops a year (both rabi and kharif) from the same lands, and of course, the yield under such circumstances is small.

Muhammad Hyat Khan, C.S.I., Judicial Assistant Commissioner, Gurdaspur.

Owing to increase in population of the Punjab, the old custom of growing only one crop or allowing land to lie fallow for one or more years, and of cultivating Banjar land has been lost sight of, or rather it
has now become impossibleto act up to it. Nearly all Banjar land has been brought under cultivation and the old fields, divided and subdivided into several parts, have passed into the hands
of the succeeding generation, who, having only a small patrimony to depend upon, cannot help cultivating the land every year, and growing more than one crop on it.

2. The zamindars suggest the following methods for improving and preserving the natural vigor of the soil: 1. occasional rest; 2. constant ploughing; 3. manuring.

None of these suggestions can be acted upon. As already stated, owing to the smallness of the estate

owned by each individual person, it is not possible to give any material rest to the land.

In regard to 3rd suggestion, it must be said that manure is not procurable in sufficient quantity. Only the land, adjoining to the villages and those irrigated from well are manured, and the rest not. With the decrease of pasture grounds there has been a gradual falling off in the breed of cattle, and consequently a scarcity of manure

Mirza Beg, Honorary Assistant Commissioner of the Jhelum Settlement,

has been employed principally in settlement work in the Gujrat, Hazara and Jhelum Districts *for 22 years past; states that the yield of land is less than it was before British rule*, for obvious reasons. Then the cultivated area was much smaller: and therefore the best lands were selected for cultivation. For the same reason more pains could be spent on them. And the large waste area enabled the agriculturist to keep more cattle, though cultivation has now doubled in extent, population has not increased in the same ratio; consequently the agriculturist's labour is divided over a large area than before. At the same time the cropping is more steady than it was in less peaceful days.

Major E. G. Hastings, Settlement Officer, Kohat states that

Native opinion asserts that the soil has deteriorated and gives the following reasons for it: increased population, and consequently more frequent cropping with fewer rests, increased uncertainty and unseasonableness of rain-fall, less careful cultivation consequent on increased employment of tenants and go-betweens. They admit, however, that the land will yield as well as ever with fair treatment."

Colonel Sleeman on the Deterioration of Indian Soil.

But the question of the diminishing fertility of the Indian soil is no new one. Even as far back as 1844, Colonel Sleeman in his "Rambles" devotes one chapter to this subject. Some portions of the conversation recorded in that chapter will prove highly interesting even at this date :—

"But in spite of all this "*zolm*" (oppression) said the old man, "there was then more *burkut*" (blessings from above) than now. The lands yielded more returns to the cultivator, and he could maintain his little family better upon five acres than he can now upon ten.

"To what, my old friend, do you attribute this very unfavorable change in the productive powers of your soil?"

"Here, sir, we all attribute these evils to the dreadful system of perjury, which the practices of your judicial courts have brought among the people."

"True, we have hardly any of us enough to eat; but that is the fault of the Government, that does not leave us enough—that takes from us as much when the season is bad as when it is good!"

"It cannot be disputed that the *burket* (blessing from above) is less under you than it used to be formerly, and that the lands yield less to our labor."

"Then why do you not give the land rest by leaving it longer fallow, or by a more frequent alternation of crops relieve it?"

"Because we have now increased so much, that we should not get enough to eat were we to leave it to fallow; and unless we tilled it with exhausting crops we should not get the means of paying our rents to Government."

Vol. II, pp. 109—112.

THE POLICY OF INVERTIBRATE DRIFT CONDEMNED.

That sympathetic observer of the low condition of Indian agriculture and manufacture struck a note of warning, but it fell flat on deaf ears. More than 70 years have elapsed since that pathetic appeal, yet the economic position of the Indian agriculturist has not been bettered as regards his command over nature. The Colonel said :—

'There is hardly anything to indicate our existence as a people or a Government in this country; and it is melancholy to think, that in the wide extent of country over which I have travelled, there should be found so few signs of that superi-

Colonel Sleeman's Rambles. Vol. II. p. 110.

ority in science and in arts which we boast of, and really do possess, and ought to make conducive to the welfare and happiness of the people in every part of our dominions. The people and the face of the country are just what they might have been, had they been governed by police officers and tax-gatherers as from the Sandwich Islands.'

AGRICULTURAL OUTTURN IN 1851 AND 1914-16.

It may be interesting to add a table of agricultural produce per acre in Bushels in England and some countries of the western continent, extracted from the *Edinburgh Review*, of July, 1851 :—*

	Great Britain.	New Brunswick.	New York.	West Canada.
Wheat ...	24	18	14	13
Barley ...	34	27	16	17
Maize ...	...	36½	25	...
Turnips ...	420	390	88	...

The yield of wheat per acre, in the Punjab was 14 maunds equal to about 18 bushels of 60 pounds each in the same year, just equal to that in New Brunswick.

But what is the yield of wheat in the Punjab now-a-days ? In the Punjab Administration Report of 1914-15 we read that 'the sown area

*Selections from the Punjab Correspondence of the Administration, Vol. I, P. 223.

of wheat amounted to 9,915,507 acres—an increase of 17 per cent. on last year and 16 per cent. better than the normal. The total outturn is estimated at 3,396,453 tons or 32 *per cent. above the normal.*" (P. 38.)

Calculating on the basis of such an exceptionally favourable year, we find that the

average yield of wheat per acre comes to 767 pounds against 1080 in 1851—a terrible decrease of 313 lbs. on one acre of land. Such is the progress of agriculture in the prosperous (?) Punjab after sixty-four years working of the cursed policies of Free-trade and *laissez faire.*

But great revelations are yet in store for us. The next Administration Report informs us that the total area under wheat was 8,991,542, and

the total yield was 2,167,561 tons or 17 per cent. short of the normal. (P. 34). This gives an average yield of 540 lbs. an acre, exactly half of 1851. It is 17 per cent. short of the normal, hence the normal yield is only 650 lbs.

EVER INCREASING PRESSURE ON LAND IN INDIA.

No civilized country on earth has got such an unbearable pressure on land as is to be seen in this poor country. The productive area in British Provinces is much too small for the actual population. The figures for the four successive censuses are given below :—

Acres per Inhabitant.[1]

	1881	1891	1901-2	1911-2
Bengal ...	1·5	0·8	1·12	...
Bombay ...	1·7	1·6	1 41	1·3
Madras ...	1·3	0·8	·68	·79
Assam ...		0·5	·78	·85
Punjab ...	1·2	1·3	1·05	1·11
Oudh ...	·81	0·7	·73	·75
N. W. Provinces ...		0·8		
Burmah ...		1·5	1·08	1·09
Central P. ...	1·67	2·4	1·9	1·79
B. India ...	1·04	1·0	0·86	0·88

This table alone is eloquent enough to reveal the economic tendencies working in India. The figures are incontrovertible proofs of the deepening poverty of the people. It is hardly possible for us to comprehend how the standard of living among the masses can go up, how greater and greater prosperity can be the result in the face of these stern and solid facts? Unless and until these calculations are shown to be wrong, we are obliged to draw the conclusion that the Indian people have been relying more and more on a decreasing share of land with a more and more reduced productive capacity.

The following Extract from the Famine Commission Report 1901, Part III, Section VI-page 106, would

1 Figures for 1891 have been taken from Mulhull's Dictionary, but others have been computed from the figures of population given in the Time's Indian Year Book, of 1914 P. 488 and tho.e of net cropped area from the Moral aud Material Progress Reports, 1911-12 (P. 226) and 1882-83 (P. 182).

throw some light on the policy of the Government on this point.

The (*Ryotwari*) system was devised for small cultivators; there was no intention to create large holdings. "There would seem," wrote Captain Wingate, one of the authors of the system, "to be few grounds for anticipating the establishment of wealthy agriculturists cultivating large farms under any circumstances in India. Our measures have to be framed from the class of small farmers who now prevail universally." Accordingly the 'field' was designed to contain "the extent of land capable of being cultivated by a pair of bullocks." This was the theory; but the facts of existing holdings and their boundaries were acccepted and fitted, as best might be, into the new scheme.

PRESSURE ON LAND IN VARIOUS COUNTRIES.

As it is by comparative study alone that we can learn where we stand and realize our actual economic condition, we will quote from Mulhull's Dictionary figures to show the *productive area* per inhabitant in various countries.

Acres per inhabitant in 1895.

Great Britain	0·91	Austria	2·05
Ireland	3·30	Italy	1·75
France	2·30	Spain and Portugal	2·90
Germany	1·70	U. S. A.	8·90
Russia	5·60	*India*	1·0

Mulhull's Memorable Evidence

Two Acres of Land Necessary for Subsistence.

As a general rule, according to Mr. Mulhull, two productive acres are required for the support of each inhabitant, and where this ratio does not exist food must be imported. It appears, thus, that Great Britain, Germany and Italy are overpopulated, while Russia, Spain and Ireland have not sufficient inhabitants.

But what About India?

·86 acres per head in India in 1895.

Just one acre of land falls to the lot of every Indian on the average and only one half acre to the lot of 5·5 million inhabitants living in Assam!

Hence India ought to import food from abroad. Her inhabitants ought to have at least two acres of land for subsistence, but with the lowest yields of wheat and rice in the civilized world, the Indians ought to have even more land, but they possess one acre alone. Yet another most wonderful fact is that India is the largest exporter of farm produce. In 1895 products worth 56 millions out of 390 millions were exported out of the country. Hence every Indian had to support himself on the produce of ·86 acre of productive area in 1895.

Taking for granted that only two acres of land even with the lowest productivity, are required for each inhabitant in India, it is more than evident that being short of 1·14 acres, he must be starving in mind, body and soul.

.6 Acre Per Head in India in 1911.

But let us not pause here. We have seen that in the years 1901 and 1911, each Indian had ·86 and ·88 acre of productive land for his support. From this, we have to deduct that large area upon which our ever growing exports of raw material are raised. The value of our total exports in 1894-5 was 1,089 million rupees but in 1911-2, it rose to 2,288, *i.e.*, it was more than doubled. Deducting twice of what we substracted before, we reach an

average of ·60 acre for the support of every inhabitant of India in 1911.

While two acres of good productivity are required for each person, every Indian had to support himself in 1911 on six-tenth of an acre on the average, while 16 years before, he enjoyed ·86 of an acre. With these sturn and solid facts before us, who would believe that India is getting more and more prosperous? Let us now look at this Incarnated Poverty of India from another point of view.

Mr. K L. Dutta has discussed this subject in another way. Although the method adopted by him is subject to weighty objections, yet his conclusions fully corroborate our enquiry. It would be safe to state his conclusion in his own words :—

"**Growth of population compared with growth of cultivation and of production of food grains.**

The following table compares the growth of population with that of production of foodgrains and the extension of cultivation :—

+ Commercial Statistics of India, 1916, P. 119.

	Average. of the quinquennium 1890-91 to 1894-95	Average of the quinqennium 1895-96 to 1899-00	Average of the quinquenium 1900-01 to 1904-05	Average of the quinquennium 1905-06 to 1909-10	1910-11	1911-12
Population	100	101·6	103·7	105·7	107.8	108·4
Total area under cultivation	100	98	103	105	108	106
Area under food grains	100	96	101	102	106	103
Production of food grains	100	18	105	99	113	109
Index numbers of Net available supply	100	99	105	100	113	...

"It may safely be concluded from the above, that population has increased by a large percentage in the period under enquiry than either the total area under cultivation, the area under foodgrains or the total production of foodgrains, or, in other words, the requirements of foodgrains for internal consumption have increased in a larger proportion than the total production of foodgrains.

It should, however, be mentioned that the total consumption of foodgrains includes not only the consumption as human food, but also consumption as seed grain and cattle food."

TRUNNIER'S EVIDENCE.

Any density of a large country approaching 200 to a square mile implies mines, manufactures, or the industry of cities. *Report on the Census of England and Wales 71871.*

In the pastoral and agricultural counties of England the number of persons per square mile even now nowhere exceeds 200, and in some it is much less. 'It would seem that Trunnier's dictum regarding Germany to the effect that agriculture alone is unable to support more than 250 persons to the square mile is equally true of England, and in fact of all parts of Europe.'

Mr. Gait then goes on to remark that 'while in Europe agriculture is unable to support more than 250 persons to the square mile, in India there are some purely agriculture tracts where it already supports three or even four times that number and others where it *cannot* support a tenth of it.'

But the worst feature of our economic life is the growing congestion on lands whose productivity is slowly diminishing. With the growth of population and inadequate extension of cultivation, the number of persons per square mile has very much increased during these forty years from 1871 to 1911. But the real pressure of population on land can be realized by observing the number of persons living on the *cultivated* area. Such figurss are not available for 1871; however, the figures of 1911 would throw a searchlight on the economic condition of the people of this country.

Mean Density per square mile in

	1871 of total area.	1911 of total area.	Of cultivated area.
Oudh ...	468	427 (Oudh and N. W. Provinces together)	829 (Oudh and N. W. Provinces together)
N. W. Provinces	378		
Bengal ...	397	551	1162
Madras ...	226	291	785
Mysore ...	187	197	600
Punjab and N.	173	177	453
W. Provinces.		165	528
Bombay ...	131	145	444
Berar ...	129	122 (Berar and Central Provinces together)	360 (Berar and Central Provinces together)
Central Provinces	97		
Assam ...	99	115	766
Coorg ...	84	111	792
British Burma...	31	53	515

India C. R. 1911, P. 25.
India Censns Reports of 1871 P. 6 and 1911 P. 48.

The consequences of this abnormal pressure on land were admirably brought out by Mr. Har Kishen Lal, in his Presidential address before the Indian Industrial Conference of 1912.

' Subtracting the land utilised for supplying foreign markets, from the total area under cultivation, we shall find that what is left does not represent more than two-thirds of an acre per head of the total Indian population. India, therefore feeds and to some extent clothes its population from what two-thirds of an acre per head can produce, there is probably no country in the world where the land is required to do so much." Further on he says: "It may also be inferred that the average income of the peasant cultivator is very small. The net profit obtainable from an acre of land seems to us altogether inadequate for one person's support; and our conclusion would be the same if we take a family of five, namely, two adults, and three children and a holding of five acres as a unit, but according to Indians' ideas and a traditional stand and of very thrifty and frugal living, five acres of good irrigated land will support such a faimly comfortably. But all the land in India is not very good, and every peasant's holding is not a five acres plot. Some peasants hold considerably more than five acres, consequently others hold less. And when we get down to the man who holds less than five acres of land, and that of poor quality, then there is want and a hard struggle for existence. That man and his household are poor even in the Indian sense of the term." "Below the peasant class there is a large class of landless folk, who also find support from the land by working for the well-to-do cultivators in return for the wage." "There are also other residents at the village who do not actually cultivate land, but yet are indirectly supported from it; such are the village blackmiths and the carpenter who make ploughs and other agricultural implements, the barber, the cobbler or leather worker, the washerman and the waterman, all these recieve doles of fixed amounts from the grain heaps at harvest time, and other dues and perquisites." "No one." The writer continued to say, "would pretend that this Indian village life is ideal, or unaccompanied by much that is distressing to the human mind to contemplate."

NOTE I—LIVE STOCK IN GERMANY.

A barometer of German agricultural prosperity is to be found in the rapid increase in German live stock.

Class of stock.		1873 millions.	1914 millions.
Cattle	...	15·77	22
Pigs	...	7·12	25*
Horses	...	3·35	4·52 (in 1912)
Goats	...	2·32	3
Sheep	...	24·99	5

While on the one hand there has been a marked reduction in the number of sheep, on the other, there has been a large increase in cattle

* Col. II. from Statesman's Year-Book, 1915.

and a striking increase in pigs. The decline in sheep is not to be deplored, because pig-keeping is twice as profitable as sheep-breeding.

DECLINE IN INDIAN LIVESTOCK.

While under the shelter of a strong tariff wall and a most active state aid, the German live stock has made tremendous strides, British and Indian live stock have suffered deplorable decreases. Mr. K. L. Dutta's conclusive words on the scarcity of cattle in India are—'These figures bear testimony to the deplorable effects of famine, the inevitable result of which has always been to reduce the number of cattle. The number of plough-cattle in the latest year (1908-09) was lower than in the commencement (1893-94'). With an increase in the national and a large increase in the agricultural populations, the result of sixteen years' progress in India has been that cattle show a percent. decrease of 4 in Bundelkhand, 3 in Agra Provinces (N. and W.), 18 in Gujarat, 20 in Deccan, 4 in Berar, 2 in Madras North and 5 in Madras West. There have been increases in eight circles, but generally they have lagged behind the growth of the agricultural classes. Agricultural India is extremely poor in pigs, sheep, goats, horses when compared with the European and American countries, her animal wealth mainly consists of cattle,—cows, bulls, bullocks, and baffaloes. But the following statements, keeping in view the German live stock which has been given here as representative of other progressive countries, reveals the low economic condition of India :—

DISTRIBUTION OF LIVE STOCK 1913.*

		Cattle in thousands.	Population in millions.
India	...	11,379	315
U. S. A.	...	69,080	107
Russia-European	...	50,588	174
Argentine	...	29,124	7
Germany	...	20,691	66
Austria-Hungary	...	16,898	50
France	...	14,298	40
U. Kingdom	...	11,826	45

CATTLE PER HEAD.

Argentine	...	4·0	Austria-Hungary	·34
U. S. A.	...	·65	Germany	·31
India ...	...	·38	United Kingdom	·26
France ...	...	·35	Russia	·23

NOTE II.

Von Bulow on Protection for German Agriculture.

"I was persuaded that vigorous agriculture is necessary for us from the economic, but, above all, from the national and social points of view" . . . "Without great and flourishing agriculture by its side, industry would soon use up the best forces of the nation" . . . . "Agriculture is the mother of the nation's strength which industry employs."

---

*Atlas of Commercial Geography 1913, P. 13

"Our agriculture needs a protective tariff. Imported agricultural products must have a sufficiently heavy duty imposed on them to prevent the foreign supply from falling below a price at which our home agriculture can make a fair profit. The reduction of agrarain duties at the time of Caprivi's commercial policy brought about a crisis in our agriculture which it was only able to weather by dint of working with stubborn energy, and hoping for a complete change of tariff arrangements within a short time. If we sacrificed the protective tariff on agricultural products in order to lower the cost of living by means of cheap imports, the danger would arise that agricultural work would grow more and more unprofitable, and would have to be given up to a greater and greater extent. We should go the way England has gone." [1]

BRITISH AND GERMAN PRODUCTION COMPARED.

The marked difference between British Agriculture under Free Trade and German Agriculture under Protection will be visible in the production on the average 100-acre farm of Britain and Germany, *

From an examination of figures relating to production, most of which are given below, the following statements would appear to be justified :—

On each hundred acres of cultivated land :—

---

1 Imperial Germany p. 209; p. 213; p. 221—222.

* This has been summarized in the Recent Development of German Agriculture P. 6. by T. H. Middleton, Assistant Secretary, Board of Agriculture and Fishries, London.

1. The British farmer feeds from 45 to 50 persons, the German farmer feeds from 70 to 75 persons.

2. The British farmer grows 15 tons of corn, the German farmer grows 23 tons.

3. The British farmer grows 11 tons of potatoes the German farmer grows 55 tons.

4. The British farmer produces 4 tons of meat, the German farmer produce $4\frac{1}{4}$ tons.

5. The British farmer produces $17\frac{1}{2}$ tons of milk, the German farmer produce 28 tons.

6. The British farmer produces a negligible quantity of sugar, the German farmer produces $2\frac{3}{4}$ tons.

NOTE III ON AVERAGE YIELD IN 1877 AND 1913.

The Average produce of principal staples of agriculture in the Punjab as reported by District officers for the 5 years ending March 1877 and 1913 as reported in the Agricultural Statistics of India, 1913-14, pp. 388-9 is :—

	1877		1913
Wheat	... 826 lbs.	per acre	726
Rice	... 869	„	688
Inferior grains	... 665	„	602(1)
Gram	... 756	„	549
Oilseeds	... 421	„	396(2)
Cotton cleaned	... 107	„	118

Punjab Famine Com. Report, 1878 79, Vol. I, Pp. 116-117.

(1) Barley, jwar, bajra and maize have been taken.

(2) This is the yield of rapeseed alone.)

CHAPTER VI.

POVERTY PERPETUATED.

Introductory Remarks—In this chapter we mean to take up the investigation of the annual earnings of the agricultural community of India including Burma.

For an exact and comprehensive estimate of the total gross income of the agricultural population, it is necessary to know the approximately correct amount and value of the output of various kinds which may be classified under the following heads :—

(*a*)	Farm produce—		Yield of all the food and commercial crops.
(*b*)	Stock	„	meat, fish, eggs, poultry, hides, wool and animals.
(*c*)	Dairy	„	milk, ghee and curds.
(*d*)	Forest	„	timber, fuel and other minor products.

Indian statistics are quite inadequate to supply the necessary data for the calculation of the manifold items included under the four main heads, but we have to build our conclusions on the available material, aided here and there by personal investigation. However inexact and rough the method followed in the estimation of a single year's income may be, it can be relied upon for comparative purposes. In the succeeding pages an attempt has been made in reckoning the gross income and in estimating the expenses of production and then by subtraction we have arrived at the total net agricultural income. The investigation is not exhaustive and accurate, yet so far as it goes, it may be accepted as a fairly correct barometer of the economic condition and progress of the vast millions who subsist on this one industry.

THE BLEEDING INDIA SCHOOL OF WRITERS.

It is essential to mention at the outset that we have not followed the method adopted by Messrs. Hyndman, Dadabhai Naroji and Digby—liberal, broad minded, honest and well-meaning gentlemen who have been cried down as outright pessimists, chief detractors of British Rule in India, writers of the bleeding India school, whose figures according to Mr. J. D. Rees, M. P. are treated by "most writers on the Congress side as if they came down from heaven, whence indeed they might have come, so little relation have they to the facts on earth?" [1] Lest they should have culled their statistics not from the publications of the Government of India or of the British Parliament but *ab nubibus.*,*

1 The Real India by J. D. Rees, P. 302.

*From the Clouds.

we have ignored these writers altogether, and based our conclusions on authentic facts and figures, yet it is to be feared that gentlemen of the creed of Mr. Rees would not relish the results of our impartial and unbiased enquiry. But we will, *au grand serieux*, request Mr. Rees and other official advocates of beaurocracy to patiently hear our case and deliver judgment on the poverty or progress of India when all the *pros* and *cons* of the case are before them.

MULHULL'S ESTIMATE.

Estimate of Income Per Head in 1895.

The distinguished statistician Mulhull, estimated the value of all agricultural and animal products for the whole of British India, excluding Upper Burmah as 320 and 80 millions sterling respectively for the year 1888. But for the year 1895, the value of the total farming products for the whole of B. India was 390 million pounds. Now, according to the census of 1891, the agricultural population of British India amounted to 172 millions, from which it would appear that "the farm products average £2·6s. or 40 rupees per head of agricultural population."*

SHARERS OF AGRICULTURAL PRODUCE.

But for a correct estimate of the gross income of the agricultural population we ought to take into consideration the following items :—

(i) *Addition of Labourers*—There were 25,467,971 general labourers in that year. But

*The Dictionary of Statistics Pp. 56 and 631.

many of them must have got their subsistence by working in fields, hence they must have shared some of the agricultural produce.

(ii) Persons whose principal occupations was agriculture but who followed other professions.

(iii) Persons whose secondary occupation was agriculture.

Adding the numbers of these three items to the population, directly supported by agriculture we get the real number of persons supported by the annual agricultural produce. But even this is an understatement, for all other persons who are not directly engaged in agriculture, but living in villages, follow occupations for the support of agriculture, as barbers, chamars, potters and carpenters, weavers, watchmen, watermen, and washermen, brahmins blacksmiths, *begaries* and beggars—i. e., *nearly the whole* of rural population cannot get subsistence from any source other than the products of the farm. Consequently, from the rural population we should exclude only 10 per cent. persons as supported by occupations other than agriculture or dependent upon agriculture. The Government of the country fully subscribes to this view in the *Indian Empire*, Vol. III, P. 2 :—

'In addition to the classes above enumerated, the village communities contain many other members whose employment depends on the cultivator, and who are therefore ordinarily supported from the produce of the village fields. Many persons too combine agriculture, as a subsidiary pursuit, with some other occupation. It has been estimated that nine-tenths of the *rural* population of India live, directly or indirectly by agriculture."

According to this view, the sharers of agricultural produce amount to 179,205,077 persons, being 90 per cent. of the rural population in the year 1891.

MULHULL'S ESTIMATE REVISED.

Thus it is more than clear that in 1891 the *value of Agricultural Produce was 380 millions* and its sharers amounted to *179* millions. Therefore, the *average gross income per head* was £ 2. 3*s* 8*d*. in 1891.

But the above estimate does not include the value of the stock, dairy and forest produce. For the year 1888 Mr. Mulhull calculated it as one-fourth of the farming products. Accepting this proportion we see that the value of all kinds of agricultural produce in the year 1891 comes up to

£	390	million	value of farming	products.
£	98	,,	,,	supplementary ,,
£	488	,,	,,	agricultural produce.

This sum of 488 million pounds divided amongst 179 million souls gives an average gross income per head of £ 2 14*s*. 6*d*.

THE METHOD OF CALCULATING NET PRODUCE.

But from the gross amount we have to deduct the following main charges incurred in raising and disposing or marketing that produce :—

(1) *a.* Share of the Government in revenue, rates and cesses.

b. Share of the proprietor of the land.

(2) Amount spent in cash or kind in paying the labour bill for ploughing, sowing, weeding, watching, harvesting and other operations,

(3) Wastage of the estimated crop in reaping, drying, disposing, stocking and marketing.

(4) Seed-grains.

(5) Manures or fertilizers purchased.

(6) Agricultural implements-buying and repairing.

(7) Charges for buying, insuring and feeding plough oxen and draught animals.

(8) Charges for buying up or providing water.

(9) Tips in cash or kind to government servants.

(10) Interest.

(11) Expenses for improvements.

(12) Expenses on litigation.

(13) Lastly it should be born in mind that the total gross value of the produce is calculated on

rates prevailing in markets. But in estimating the *value of this produce to the agriculturist* some deduction must be made from its market-value on account of the cost of carriage and the profits of the grain-dealer or salesman. A deduction, on these accounts, of 10 per cent. ought to be allowed at the least.

"*Improvement*," according to the Government, means any work which adds to the letting value of land, and includes the following, namely :—

(*a*) the construction of wells, tanks and other works for the storage, supply or distribution of water, for the purpose of agriculture, or for the use of men and cattle employed in agriculture.

(*b*) the preparation of land for irrigation.

From among the 13 items, we ought to ignore the following two very big factors :—

(*a*) rents and other dues received by landlords, and

(*b*) wages obtained in kind or cash by all sorts of labourers who have directly helped to raise the produce, because these two classes of masters and servants share the produce which a cultivator has raised on his land. The other items of the expenses of production are either spent in raising that produce or handed over to the state and the non-agricultural classes.

The items of interest and litigation deserve particular attention, because the fact of the extreme indebtedness of a large section of agriculturists has been conclusively established by all observers. It cannot be denied that at the time of the sowing, most of the tenants and small peasant proprietors are greatly dependent on these money lenders, and if at this period any delay in getting a loan occurs, the proper time goes away and proper crop cannot be ensured. Somewhere it has been truly said that 'the profit of farming goes to whoever lays out the capital.' The extent of the intensive indebtedness of the Indian peasant has been thus acknowledged :—

Extract from the Famine Commission Report, 1880.

(Part II, Chapter III, Section IV—page 131)

We learn from evidence collected from all parts of India that about one-third of the landholding class are deeply and inextricably in debt, and that at least an equal proportion are in debt, though not beyond the power of recovering themselves.

Much can be written on the point how, when a cultivator becomes entangled in the meshes of even a small debt, as he inevitably does every year, he cannot get freedom from it for years together. If a cultivator contracts a debt of Rs. 100 and pays off Rs. 25 per year, he will clear off this debt at 12 per cent. only in 6 years and a debt of Rs. 200 at 9 per cent. in 14 years !

But to meet all the expenses of production detailed above, the cultivator has to borrow money on exhorbitant rates of interest which are generally above 20 per cent. per annum. Hence a very large margin ought to be allowed on this point.

RATIO OF COST TO PRODUCE.

Now a very rough idea of the proportion which expenses of production bear to total produce can be had from a table given in Mr. W Digby's 'Prosperous' British India—

It will be observed that the items of the money cost of production of Digby's statement do not include such large and important charges as those incurred in wastage and the last four factors of our list. Hence an addition is to be made for these items and a subtraction is to be affected for the important item of the wages bill of labour. That statement can be summarized as below :—

ESTIMATE OF SETTLEMENT OFFICERS.

Expenses including land Tax but excluding wages for labour-	estimated charges, for the 5 items ignored.	In-rupees. Total Expenses	Produce.
10·8	3	14	25.
8·3	2	10·3	20·
6.4	2	8·2	16

It is evident, therefore, that according to this corrected estimate, the cost of production is a little more than half the gross produce.

ESTIMATE OF RYOT.

(In rupees.)

Expenses including land-tax but excluding wages for labour.	Charges for the five items ignored.	Total expenses	Produce.
9·2	3	12·2	20
8·15	2	10·15	18
6·75	2	8·75	14

The Ryot's estimate shows that expenses of production are 60 per cent. of the gross produce, but a deduction of 10 per cent. as the difference between market and village prices from this produce has to be made to arrive at the value received by *the producers* of the produce.

FURTHER EVIDENCE.

The estimate of the money cost of production is strongly corroborated by our personal observations in the surrounding villages. A tenant holding 50 bighas of land (a bigha =20 ×20 chains has to incur the following money cost on three items alone :

	Rs.	a.	p.	
Rent to the landlord ...	0	11	0	per bigha.
Seed for the *wheat* crop 5 seers per bigha ...	0	8	0	,,
Seed for the autumn crop ...	0	4	0	,,
Wages	0	9	0	,,
	2	0	0	
Cost for 50 Bighas ...	100	0	0	
Price of produce ...	200	0	0	

Hence, 100 rupees are the maximum share of the tenant for the whole year. He has to meet all the other charges which we detailed before out of this sum and feed all the members of his family. If we take those 'other charges' to be equal to $\frac{1}{15}$ of the total charges above calculated as Rs. 100 for 50 Bighas we see that the total cost of production (deducting wages even) appreciably exceeds the value of half the gross produce to the producer.

In the M. and M. Progress Report, 1882-83, p. 194, the Government calculates the cost of growing *wheat* on manured and irrigated land at 1*s*. 6*d*. per 31 *seers*, inclusive of rent, *i. e.*, comprising all charges from the purchase of the seed to the threshing of the crop. "A market rate of 18*s*. 6*d*. the quarter implies village prices not exceeding 15*s*. or 16*s*." Thus $\frac{12}{15}$ or $\frac{12}{16}$ part of the produce is the cost of production and $\frac{3}{15}$ or $\frac{4}{16}$ is the profit of the cultivator.

Again a very large confirmatory evidence on this point is to be had in the Punjab Famine Commission Report, 1878-79. Therein typical instances of the economic condition of the agricultural population are given for each district of the Punjab. If we look to the first pages of the second volume, we find that the income and expenditure of eight cultivators stand thus:—

I Total income from all sources.		II Government share and customary charges of village menials and hired labour of all sorts.		III as per cent. of I.
574	...	325	...	58
786	...	342	...	43
65	...	46	...	72
737	...	390	...	53
93	...	101	...	109
100	...	112	...	112
1640	...	906	...	55
100	...	30	...	30

Average of these eight cases = 65½

It is evident that the two charges mentioned above cost on the average 66½ per cent. of the total income from all sources. We have still to add to the above estimate the cost of seed grains, charges on account of feeding, buying and housing cattle ; expenses incurred in procuring manures and implements, in improvements and litigation ;

and money spent on tips and as interest. All these items will mightily swell the expenditure bill and leave a small margin to the cultivator for supporting his family. On the basis of this incontrovertible evidence too, we are justified in taking the expenses of cultivation excluding the ordinary labour bill, as half of the gross produce.

NET PRODUCE.

We can now easily calculate the net produce per head of rural population.

	Million pounds.
I.—**Estimated Gross value of the produce**=	488
II.—**Ten per cent. deduction** as the difference between market and village prices=	48·8
III.—**Gross value to the producer**=	439·2
IV.—**Value when 50 per cent.** deduction as expenses of production is allowed =	219·6
V.—**Value when 60 per cent.** deduction as expenses of production is allowed =	175·7

INCOME PER HEAD.

As the net proceeds of the produce are to be shared alike by 179 million persons, we have to divide items IV and V by 179. It means that according to the first estimate

Income per head of the Agricultural Community pproximately

One pound and five shillings.

The second estimate reduces it to

Less than One pound.

Considering that the truth lies between the two and in so doing we cannot be far from the right limit, **the Average Annual Income per head of 179 Million Agriculturists amounted to seventeen Rupees in 1891.**

AGRICULTURAL INCOME IN 1880 AND 1900.

Lord Curzon, the ex-Viceroy of India in his Simla speech of October 19,1900 declared that the annual agricultural production of India and Burma averaged in value between 350 and 400 crores of rupees. But the agricultural income of India in 1880 was calculated as 350 crores, therefore it meant that the agricultural wealth of the country had remained stationary for twenty years, while the population had gone on increasing by leaps and bounds. Consequently it was pointed out that the average income *of every inhabitant of India had sunk* from Rs. 27 in 1882 to Rs. 22 in ordinary years, and to Rs. $17\frac{1}{2}$ in 1900. In order to dissipate the too pessimistic views prevailing in some quarters, His Lordship got his estimates revised and that revised total swelled to 450 crores or 300 million pounds sterling! He did not place before the public his data for calculating, revising and swelling his estimates on the two occasions, but made a bare statement that he had in his desire to be on the safe side underrated the total in his Simla speech.

The highest functionary of the state, having the whole available data and the services of great statisticians at his disposal and then underrating the agricultural income of the community by 100 crores, presents a very sorry spectacle. However, accepting these exaggerated * figures as correct we find that the average income per head in 1900 comes up to Rs. 20, or Rs. 2 higher than in 1880.

How insignificant is this *money* income of the people need not be commented upon. But this growth in the mean income of the people is really fictitious. His Lordship ought to have shown that the purchasing power of the rupee remained constant after the lapse of twenty years. If, as we know it for certain from the Price Reports, that the value of the rupee had considerably declined, how could the people buy with Rs. 20 the same amount of goods in 1900 as they could in 1880? In fact, the situation stands thus—

	1880	1900
Index No. of Income—	100	111
Index No. of Prices—	100	131 (*a*)
	100	176 (*b*)
Index No. of Purchasing	100	85 (*a*)
Power—	100	63 (*b*)

(1) Lord Curzon in India, pp. 91 and 382.

* (*a*) Lord Cromer's estimate of the average income was 27 rupees, as against the 30 rupees of Lord Curzon's Government.

(*b*) Mr. F. J. Atkinson's calculations were too far-fetched. He calculated that between 1875 and 1895 the agricultural income increased from 26 rupees to 35 rupees or 39 per cent.; the non-agricultural income from 28 rupees to 34 rupees, or 18 per cent.; the average annual income of the masses had risen from 27 rupees to 35 rupees, or 28 per cent.

It need not be mentioned that these statements go against all the evidence produced in the preceding pages.

Thus the rise in Agricultural incomes was 11 per cent., but (*a*) the rise in prices on the basis of the Atkinson's Index No. for silver prices was 31 per cent., while (*b*) on the basis of the weighted arithmetic average of index number of food grains and that of imported articles (*Variations in India Price Levels from 1862 to 1912, p. 16*), weights being 5 and 1 respectively, the rise during these twenty years alone amounted to 76 per cent. The conclusion is inevitable that the purchasing power of the community did decrease either by 15 or 37 per cent. during the same period, in spite of the rise in money incomes.

VALUE OF INDIAN FARM PRODUCE IN 1911.

Preliminary remarks—We have endeavoured to calculate the *total value of the farm products raised in the whole of India including Burma in the year 1911-12*. For this purpose, the yields of the principal crops as given in the estimates of Area and Yield of Principal Crops in India, 1914-15 have been adopted. This report contains the outturns of rice, wheat, raw sugar, tea, cotton, jute, linseed, rape and mustard, sesamum, groundnut, indigo, barley, jwar, bajra, maize and gram.

Their Prices for the year have been taken from the report on Prices and Wages in India, 1917. The prices of the first eleven * articles are wholesale export prices at Calcutta, while export prices of the latter five

Each price in the following table is the average of July, and January prices of 1911 and 1912 respectively.

being not available for that city, their wholesale prices have been taken as ruling at *Delhi*. The whole process stands thus :—

* * * *

Wholesale Export Prices in 1911-12.

	Rs.	a.	p.					
1. Rice	4	1	9	per maund	∴111	13	10	per ton
2. Wheat	3	6	6	,,	∴92	11	7	,,
3. Sugar	31	0	0	per candy of 500 lbs.	∴138	14	1	,,
4. Tea	0	7	7	per lb.	...			...
5. Cotton	288	0	0	per candy of 784 lbs.	∴146	15	0	per bale
6. Jute	50	4	0	per bale of 400 lbs.				
7. Linseed	8	14	0	per maund	241	9	7	per ton
8. Rape and mustard.	6	4	0	,,	170	2	3	,,
9. Sesamum	6	8	0	per maund	176	15	2	,,
10. Ground-nut	5	0	0	,,	136	8	0	,,
11. Indigo	140	0	0	per maund	138	14	1	,,

Wholesale Prices.

	Rs.	
12. Barley	2·59	,,
13. Jawar	2·808	,,
14. Bajra	3·039	,,
15. Maize	2·378	,,
16. Gram	2·257	,,

One maund = 82·286 lbs ; one ton $\frac{82}{3}$ maunds = 2240 lbs.

PRINCIPLES OF ESTIMATION.

The estimates for *cotton*, *wheat*, and *jute* relate to *all tracts of India* where these crops are grown to any extent, excluding certain unimportant outlying tracts, such as Baluchistan, Kashmir, Nepal and Sikkim. *For other crops*, (up to 16th item) however, the estimates, though relating to all the British provinces where they are grown to any considerable extent (excepting Burma in the case of sesamum), still exclude the Native states, except those in the Bombay Presidency and the states of Hydrabad and Baroda in certain cases. The yields of crops referred to in items 17 to 20 are approximate estimates for the whole of India. The Decennial Report on the Moral and Material Progress of India, 1911-12 gives the territorial distribution of the principal crops in 1911-12 for British India. We have adopted the following figures for the succeeding four items :—

	British India. (As given in Report).	India. (As adopted).
	Acres.	Acres.
1 Coffee ...	95,000	220,000
2 Other fibres ...	689,000	900,000
3 Other food grains, ragi and pulses.	33,803,000	40,000,000
4 Sundries ...	15,626,000 (cotton-seed not included).	20,000,000 (cotton-seed included).

1 M. and M. Prog. Report, P. 277. To the area sown in B. I. and Mysore, 18,400 acres have been added for Travancore.

The yield and price of coffee have been taken as equivalent to those of tea, of other fibres equivalent to jute, of food grains and pulses equal to gram and of sundries equivalent to wheat.

OUTPUT OF FARM PRODUCTS IN 1912.

		In thousand.		*Value in Rs.*
1	Rice ...	28,485	tons	3,330,382,507
2	Wheat ...	9,925·5	,,	920,238,925
3	Sugar ...	2451·1	,,	310,419,279
4	Tea ...	268,602·7	lbs.	127,306,488
5	Cotton ...	3,288	bales	483,339,795
6	Jute ...	8,234·7	,,	413,791,940
7	Linseed ...	644·9	tons	155,806,993
8	Rape ...	1,325·7	,,	225,455,512
9	Sesamum ...	397·6	,,	70,395,200
10	Grundnut ...	605·7	,,	82,678,050
11	Indigo ...	47·7	,,	9,089,750
12	Barley ...	975	,,	68,920,250
13	Jawar ...	2,459	,,	187,703,666
14	Bajra ...	1,158	,,	96,190,428
15	Maize ...	1,893	,,	11,895,000
16	Gram ...	4,356	,,	268,725,996

2 More than ⅓th added.

3 A little less than ⅓th added (4) ½th added, the rest for cotton-seed.

5 The sundries include condiments and spices, tobacco, cinchona, orchards and garden produce, and other very minor crops. Although high priced articles are included in this item, yet very cheap fodder crops and low-priced food or non-food crops also fall under this head. Their yields have not been found out by us in any Report for that year, hence their total production has been taken as equal to that of wheat.

VALUE OF FARM PRODUCTS.

Value of these 16 items ...	= Rs. 7,908,097,779
$\frac{1}{10}$ *of this value added* to complete the estimates for the whole of India	790,809,778
∴ Value of Principal crops	**= 8,698,907,557**
17. Coffee ...	48,742,515
18. Other fibres ...	125,398,032
19. Other food grains and pulses...	657,237,895
20. Sundries ...	613,492,616
Total for these four	= 1,434,865,058

Value of All Farm Products for the whole of India

= 10,143,772,615 Rupees.

But the value of the first eleven articles were calculated on the basis of the average wholesale export prices prevailing at Calcutta, of the succeeding five on the wholesale prices ruling at Delhi, while of the remaning four items on the basis of both. It is no secret that export prices at Calcutta are very high as compared with prices received by agriculturists; a large reduction ought, therefore, to be made for the difference between the Calcutta market and Village prices. Hence these Culcutta prices can be taken as 25 per cent. higher than those pocketed by Villagers. The Delhi wholesale prices may generally be considered as 15 per cent. higher than Village prices. Moreover, articles are not of the same quality. Prices of superior kinds are generally quoted, but those of middling and inferior grades are ignored. If we too should disregard a large reduction in the above estimate on this score, and deduct only 15 per cent. to arrive at an approximately correct estimate of the gross value of the Indian farming produce, we get the following interesting results :—

		Rs.
Gross value of Farming Produce	...	**10,143,772,610.**
15 per cent. Deduction		**1,521,460,892.**
Real value	...	**8,622,306,723**

VALUE OF SUPPLEMENTARY PRODUCE.

The above estimate, does not of course comprehend the whole of the produce of the rural population. Straw, hay, fish, eggs, poultry, cattle, milk, hides, horses, dairy and forest produce being evaluated would add enormously to the incomes of the rural population. Mr. Cunningham would like to make an addition of one-third of the value of gross agricultural produce for the annual value of the stock, dairy and forest produce. Mr. Mulhull has adopted one-fourth of the value of the agricultural outturn as the value of animal products. We accepted the last estimate in our preceding calculations and the same would be done here.

Adding the value of the supplementary produce which has been taken as $\frac{1}{4}$th of the value of farm products, we will have the total gross income of the agricultural community. It will therefore amount to

			Rs.
Farming Produce	=	...	**8,622,306,723.**
Supplementary ,,	=	...	**2,155,576,681.**
Total Agricultural ,,	=	...	**10,777,883, 404.**

PRODUCT PER HEAD-VALUE.

It is perfectly evident from what has been written before (P.135) that nine-tenth of the rural and not of agricultural population alone, must have shared that produce. The former being 90 per cent. of the total population comprised 285·5 million persons. Hence 9/10th of these amount to 256·95 million souls. It appears, therefore, that without excluding any item of the tremendous money cost of production incurred in raising that agricultural produce worth 10,777·88 million rupees, the Gross Annual income per head of the 256·95 million persons dependent on agriculture in India was Rs. 42. The value of all agricultural products is approimately 10,777·8 million rupees, and the ratio of gross product to net produce is as already shown, about 100 : 50 or 100 : 40. Hence the net income per head from all sources comes up to

(1) Rs. 21 or

(2) Rs. 16-8. as.

Supposing that truth lies between these two highest and lowest limits, we see that

in 1911 the average annual income of 257 million persons was not above nineteen rupees.

RISE IN MONEY INCOME.

It should be remembered that Lord Curzon's exaggerated estimate gave an average income of Rs. 20 per head, while our *ultima thule* shows the mean income per head in 1911 at Rs. 21. Taking Rs. 19 as the true average in 1900, we see that the average earning has remained stationary even after the lapse of eleven years.

The *money income* of the agricultural people has not decreased as compared with 1900, while it has surely advanced in comparison with that of 1891.

In other words, measured in terms of money the average annual income per head of agricultural classes has risen by Rs. 2 or 11 per cent. during these twenty years.

VARIATION IN PURCHASING POWER.

Looking at the surface it seems to be a satisfactory advance in a stagnant country like India. But the vital problem lies beneath the surface. Rupees and pounds are not to be consumed by the agricultural population. Money is only a medium of exchange and as such we have to examine its purchasing power in the two years, 1891 and 1911. This variation will be apparent from the index numbers of wholesale rupee prices of several groups of articles.

TABLE 1 (*a*)

Year	Cereals	Pulses	Sugars	Other articles of food.	Oil seeds.	Cotton.
1891	99	100	100	97	98	94
1911-12	143	141	111	136	156	150

TABLE II

Other Raw and Manufactured Articles.

1891	...	98
1911-12	..	132

(a) Enquiry into the Rise of Prices, Vol. II, P. 51.

Taking averages of the six groups of Table I in both the years we arrive at 98 and 139.

Finding out a weighted arithmetic average of these averages. when the weights for I and II are 5 and 1 respectively, we arrive at 98 and 138 as the index numbers for the years, 1891 and 1911.

The net result is that prices in 1911 were 41 per-cent. higher than in 1891, but the money income of the agriculturists rose by 11 per cent. during the same period. Hence they ought to be very much worse off in the year 1911 as compared with 1891.

POVEETY PERPETUATED.

The following statement would visualize the results :—

	1891	1900	1911-12
Index No. of incomes	100	112	112
„ of prices	100	124	141
„ of purchasing power	100	91	80

It other words, a rise in the money income of the agricultural community can not be a sure index of their growing prosperity. When we look at the rise in prices during these twenty years from 1891 to 1911, we find that there have been phenomenal variations for the worse, so far as the great mass of the community is concerned. A rise in prices of 24 per cent. in 1900 and 41 per cent. 1911-12 means a very much reduced purchasing power of the rupee. The advance in the money income has not kept pace with the rapid rise in prices, but has lagged very much behind. Hence the net result is the deepening poverty; helplessness and resourcelessness of the people. 257 crores of people whose average money income did increase by 11 per cent. during these twenty years, find themselves the masters of lesser articles than they could command in the year 1891. They could command 9 per cent. less commodities in 1900 and 20 per cent. less in 1911-12 compared with 1891.

Is this improvement or impoverishment, prosperity or poverty, development or degradation? Is there any iota of doubt left now that the perennial poverty of India is being perpetually perpetuated? In the light of these figures can Lord Curzon, or anyone of His Majesty's Satraps in this country declare that 'it is not a stationary, a retrograde, a down trodden, or an impoverished India that I have been governing for the past five and half years'? His Lordship does confess that

'Poverty there is in abundance.'

There is enough, and far more than enough. There is a great deal more than any one of us can contemplate with equanimity or satisfaction. There is, God knows, enough of poverty and affliction in India,' but he does not believe

that the people are getting poorer; on the contrary he holds that they are making slow but sure advances. But we hope that His Lordship, being not impervious to the evidence of facts, can not now decline to be convinced that the poverty of the peasant is not only being perpetuated but deepened forthwith, because his earnings are not keeping pace with the rise in prices.

Mr. Dutta's Enquiry into Agricultural Incomes.

But the results of Mr. K. L. Dutt's enquiry, although they go a large way to confirm what we have written, do not fully coincide with our conclusions: He his followed a different methcd in finding out the growth or otherwise of the agricultural income in India.

How index numbers of agricultural income have been constructed.

In constructing index numbers of agricultural income the following procedure has been followed: The first step has been to estimate the surplus quantity of food grains which the agriculturists have for sale. To estimate this surplus, imports of foodgrains have been added to and exports deducted from the total production, the result being the net availabe supply; and two-thirds of this quantity have been held as consumed by the agriculturists themselves. The surplus available for sale has been taken as the total production less the quantity consumed by the cultivators. It is the income from the sale proceeds of this surplus grain as well as the sale proceeds of other crops, *e.g.*, jute, cotton, oilseeds, sugar, tobacco, etc., practically the whole of which is sold by them, that generally enables the cultivators to meet their obligations in the way of rent, interest on debt, etc., and to purchase the other necessaries of life. The income of the agriculturist depends, therefore, on the quantity of surplus foodgrains and on that of other crops and their price.

In considering the relative material condition of the community in each province, it is necessary to obtain a measure of the changes in the income per head of population in that community in the several provinces. It has already been explained that the distribution of the population by occupation is not quite reliable; index numbers of the income per head of agricultural population has, therefore been calculated on the assumption that the agricultural population has increased at the same rate as population as a whole.

The following table compares in index numbers, the total agricultural income, the average income per head of the agricultural population and the retail prices of the commodities which the agriculturist ordinarily purchases. For the present purpose, index numbers of wholesale prices of cotton manufactures at the nearest port from which the province or circle generally obtains its supply has been taken in constructing index numbers of prices of commodities purchased by the cultivators, as statistics of prices of this class of commodities, wholesale or retail, could not be obtained for the cricles other than sea-ports:—(P.158)

Agriculturalists in different circles.

From an examination of the above table it will be seen that in Assam the rise in the agricultural income has throughout the period been more than the rise in the cost of living, indicating that the material condition of the agriculturists has been improved by the rise of prices.; In the Provinces of Bengal and Bihar however, the rise in the cost of living has been all along more than the rise in the agricultural income, showing that the cultivators in these parts have been adversely affected by high prices; this, however, is not true for all parts of these provinces—specially of Northern and Eastern Bengal—where the cultivators have obtained very large profits on jute and are substantially better off than before. The flourishing condition of these well-to-do tracts is not clear from the figures in concequehce of their combination with the poorer areas of Bihar and Chota Nagpur, the agricultural population of which are in more or less deplorable condition. In Bundelkhand also, the cost of living for the agriculturist has throughout the period risen more than his income. In the other parts of United Provinces the agriculturist fared badly in the quinquennia 1895—99 aad 1900—04, but in the quinquennium 1905—09—the period of high prices—his condition has improved,.

Province or Circle.	Average index number of agricultural income per head of population. 1890 to 1894	1895 to 1899	1900 to 1904	1905 to 1909
Assam ..	100	134	136	155
Bengal and Bihar ..	100	107	102	116
United Provinces ..	100	103	106	130
Punjab and North-West Frontier Province ...	100	89	112	144
Sind	100	97	106	166
Bombay Presidency (excluding Sind ...	100	89	105	123
Berar ...	100	101	168	149
Central Provinces ...	100	96	132	160
Madras Presidency ...	100	101	132	141

Circle.	Average index numbers of the retail prices of commodities which an agriculturist generally purchases. 1890 to 1894	1895 to 1899	1900 to 1904	1905 to 1909
Assam ...	100	100	109	120
Bengal North East	100	100	110	121
Bengal South West	100	103	111	124
Chota Nagpur ..	100	106	112	123
Bihar ...	100	101	109	126
Agra Provinces East	100	102	110	127
Bundelkhand ..	100	106	115	132
Agra Province ...	100	102	110	125
Nort and West ...				
Punjab East ...	100	103	111	127
„ West ...	100	106	106	121
Sindh ...	100	105	109	119
Gujarat ...	100	100	105	114
Konkon ..	100	103	108	118
Deccan ...	100	104	106	119
Berar ...	100	102	108	118
Central Provinces .	100	102	104	118
Magras North East	100	103	107	118
„ North East ..	100	99	105	113
„ South ...	100	104	109	119
„ West ...	100	103	106	120

the rise in his income having overtaken or rather exceeded the rise in the cost of living. In the Punjab and North-West Frontier Provinces, the agriculturist suffered in the quinquennium 1895—99, but in the next quinquennium his condition improved. In the quinquennium 1905—09 there was further and considerable improvement in his condtion. In Sind, the agriculturist's material condition deteriorated until the quinquennium 1900—04, after which his income by far exceeded the cost of living. In the other parts of the Bombay Presidency also, the condition of the agricultrists was worse up to 1904 than in the basic period. In the quinquennium 1905—09 however, his conditon improved, but not to the extent as in Sind. In Berar and the Central Provinces, the cultivators were adversely affected only in the quinquennium 1895—99, but since then their condition has remarkably improved. Throughout the period under investigation cultivators in the Madras Presidency have considerably benefited by the rise of prices."

CRITICISM OF MR. DUTTA'S RESULTS.

His conclusions are highly vitiated by the two large assumptions made by him. He has taken for granted that the agricultural population has increased at the same rate as population as a whole. We have seen in Chapter II that in no province of India such a thing has happened. Everywhere the agricultural population has grown more than the total population. Tables 12 and 13 of Chapter II are more than sufficient to upset the validity of his conclusions. Need we see that he has trampled upon the whole evidence of census statistics and ignored his own conclusion stated on page 85 *supra*. His second assumption is no less strange. The whole produce of cotton, jute, oilseeds, sugar, tobacco, etc., is according to him, practically sold by the agriculturists. Nothing can be more gratuitous than this assumption. It passes our comprehension that such an assumption could ever be made by a gentleman of Mr. Dutta's wide experience. How can it be possible that four-fifths of the inhabitants of this country who raise such necessaries of daily life as cotton, tobacco and sugar from their lands and yet they sell them all to the non-agricultural classes or to the foreigner and keep nothing of these articles of utmost necessity with themselves?

If the results of Mr. Dutta were consequently to be corrected in the light of the preceding criticism, the condition of the agricultural community taken *en mass* will not be inspiriting. Our results though arrived at without any pretence to accuracy, faithfully depict the deplorable condition of the rural community that is falling more and more upon land which is being steadily exhausted. If our calculations are approximately correct, then it is more than obvious that the mass of the population has not sufficient means to support a healthy existence, that pauperisation and impoverishment have come to stay with the people, and that India is on the high road to Bankruptcy and Ruin.

POVERTY UNVEILED.

We have seen that the average annual income of the agricultural community in 1911 was Rs. 19. It means that

The Income Per Diem Per Head of 257 Million Indian Agriculturists

Was Ten Pies, or
6⅔ Farthings!!

Mind reader! it is but an average. Only a few million persons must be engrossing and appropriating a comparatively large portion of the annual produce, while the countless masses must, of necessity, be getting less than ten pies a day!

And yet India seems to be happy, prosperous, contented, and progressive to our bureaucracy!

257 Millions of men, women and children have $6\frac{2}{3}$ farthings a day to satisfy the innumerable wants of human existence. All the physical, mental, moral, religious, social, and political wants of $25\frac{1}{2}$ crores of people have to be fulfilled with

$\frac{5}{6}$th part of a penny a day!

But let us see what does an income of $\frac{5}{6}$ penny a day or 19 Rs. a year mean? Let us calculate how much wheat, rice, or inferior grains such as barley, jwar, bajra, maize and gram an Indian could buy with his $6\frac{2}{3}$ farthings in the year, 1911? We know the wholesale prices of these food grains in that year (P. 147). We will deduct 15 per cent. from these in order to reach the prices at which a member of the agricultural class could buy his food grains in his own village.

Even with this necessary correction we find that the daily income of $\frac{5}{6}$ penny per head could buy

15 chhataks of inferior grains

$11\frac{1}{2}$ „ wheat and

$9\frac{1}{2}$ „ rice!

Every man and woman could get grain just sufficient for his daily bread but none of the other articles of food, no shelter, no light, no clothing, no comfort, no luxury and in fact, none of the primitive wants of the human animal even except bread. Either he must fill his belly with coarse grains, and go without ghee, oil, spices, vegetables, eggs, meat, tea, drink, remain without house and raiment, without religion and culture, without fulfilling any duties towards the family, the tribe, the village, the country and the state ; or if he were foolish enough to buy some of these things, he must go without food. These persons must, in the words of Mr. Rowntree, 'never spend a penny on railway fare or omnibus; they must never purchase a half-penny newspaper or spend a penny to buy a ticket for a popular concert. They must write no letters to absent children, for they cannot afford the postage. They must never contribute anything to the church or chapel, or give any help to a neighbour which costs them money. They cannot save nor can they join sick club or trade union, because they cannot pay the necessary subscription. The children must have no pocket money for dolls, marbles, or sweets. The father must smoke no tobacco and drink no beer...should a child fall ill, it must be attended by the parish doctor; should it die, it must be buried by the parish. Finally, the wage earner must never be absent from his work for a single day."

Thus according to Mr. Rowntree some seven and-a-half millions of people in England are living below the poverty line, in a state which "does not allow of anything but the primitive wants of the human animal-food, shelter, light and warm clothing." But what about India? ·257 millions have an average income of $6\frac{2}{3}$ farthings a day! Supposing that 57 millions are above that average, even then we have got 200 millions earning less than $6\frac{2}{3}$ farthings per diem!! Thus millions upon millions have to support themselves on less than a penny a day! $25\frac{1}{2}$ crores of men, women and children can get nothing but the coarsest bread. They cannot buy any clothing, cannot provide themselves with any house that costs them any money or with any other primary necessity of life! If they buy as they really do because living in society man can never live without those minimum necessities that society has sanctioned for its various elements—these poor souls can never have enough to eat. Thus they are starved in body and soul. They are underfed, underclothed and underhoused. Living in such an abject want they deteriorate in body and are ever a prey to innumerable diseases of body and mind. Destitution, depression, dejection, degradation, disease, deterioration, suffering, starvation and sorrow are indelibly written in letters bold and black on their faces.

INDIAN STARVATION.

Nothing is being written here in a vein of pessimism and exaggeration. These things have been frankly confessed in official publications. Thus even Sir William Hunter, K. C. S. I., the well-known Historian of India said in 1880 that '40,000,000 of Indians went through life on insufficient food.' This according to Mr. J. D. Rees, the well-known Parliamentary bureaucrat, is a dogmatic assertion and utterly unsupported, and therefore mischievous, statement. But what would he say to Sir Charles Elliot's estimate that 'one half of the agricultural population never satisfied hunger fully from one year's end to another?' * How does Mr. Rees relish the remarks of Mr. Macdonald ?

"From thirty to fifty million *families* (*i.e.*, from 150 to 250 million persons) live in India on an income which does not exceed 3½d. per day. In July, 1900, according to the *Imperial Gazetteer*, famine relief was administered daily to 6,500,000 persons. The poverty of India is not an opinion, it is a fact. At the best of times the cultivator has a millstone of debt around his neck."

Has Mr. Rees paid attention to the following words of his parliamentary colleague ?

" For days and days one goes through the land and sees nothing but thin bodies toiling, toiling, toiling, trudging, trudging, trudging, ; or pinched bodies worshipping, worshipping, worshipping with a sadness that one sees in no other temples.

India is the home of the poverty-stricken." The Awakening of India, P. 91.

---

* Quoted from J. R. Macdonald's Awakening of India, P. 102.

Mr. R. C. Dutt's remark that 'The poverty of the Indian population is unparalleled in any civilized country'

is again a sweeping statement according to Mr. Rees but has he any authentic evidence to contradict the views of his brother Englishmen ?

"The Government assessment does not leave enough food to the cultivator to support himself and his family throughout the year." *Sir William Hunter in the Viceroy's Council, 1883.*

(1) "There is no more pathetic figure in the British Empire than the Indian peasant. His masters have *ever* been unjust to him. He is ground until everything has been expressed, except the marrow of his bones." Mr. Herbert Compton in Indian Life, 1904.

SIR JAMES CAIRD ON THE CONDITION OF THE CULTIVATING CLASSES.

(2) "Three-fourth of the cultivators have no capital. In a good year they have enough for their *simple* wants ; in a year of abundance they barter something to apply in reduction of their debt ; in an unfavourable year they live very poorly, and partly by help of their credit ; in a year of famine that is withdrawn, an they have no means left of employing labour, and the poorest of them and their labourers are equally destitute."

Sir H. J. S. Cotton, K. C. S. I., has admirably summed up the bitter controversy on Indian poverty in his 'New India,' P. ~~95~~ in these words :—

(1) The Causes of Present Discontents in India by Mr. O'Donnell.
(2) "India", the land and the people," Pp. 212—213.

But all this is not inconsistent with the growing poverty of the people to which the unanimous testimony of Indian observers bears witness. This has been the theme of every National and Provincial Congress for the past nineteen years. It is supported by the evidence of Indian merchants and traders who are convinced from their business experience that the struggle for existence is greater than it was before. Official opinion admits this in regard to artisans, but denies it in respect of the great mass of the population, the agricultural classes. The official verdict affirms that the material prosperity of the people generally has improved. This verdict is directly opposed to educated Indian opinion, and a battle royal rages between the contending camps. In any case, there is no question that the people of India are miserably poor. They are absolutely and relatively poor.

The increasing poverty of India is due to many causes, but primarily I trace it to the decay of handicrafts and the substitution of foreign for home manufactures. It is due also to the extension of agriculture Every exertion is made to augment the area under cultivation with staple crops, and the increase in the amount of agricultural produce exported is pointed to as irrefragable proof of increased national prosperity. It is a proof of the reverse.

1 A general aurvey of the Empire led Sir Robert Giffen. the most distinguished statistician who was neither a sentimentalist nor a detractor of British rule in India, in his address to the British Association in 1903, to consider **How vast must be the economic gulf separating the people of the United Kingdom and the self-governing colonies from India and like parts of the Empire occupied by subject races, when we find that forty-two millions of people in the United Kingdom consume in food and drink alone an amount equal to the whole income of three huudred millions of people in India."**

O'DONNELL ON PERENNIAL POVERTY.

" The number of human beings who subsist in a perennial hunger, usually on one meal a day, was estimated a few years ago by the Pioneer at one hundred millions.

India is rapidly becoming a land steeped in perennial poverty. The evil is fortunately at present confined in its worst form to Southern and Central India, to Bombay, Madras and the Central Provinces. But the pressure of the land revenue is severe in the North-Western Provinces, in Oudh, and in the Punjab. There are not wanting, however, many signs that impoverishment, pauperisation in fact, has made much progress."

MR. REES ERRING INTO TRUTH.

Let these evidences alone. The reader will be startled to see how Mr. Rees himself has erred into truth on this point.

'A coolie on an Indian Railway, for example, will get probably 3*d.* a day himself, while his wife and family will earn 2*d.* and a *penny a day is more than enough to maintain each individual* *member of the average family of five persons.* The coolie pays nothing for rent and fuel, and very little for boots and clothes, and his penny for the food he wants goes *at least* as far as 1*s.* a day for the British workman's tea, bacon, meat, bread, etc.'*

The unbiased reader in going through the above passage must have realised the heartlessness, poignancy, calousness and grim satisfaction with which Mr. Rees has described the condition of a coolie family. Such a family spends very little for boots and clothes, *i.e.*, the whole family of five souls goes without boots and clothes, or remains naked through winter and summer and rains alike. Then a penny of the coolie goes *at least* as far as 1*s*. a day for the British workman.

There could be nothing preposterous than this. A coolie living in a town or in its neighbourhood and buying articles at a retail shop can never get more than 1½ lbs. of inferior grains, 1¼ lbs. of flour or 1 lb. of rice. These are hardly sufficient to keep this body and soul together. Mr. Rees has allowed tea, sugar, bacon, meat and *etc*, *i.e.*, beer, coffee, sauces, and vegetables, boots and warm clothing to his English workman, but he has allowed nothing but course bread to an Indian labourer and yet he poses to be a friend of India !

Mr. C. J. O'Donnell M. P., in the Causes of Present Discontents in India, P. 105.

*The Real India, P. 316. Italics are ours.

Can any honest gentleman aver that *any* of the things allowed to an Englishman can ever in India be had with an income of penny a day per head?

If not, how does an army of 50 million labourers or 257 million agriculturists live in India?

Dear Mr. Rees! allow the curtains of casuistry, sophistry and sycophancy, of convential lies and parliamentary prevarications to rise, allow the virtual vision of Real India to come before your eyes, yes, the real view of India—your mother for thirty years—as she lives, breathes and has her being in her villages and labourers' cottages.

See how her sons seem poverty-stricken, how want abounds, how millions live on one coarse meal a day, how thousands can eat food once in two or three days, how thousands have to starve, how millions die for lack of food and medicine!

See an army of about 50 million men, women and children with battered bodies, shattered health and tattered clothes, uncultured souls and untutored minds, weary and care-worn, toiling, tramping, trudging and marching along the dark and dreary road to ruin and bankruptcy! If you have seen this army, then let us part. Farewell!

CHAPTER VII.

THE PROSTRATE PUNJAB.

When a student of political economy studies the economic condition of India in the light of preceding facts and figures, he finds himself face to face with important problems crying out for immediate solution. Yet he cannot but be shocked at the apathy, indifference and grave-like silence with which the Indian peoples *have been* looking on them without realising their supreme importance. He sees that the inhabitants of this vast peninsula *have been* letting economic forces run their tortuous course with the one thought that Providence will in all probability step in at last to mend and mould things in the best manner possible.

Such an irrational and stoic indifference of the people on one side and on the other the state policy of invertibrate drift based on the accursed doctrines of *Laissez-faire* and

Queita non movere

(Let sleeping dogs lie) have more than paralysed the economic development of this country. We have briefly indicated that industrial stagnation and progressive ruralization are not limited to any one portion of this British Empire. They are as extensive as the country itself. But the vastness and diversity of the varying phenomena have rather blurred the picture. The real nature of these saddening variations in the complicated structure of the Indian economic organism can only be disclosed by a special study and delineation of the transition in each part separately. In this chapter we have endeavoured to bring out the principal facts bearing on the economic transformation of the so-called Prosperous Punjab—the province of peasant proprietors.

We have extracted from the Punjab Census Reports the following figures relating to the percentage increase in provincial as well as in agricultural population :—

TABLE I.

PROGRESS OF PROVINCIAL AND AGRICULTURAL POPULATIONS COMPARED.

1881—1891.		1891—1901.		1901—1911.	
Per cent. Increase in population.	Per cent. Increase in agricultural pop.	Per cent. Increase in population.	Per cent. Increase in agricultural pop.	Per cent. Decrease in population.	Per cent. Increase in agricultural pop.
1	2	3	4	5	6
10·7	12	7·26	Apparently 6·4 Really 10·8	—1·7	2·5

The foregoing figures prove that there has been a proportionally greater increase in the agricultural classes than in the total population, that while the rate of increase in the population of the province was 10·7, 7·26 and 2 per cent., the cultivating classes increased by 12, 10·8 and 2·5 percent. at each succeeding Census, that is, the people goaded by some extreme necessity have migrated more and more to agriculture during the thirty years under review. In column 4 we see that the rate of increase in the agricultural population is given as 6·4, but the virtual rate was 10·8 per cent. as will be seen from the following words of the Census Report, 1901, Part I, page 360:

"Agriculture alone shows a slightly higher increase of 6·4 per cent., but the increase would have been *greater* had not 'agricultural labourers' decreased considerably, for taking land-owners and tenants alone, we have now 14,770,000 souls, including dependants, as against 113,330,000 in 1891, *an increase of* 10·8 *per cent. in these two occupations.* This increase is significant of the development of canals and the colonization of uncultivated tracts in the past decade."

PROPORTIONALLY PROGRESSIVE INCREASE OF AGRICULTURAL POPULATION.

In the Decennial Report on the Material Progress of the Punjab, 1881—1891, page 1, we read "The proportion borne by agricultural and pastoral classes to the total population according to the Census of 1880-1881 was 53·6 per cent. In the

Census of 1891 the figures for these classes are 54·1 per cent." Then in the Census Report, 1901, Part I, page 314, we see that 58·05 per cent. of the total population were engaged in pasture and griculture, but lo ! the next decade again tells the ame sorry tale of the constantly increasing Ruraization of the Province, for pasture and agriculture claim 60 per cent. of the people in their folds!

In brief, the last four censuses reveal an inevitable tendency for migration to the land which is now more than ever subject to the law of diminishing returns, and for the desertion of native handicrafts and indigenous arts and industries which were handed down from father to son, from times immemorial; 53·6, 54·1, 58·05, 60 per cent. was the proportion of the agricultural classes to the then total population of the respective censuses of 1881, 1891, 1901 and 1911. In short, there has been a rise of 6·4 per cent. in the proportional strength of the agricultural community. Such is the prosperity, progress and economic development of the Punjab!

The same aspect is emphasized by the following table of the Functional Distribution of population during the last three decades .—

TABLE II.

Serial No.	Occupation.	1891.	1901.	1911.
1	Government ...	2·4	2·1	1·7
2	Professions ...	3·2	2·21	2·5
3	Agriculture ...	58·5 really 54·1	58·05	60·
4	Artisans ...	21·7	19·37	20·4
5	Commerce ...	3·3	4·54	9·5
6	Personal ...	6·4	6·88 3·56	6·56
7 8	Unskilled } Independent }	4·6	3·29	·24
		100	100	100

Native manufactures have constantly been pushed out and cruelly ruined by the relentless competition of cheap and showy foreign goods, hence many industries are every day becoming decadent, while their place is not being taken up by mechanical industries. It is evident, therefore that the Punjabis like their brethren in other Provinces are fast becoming a nation of agriculturists and of distributors or suppliers of Western commodities and that they are losing their position in *professions*, liberal arts and State service.

RESULTS OF THE ECONOMIC TRANSITION.

It appears from the Census figures for 1891 and 1901 that *two million people who amounted to ten per cent. of the total population of the Punjab were turned within one decade into lower grades of labour* and some of them must have unfortunately joined the tribes of menials and servants. Professor Nilcholson speaking on the criteria of the progress of a nation says :—

"One of the decisive marks of economic progress is found in the increase of the numbers of the classes with higher earnings relatively to those with lower incomes."

But alas ! in the Punjab, within one decade alone, there has be an enormous decrease in the numbers of the classes with higher incomes, while full two million persons have been undeservedly doomed to lower grades of labour and some to perpetual starvation ! Such is the evidence of the Economic Retrogression or the Progressional Ruralization of the Province during the last decade of the 19th century !

Proofs of a similarly disastrous character can be multiplied to an indefinite extent, but the constant deterioration of the old industries of the Punjab and the slow increase of the new mechanical industries would be still more visible from the declining urbanization of the province.

TABLE III.

DISTRIBUTION OF THE PROVINCIAL POPULATION BETWEEN TOWNS AND VILLAGES.

British Territory	1881	1891	1901	1911
Rural Population	87·06	88·43	88·44	89
Urban Population	12·94	11·57	11·56	11

In the census of 1881 the rural population of the Punjab was said to amount to 87·06 per cent. of the whole, but in the year 1891 it was stated to amount to 88·43 per cent.* "In this way we find that the urban population has increased in the last decade at the rate of 8·7 per cent., whereas the rest of the population has increased by 11 per cent. *Contrary therefore to ordinary experience in developing countries the rural population is here found to be increasing faster than the urban.*" Indeed, as will be seen from the figures below, the rate of increase in the smaller towns has been even smaller than would appear from what is said above :—

TABLE IV.

PERCENTAGE OF TOTAL URBAN POPULATION.

		1881	1891
Towns under 50,000	...	67·3	59·0
Towns over 50,000	...	32·7	41·0

That Decline of industries is the cause of this lamentable decrease of the Urban population living in towns of less than 50,000 inhabitants has been frankly admitted by the Government:—

"The decline of the shawl industry has caused a decrease in Nurpur, and the diversion of the cotton trade has crippled Firozpur Jhirka in Gurgaon."

---

* Material Progress of the Punjab, 1881—1891, Pp. 1, 33, 34.
M. Prog. of the Punjab 1881 – 1891, P. 34.

REMARKABLE REVELATIONS ON THE ECONOMIC CONDITION OF INDIA.

What follows from the Decennial Report of the Punjab is applicable to the whole of the country and deserves to be carefully studied :— "It seems probable that the reason why *the rural has increased faster than the urban population* is the nature of the trade which has flourished within the last decade. The export of cereals and pulses, and more especially of wheat, has increased very remarkably of late years and forms by far the most striking feature of the present trade of the country. *The higher prices involved, by this large export of the food staples of the country have* **naturally** *tended to favour* the increase of rural population".

TOWNS FROM 1881 TO 1911.

A comparative statement of the number of towns falling in each class at the four censuses remarkably corroborates the incessant tendency of urban decadence in the Province;—

TABLE V.

Class		1911	1901	1891	1881
I 100,000 and over	...	3	3	3	3
II 50,000 to 1,000,000	...	6	6	7	5
III 20,000 to 500,000	...	13	13	13	14
IV 10,000 to 20,000	...	30	34	32	30
V 5,000, to 10,000	...	77	99	97	107

The following table is still more telling than the preceding one as it fully reveals the declining proportion of the urban population in the various parts of the Province. The figures are taken from the Punjab Census Report, 1911, page 17. The provincial figures differ a little from those given by us in Table III culled out from the various Government reports; however, the tendency is unmistakable.

TABLE VI.

DECLINE OF URBAN POPULATION.

	1881	1891	1901	1911	Decrease.
Province ...	13	11	11	11	2%
Indo-Gangetic Plain	16	14	15	14	2%
Himalayan Tract ...	4	4	4	3	1%
Sub-Himalayan Tract	10	9	9	9	1%
N. W. Dry Area ...	10	9	8	7	3%

Another proof of a proportionately smaller urbanization is to be seen in the rates of increase in the urban and total populations during the period of 30 years from 1881 to 1901. The period is fairly long and representative of circumstances conducive to development and decay. For the whole province, the rate is about

12 per cent. for 30 years, but the total population has increased at the rate of 15. 6 per cent. during the same period.

This fact can be presented in greater detail the following table :—

TABLE VII.

Year of Census	Variation per cent. in	
	Total population.	Urban population.
1911 ...	−1·7	—1·7
1901 ..	+6·9	+4·7
1891 ...	+10·0	+7·4

Still another evidence is to be found in the increase of the number of villages with a concomitant decrease in the number of towns as shown in Table V. The number of cities and towns with inhabitants of 100,000 and over and 10,000 to 20,000 has remained constant, the second class of towns shows a positive decrease of one and the third class an increase of one. Curiously enough the total of the first four classes has remained stationary, but the fifth class of towns increased by 30.

The causes of this urban decline, according to the writer of the Census Report 1911, are to be found in the improvement of communications which tend to encourage. the opening of local shops, thereby reducing the trading population at the larger centres, and in the insufficient industrial development which has not neutralized these losses. It will be found on a slight consideration that in spite of the rapid and mighty improvements of communications in western countries there has been an ever-swelling exodus into urban areas. Why? because the industrial development of those advancing countries has outstripped the losses due to the first cause. But the indigenous industries of the province, as of the whole of India, are in a declining condition, hence * 'the proportion of the urban population has been gradually falling during the last thirty years.'

India Census Report, Vol. I, P. 30.

If the reader will carefully study the Punjab census tables of the last two decades, wonderful things will be revealed to him. Since 1881 and in fact long long before that year there has been a strong tendency towards the transformation of an industrial Punjab into a purely agricultural country; but that tendency was *mightily visible* in the last **decade of 1901-11, because in spite of a positive decline of 1·7 per cent. in the population of the Punjab during that decennium agriculture, pasture and farmstock breeding claimed more people in 1911 than in 1901. On the whole, there were 349,502 agriculturists more after the lapse of ten years, though, the actual reduction of population amounted to 566,985 souls.**

If the population of the Province had increased, there would have been no misgivings, but now that we had lost nearly 2 per cent. in numbers, the addition of 349,502 hands to the already crowded agriculture is virtually the most disastrous event of the decade.

DISAPPEARANCE OF 8,300,000 LANDLORDS AND THEIR DEPENDENTS.

Another fact of tremendous importance is that during these ten years 8,289,800 men who were receivers of income from rent of agricultural land, have disappeared. Where? nobody knows. In the year 1901 the number of these landlords was 8,915,669, but in 1911, it was only 625,869—there were in 1911, only seven landlords instead of 100 in 1901. It is well to remember that the numbers 625, 869 and 8,915, 669 represent actual workers as well as their dependents. If we were to exclude the direct dependents of the landlords, then there were in 1911, 239, 772 landlords of both sexes. These rent-receiving landlords belonged to many and varied classes. They comprised agriculturists, Government employees of all kinds, money-lenders, grain-dealers, other traders of all kinds, priests, clerks, school masters, lawyers, estate agents and managers, medical practitioners, artisans of all kinds and men of many other sundry occupations.

We have looked in vain throughout the Census Report for some explanation of this uncommon phenomenon, of this extraordinary, and almost sudden change in the functional distribution of the Punjab population. The silence of the Census Commissioner on this momentous problem when he has enlightened us on many other points of far less importance is very remarkable. But a partial explanation of this violent change is to be found in the different systems of classification, because in this decennium, there has been a net addition of

7,650,711 persons to this class of peasant proprietors, while the net decrease in the class of landlords was 8,289,800. If, however, there has been a real change, then the following important questions occur to us:—

(*a*) Whas has become of the people who have been dispossessed of their landlordship, *i. e.* what main occupations have been adopted by them?

(*b*) What classes have been ousted from the ownership of land?

(*c*) Men of what classes and religions have come to possess that ownership?

(*d*) What was the approximate income of 8,915,669 landlords and their direct dependents and how is that income now distributed?

FORTY-FOUR YEARS OF RURALIZATION.

The second persistent tendency is to be observed in a

Marked Decline of Proprietary Cultivation.

The subject can best be presented in the words of the Decennial Report on the Material Progress of the Punjab.

"The area cultivated by the owners of the soil has decreased since 1891-92, both relatively to the total cultivated area of the Province and absolutely.

Owners now cultivate 44·7 per cent. of the total

cultivated area compared with 53·7 per cent. in 1891-92; the actual figures being :—

TABLE VIII.

	Total cultivated area.	Area cultivated by owners.
	Acres	Acres
1891-92 ...	25,774,262	13,848,825
1900-01 ...	28,279,983	12,661,827

This decline in proprietary cultivation has been mainly due to the alienation of land to non-agricultural classes, who let the land to tenants. The indebtedness of the old land-holding class, and the great extent to which the land was falling into the hands of the money-lenders, led to the passing of the Punjab Alienation of Land Act, XIII of 1900."

But was this sharp decline arrested or accelerated in the next decade? This important question cannot be satisfactorily answered on account of the most faulty classification adopted at the next census, however, the marked decrease of the landlord class points out to an accelerated tendency.

From the Punjab Census Report of 1867 we learn that the agricultural classes numbered 9,683,580 and the non-agricultural classes, 7,927,918, that is, *they were respectively 55 and 45 per cent.*

Comparing these results with the year 1911, we see that after the lapse of 44 years, the proportion of the agricultural people has risen by 5 per cent.!

The actual numbers of the various industrial classes in 1867 were as below:—

TABLE IX.

Industry		*Males*	*Females.*
Calico Printers	...	15,980	13,638
Weavers	...	493,517	430,641
Dyers	...	36,470	30,774
Woollen manufacturers	...	22,604	19,444
Shoe-makers	...	159,660	138,560
Cotton cleaners	...	69,778	57,477
Tanners	...	136,449	119,386
Oil-makers	...	23,943	20,744
Blacksmiths	...	84,879	73,038
Cutters	...	1,763	1,577

OCCUPATIONAL DISTRIBUTION IN 1881.

The occupational statistics of 1881 would also prove interesting so far as they go:—

TABLE X.

Occupation		(per. thou,) *Males*	*Females.*
Agriculture	...	551	405
Total village menials	...	106	134
Workers in fabrics	...	75	224
,, food ...	...	14	68
Miscellaneous Industries	...	27	15
Labouring class ...		57	112
Merchants ...	...	54	5
Unproductive class ...	...	92	88

Punjab Census Report, 1881, Pp. 380 and 388.

Thus the actual workers engaged in various industries were 222 males and 391 females per one thousand.

Ten years after, the schemes of classification differed from those of 1881; however, with some minor manipulations it has been possible to institute some necessary comparisons.

TABLE XI.

CHANGES DURING 1881–1891.

(No. of Employed persons over 15 years)

(in thousands.)

Occupation	1881	1891
Agriculture	3,864	4,711
Personal Service ...	512	492
Preparation and supply of material substances ...	1,572	1,650
Com., Trans., and storage ...	210	281
Professional	176	274
Government	207	258
Indef. and Independent ...	614	413
Grand Total ...	7,168	8,082

DECLINE OF VARIOUS INDUSTRIES DURING THE DECADE 1881–91.

The succeeding figures of the actual workers engaged in various industries at the three Census enumerations are eloquent testimonies for the sure and steady decline of the provincial industries. Although the population had increased by 1,734,771 persons, yet the following important industries showed dismal decreases *not in percentage proportions but in the actual workers* who followed those professions :—

TABLE XII.

Industries	1881	1891	1911
Wool workers	17,879	11,887	8,586
Silk ,, ...	9,785	9,017	6,372
Cotton ,, ...	413,858	412,400	401,820
Brass, copper and bell-metal workers ...	13,897	7,547	...
Steel workers ...	72,262	61,235	...
Metals	139,055	131,310	82,769
Wood, cane and leaf workers ...	166,562	150,907	178,894

We will have to speak of the decadance of many industries afterwards, but here we cannot refrain from pointing out the steady decline of our woollen, indigo and sugar industries.

DECLINE OF WOOLLEN MANUFACTURES.

While in 1867, there were 22,604 males and 19,444 females engaged in this work, even with an appreciable increase in the total population of the province, the number of male *workers* dwindled to 11,887 in 1891. Ever since that time, the industry has highly suffered from foreign competition. The total number of *persons supported* (workers and their dependents) by it fell from 32,361 to 17,023 or by 47 per cent. during the decade of 1901 to 1911.

CAUSE OF THE EXTINCTION OF WOOLLEN INDUSTRY IN THF PUNJAB.

The Government of the Punjab in its Punjab Administration Report, 1901—2, P. 107 has fully confessed that imported piece-goods have thoroughly destroyed the once flourishing industry of this province :—

" Woollen industry has almost disappeared in most of the districts in which it was carried on, on a small scale, while the two great centres Gujarat and Ludhiana appear to have *suffered materially from the competition of imported piece goods.*"

*Again in the Census Rep. of 1911, we read :—
The wool industry is still of importance in this province, *although it appears to be on the wane.* Like other spinning and weaving industries, silk also shows a decline of 19·5 per cent. The strength of spinners, sizers, and weavers of cotton has decreased 8 per cent. from 959,688 to 883,156. The high prices together with the *keen competition with the piece goods of foreign manufacture* have also proved prejudicial to demands on power-worked and hand industry.

Inspite of all these admissions, the Indian Government fettered by the fiscal policy of England has been obliged to keep its ports open to all the traders of the world.

---

* Pp. 500,501, and 499.

DISASTROUS DECLINE IN COTTON INDUSTRY.

The decline of the Punjab Cotton Industry can be measured by the following figures which relate to all the textile occupations:

TABLE XIII.

	1867	1901	1911
No. of Persons supported	1,585,721	1,305,006	1,088,481
Total population	17,612,321	20,330,337	19,974,956

Per cent. *Increase* in population from 1867 to 1911 ... 13
Per cent. *Decrease* in Textiles ... 31

Textile workers instead of increasingly 13% with the growth of population have declined in actual numbers to 69% of what they were in 1867. Hence the ratio that they bore to total provincial population could not be maintained. The consequence is that in 1911 they were 4·5 per cent. against 9 per cent. in 1867. But why ? Only because of the fatal policy of Free Trade thrust upon us by Lancashire !

Mr. H. A. D. Phillips of Bengal Civil Service and author of Our Administration of India says on this subject :—

'The terrible competition of Manchester has crushed out a multitude of minor handicrafts, and cotton manufacture especially has declined and deteriorated. It is melancholy to contemplate the decay of the weaver class, and their struggles to bear up against the inevitable. The abolition of all import duties has doubtless benefited the general consumer, but it has ruined the weavers and a few other castes. (Page 210).

The abolition of customs duties and the competition of Manchester has ruined the weavers and crushed out some minor handicrafts. Should any portion of such duties be re-imposed? This is a broad question of Imperial policy, which can only be fitly decided by the Government of India." (Page 222).

That the regeneration of India lies in her economic development has well been expressed in the following remarks of a distinguished officer.

* Cotton and woollen mills have not yet been started in the Punjab. But if European enterprise and capital is once attracted to the richer Districts of the Punjab, there is a little doubt that in sugar, cotton, wool, silk and other products, it will find abundant field for profitable employment. The bearing of such enterprises on the prosperity of the agriculturists who supply the mills with raw products is patent. And it is in the development of such enterprise, whenever practicable, rather than in legislative schemes and systems of Local Government, that the true remedy is to be found for the indebtedness, the poverty, and the unskilfulness of the native agriculturist.

DECAY OF INDIGO INDUSTRY IN THE PUNJAB.

Indigo plantation must have decreased a good deal, *because in 1911 there were only 11·3 men supported by this industry in place of 100 in 1901.*

* Punjab Famine Commission Report, of 1879 Vol. I, P. 295.

The Punjab Administration Report of 1903-04 gives us a very important clue to the decline of this industry. "The indigo factories formerly existing appear to have ceased working." P. 24. The production of Indigo was a very lucrative industry. From times immemorial India has been renowned for this product. The very word *indigo* (English and German) comes from L. *Indicum*, that which is Indian (L. *Indicus*) or that which has been imported from India. The Greek word for indigo is *Indikon*. The indigo colour was fondly used by the ancient Phœnicians, Egyptians, Assyrians, Greeks and Romans, but now like many other things we have lost our market even for this article in the world.

THE FATE OF INDIGO SEALED.

'*The rapid decline in this valuable crop is one of the tragedies of Indian agriculture.* Twenty years ago the area was well over a million and a quarter acres; it is now only 131,700 acres; and steadily decreases. The reason for this is the discovery and manufacture of synthetic indigo in Germany, and the *difficulty which the natural indigo has had in competing with this substitute at the price at which the latter can be put on the market.* The effects of this discovery were at once felt, and, since 1897, the indigo industry of Bihar has steadily gone from bad to worse. Heroic efforts have been made by the Bihar Planters' Association, with the assistance of Government, to rehabilitate the drooping industry." (Agriculture in India, P. 66). But they were all of no avail in the face of the free importation of the cheap synthetic German indigo. Even the most enterprising Britishers who largely control the production of Indigo in Bihar and Madras could not save their lucrative industry from being strangled by the Free Trade policy of the State.

The sharp decline of this most ancient, important and profitable industry in Madras has been described by Mr. A. Chatterton in the Madras Census Report 1911, as below :—

'In 1900-01 the area under indigo was over 250,000 acres, and the production of the dye was estimated to be 46,100 cwt., whilst by 1910-11 the area had dwindled down to 72,000 acres, with a yield of 12,600 cwt. It is hardly necessary to point out *that this is due to the competition of artificially-produced indigo*, and it seems not unlikely that the cultivation of the plant for the purpose of producing dye-stuffs *will in time cease altogether*. This has been the fact of madder." P. 210.

The reader will see many more evidences of the decadence of these staple industries in the suceeeding pages, hence we need not dwell at length on this point here.

DECAYING SUGAR INDUSTRY.

Such is the enormous reduction in the production of indigo, but the same lamentable fate is reserved for the provincial sugar industry, because makers of sugar, molasses and *gur* have decreased by 39·6 per cent. during one decade 1901-1911 (group 23, Schedule II, Table X). Sugar from Java, Mauritius and Germany is ousting the native product from Indian market on account of its cheapness. Its import increased from £3,933,481 in 1901—02 to £8,777,310 in 1910—11, that is, within one decade there has been an increase of 123 per cent. in the importation of sugar.

THE TABLES TURNED.

India, the original home of sugar industry, India, once the greatest sugar producing country in the world, India that gave its very word to the various nations for expressing that sweet article of every day consumption, *India, once the sole monopolizer of the world market*, is to-day impotently looking to foreign countries for the supply of that very product. Now that the war has dislocated foreign trade, India being incapable of producing sugar sufficient for her home market is suffering from a phenomenal rise of prices which have actually doubled during the first two years of war. Its exports have constantly been dwindling, its output and acreage have been remarkably decreasing, but its imports have been steadily growing, in volume to the detriment of the Indian industry. Sometimes the Indian market has actually groaned with heavy stocks of Java and German sugar, which has led to a serious fall in prices and thus not only arrested the development of the industry but has actually strangled it. The country has thus become more and more dependent on foreign supplies.

'The total area under sugar cane in 1913-14 was 2,519,800 acres of which the United Provinces contributed 1,379,900 acres and the Punjab 611,200 acres. The total yield of the crop was estimated at about 2,000,000 tons of sugar and *gur* and 460,000 tons of palm sugar, of which only 16,000 tons were exported—mostly to the United Kingdom. On the other hand, over 800,000 tons of a value of nearly 10 millions sterling were imported. Although, therefore, India is the greatest producer of cane sugar in the world she cannot meet her own needs.' P. 52, Agriculture in India.

TABLE XV.

FOREIGN TRADE IN SUGAR.

(*Value in £*)

	1872-3	1882-3	1891-2	1913-14
Exports ...	492,743	989,069	...	91,666
Imports ...	440,146	1,086,961	2,516,803	9,991,266

Such a rapid decadence of an exceedingly ancient and important indigenous industry by the continuous growth of foreign imports is remarkable when it is remembered that foreign sugar has to pay five per cent. import duty and also bears the heavy burden of ocean freight from 12 to 15 shillings per ton. It means that we are succumbing to our competitors only because we are following antiquated methods of production. * Our *yield of cane* per acre is 25 at the utmost, while Javanese average is 36 and the Mauritius output goes up to 40 tons per acre. Again, the *average yield of sugar* per acre in tons is 1·25, 3·6 add 4·4 respectively in the three countries named above.

It is a matter of great delight that the Indian Government has at last awakened to its sense of

---

*The present state of things in India is due to three causes, first, wrong and wasteful methods of manufacture, secondly, poor varieties of cane; and, thirdly, bad cultivation.

J. Mackenna in Agriculture in India. P. 45.

duty, has shaken off its lethargy and come to the rescue of this dying industry. The memorable words of the Director of Statistics should be most carefully read. "Serious attempts are being made to improve the Indian sugar position, and to *remove the stigma that India (which is the largest producer of cane sugar* in the world) is importing increasing quantities of cane sugar from other countries *at the expense of her home industry.*"*

But it is also abundantly clear that this free expert aid for the resuscitation of a dying industry cannot be adequate without a strong tariff wall. Even the late lamented Lord Minto, an ex-Viceroy of India nobly said:

"If Indians want to create great industries, he did not see how this could be done without some thing being done in the way of tariff-reform."

RURALIZATION OF KASHMIR.

Leaving the province as a whole, let us now look to an important part of it. The Native state of Kashmir with an area of 84,432 square miles presents strange features. Its ruralization is proceeding apace much more intensely than that of the British Punjab. It is mainly an agricultural state, as many as 7,979 persons out of 10,000 being engaged in the exploitation of land Although the total population of the State increased by 8·7 per cent. during the period of 1901-1911, yet the people employed in the production

* Trade of India 1914—15. P. 40.

of raw materials increased by 13·2 per cent. and industry and trade suffered a decrease of ·7 and ·1 per cent. respectively. These figures are presented in the following table :—

KASHMIR FROM 1901 TO 1911.

	Increase + or Decrease — %
Entire state	+8·7
Production of Raw materials	+13·2
Transport	+29·4
Industry	—·7
Trade	—·1

PAUCITY OF MILL INDUSTRY IN THE PUNJAB

The number of factories subject to inspection under the Act was 201, of which 197 actually *worked for some periods* of the year. The average daily number of employees in all the factories in question was

31,243 compared with a total number of *31,709* last year, the figures for adult females and child workers being 3,749 and 1,132. Out of a population of 20 millions which is just half of that in Great Britain, about 31 thousand persons alone were employed in mill industries, while in the United Kingdom, according to the Census of Production of 1908, the hands engaged in mill industries were 5,242,870. Such is the

Kashmir Census Report, 1911.

paucity of the Punjab mill industry, when in the words of the writer of the Punjab Census Report of 1911 'all attention has, however, for the time been diverted to machinery using some kind of power, and the indigenous handicrafts are either being neglected or are being driven out of the market by machine-made goods.' (P. 56.) Had exclusive attention been not devoted to the development of mill industries, we do not know where we would have stood in any comparison with other countries!

THE PUNJAB AT A GLANCE.

GROWTH OF POPULATION.

		Per cent. variation.	Annual Rate.
1868 ...	16,255,456	...	...
1881 ...	17,274,597	+ 6	·47
1891 ...	19,009,368	+10	·96
1901 ...	20,330,337	+ 6·9	·67
1911 ...	19,974,956	— 1·7	—·18

The Census of 1868 was not complete and accurate, hence the population in that year was really underrated by about one million, so that the Census enumeration of 1881 does really show no increase at all and that was entirely due to the severe famine of 1878-79. Allowing for some inaccuracy even in the Census of 1881, we find that

Punjab Administration Report, 1914=15, p. 43.

during thirty years from 1881 to 1911, the population of the Punjab increased by 15 per cent. alone, or during 54 years from 1867 to 1911 it grew only by 16 per cent. and not by 23 per cent. as the Census figures show.

This increase of 16 per cent. is extremely insignificant. Indeed the Punjab is far behind every other province except the contiguous Provinces of Oudh Agra and in the rate of the growth of its population. This trivial increase is really contemptible when compared with that of other nations. (P 204.)

MEAN DENSITY PER SQUARE MILE.

The density of population went on increasing up to 1901, but received a set back in the next decade on account of the 2 per cent. decrease in provincial population. In 1911 the density was 200 against 156 in 1855, the latter figure is no doubt much less than the truth, for the Census of that year was extremely inaccurate. Yet there has been a good increase in density as well as in the proximity of the people which has risen from 173 in 1871 to 177 in 1911.

Year		1855	1911	1871
Density	...	156	200	...
Proximity	...	...	177	173

CULTIVATED AREA PER INHABITANT.

There has been a remarkable extension of agriculture in the province, yet it is a fact that it has not kept pace with the growth of the provincial population. A comparison of 1911 with 1881 fully reveals the virtual position of the Punjabis in this respect:—

	1881	1891	1901	1911
Cultivated acres per inhabitant	1·2	1·3	1·07	1·11

Although the Punjab has not suffered as much as other provinces, yet the great danger of an increasing pressure on land subject to the law of diminishing returns in the absence of any improvements in agriculture cannot be safely ignored.

CHAPTER VIII.

RETROGRESSION IN THE UNITED PROVINCES. DECLINE IN POPULATION.

The first censual decade of the twentieth century is full of interesting revelations regarding the United Provinces of Oudh and Agra.

While the total population of the two provinces was 47,692 thousands in 1901, ten years after instead of increasing by a single soul it dwindled to 47,182 thousands.

Who would believe us in progressive Europe and the rapidly developing America and Japan when we should inform him that

There were in 1911 actually 510,233 persons less in number as compared with those of 1911 in a province

whose population is about 2 millions more than that of the United Kingdom ?

The annual rate of increase for the province was only 3·1 per *mille* per annum up to 1901, when during the same period the rate of the increase of the populations of other countries has been four times as much. The succeeding table would fully reveal the very low rate of increase for this province when compared with the rates of other countries :—

TABLE I.*

RATE OF INCREASE PER MILLE PER ANNUM FROM 1870 TO 1900 IN CERTAIN COUNTRIES.

Country.	Rate.	Country.	Rate.
England & Wales	12·0	Switzerland ...	7·2
Holland ...	12·0	Sweden ...	7·2
Germany ...	10·8	Italy ...	6·6
Denmark ...	10·3	Spain ...	4·0
Scotland ...	9·6	**U. Provinces**	3·1
Belgium ...	9·6	France ...	1·9
Norway ...	8·5	Ireland ...	6·5
Portugal ...	7·3		

Thus, while England herself has been adding to her existing population at a fourfold rate, while in the decennial period of 1901 and 1911 there has been an increase of 3,757,944 persons or 9·1 per cent. upon the number returned in 1901, the United Provinces show a lamentable decrease of 510,233 persons or one per cent. *The provincial "population is 4 per cent less than it ought to be,"* is the conclusion of Mr. Blunt, writer of the Census Report of the United Provinces. In other words, calculating at the basis of 3 per mille per annum increase, the population of 1901, numbering 47,692,000 would have normally become 49,122,760, had normal conditions prevailed during these years. These facts, can more explictly be presented in a tabular form thus :—

* U. P. Census Report, 1911, Part I, p. 40.

TABLE 2.

Population of U. P. in 1901 ...	**47,692,277**
Population in 1911 as it ought to have been on the basis of the actual increase of ·3 per cent per annum during the last 29 years before 1901 taken as normal ...	**49,122,760**
Enumerated population in 1911 as it actually was	**47,182,044**
Actual loss sustained during the decade	**1,940,716**

LOW CAUSES OF THE VITALITY OF THE PEOPLE.

The chief causes of this abnormal decrease have been summarized by the writer of the census Report in these words :—

" *There is firstly the effect of plague*, resulting in a great loss of life and chiefly to female life, which indirectly must also have contibuted to lower the birth-rate to some extent. There is secondly the *epidemic malaria* of 1908, the effect of which was similar to that of plague. There is thirdly, *famine*, though this had little direct effect on mortality, *it lowered the vitality of the people* and consequently the birth-rate, and as will be seen it acted in some parts as an incentive to migration. There is fourthly *migration*."

Admitting that these are the direct causes of that abnormal decline during the decade, can it be denied that the one effective and comprehensive cause is the low economic condition of the people? They were living on the very verge of poverty amidst starvation and misery with poor physique and low vitality and hence could not overcome the adverse conditions of the decade. While hundreds and thousands were thrown out of their traditional and lucrative employments and forced to adopt the simple, low-paid, primitive agriculture, millions died from fever, famine, and pestilences like malaria, cholera and plague, while others in thousands deserted their hereditary hearths and homes for ever and ever to live in lands new and strange.

LOW RATE OF INCREASE FROM 1872 to 1901.

The decade, it would be remembered, was declared abnormal, hence the conditions prevailing in it must of necessity have been temporary. But does the Province present any features of prosperity during the preceding decades or have abnormal conditions alone been looked upon as normal in India? Let the reader judge it for himself from the rate of the increase of the provincial population whose variation at the last five censuses has been as below :—

TABLE 3.

	Actual Population.	*Percentage of Pop. In 1911—100* Actual	corrected.
1872	42,002,000	89	92
1881	44,150,000	93	94
1891	46,903,000	99	99
1901	47,692,000	101	101
1911	47,182,000	100	100
Gross increase From 1872 to 1911	= 5,180,000	11 %	8 %

Thus the total gross increase during the 39 years under review is 5·18 millions, or 11 per cent. for the whole period, but making allowance for the inaccuracies of the first two census enumerations Mr. Blunt gives corrected per centages as recorded in the last column of the preceding table. It is evident from these **that the increase for the United Provinces has been only 8 per cent. during the 39 years under review.**

COMPARISON WITH PROGRESSIVE COUNTRIES.

That this is a very slow growth will be conspicuously revealed by the following table which presents the relative growths of the populations of four countries with a percentile increase for each :—

U. P. Census Rep., Vol. I, P. 39

TABLE 4

	Country.	1872	Percentage when the pop. of 1911=100.	1911
Popu.	of U. P.	42,002	92	47,182
„	U. Kingdom	32,000	70·77	45,216
„	Germany	41,000	63·54	66,096
„	U. States	40,596	43·28	93,792

Thus while within 39 years from 1872 to 1911, the population of Germany and the United States have tremendously increased and even the already densely peopled United Kingdom has added considerable numbers to its then existing population, there has been comparatively slight development in one of the most populated provinces of India !

If the year 1911 be taken as a base for comparing the relative growths of the populations of these four countries, then thirty-nine years before, their strength was 92, 71, 63½, 43 per cent. respectively. Thus, the United Provinces of Oudh and Agra have made comparatively *little progress.* This slow increase of population is sure to give us a rough estimate of the slow rate of economic progress of this Garden of India.

COMPARISON WITH GERMANY.

A comparison with Germany fully reveals the most insignificant growth of the population of the United Provinces. In 1872 there were just *one million souls less in the German Empire,* but the passing of 39 years has seen about

Nineteen Million persons more

than those of the United Provinces. Such has been the miraculously rapid growth of the one and the comparatively stationary condition of the other!

PORTENTOUS INCREASE OF AGRICULTURAL POPULATION

The first decade of the 20th century has seen a great revolution in the relation of the different classes of the population. Such a mighty cataclysm has never been seen in the civilized world. A mighty transition is over the land, not for its ultimate or transitory good but for its sure ruin and destruction. The distribution of the people among the manifold occupations has been fundamently overturned. The province is, without doubt, adopting some Western methods of living and production, **hence the workers and their dependents who are being supported by such occupations as building, transport, post office, telegraph telephone, medicine and instruction have increased by 91,905 persons during the ten years from 1901 to 1911, but the greatest increases have been in pasture, agriculture, forestry raising of farmstock and trade in fuel. Into these low paid, primitive unskilled, extractive industries which are being diligently deserted by the Western nations, 3,045,432 or** *more than Three Million Persons have been shouldered within one decade.*

These miserable millions had to give up their traditional, well-paid, highly-skilled, honourable professions by the force of unavoidable circumstances. Being turned out of their lucrative occupations, they have been hurled upon the land which is more like a sucked-up orange than the mine of wealth that it once used to be. The richest soil of this province lies undeveloped on account of the insufficient means for the irrigation of the fields. Agriculture mostly depends upon precarious rains. For instance, in the year 1909-10 which was somewhat better than usual as regards the area sown which exceeded the normal by 2·4 per cent. over the whole province, the cultivable land being 72·2 per cent. of the total area, the net cultivated land was only 53·1 per cent;* but out of this whole gross cutivated area, the irrigated lands amounted to 27·9 per cent. alone *i. e. 72 per cent, of the cultivated lands were absolutely dependent upon uncertain rains!* We will put these facts in a distinct form thus:—

TABLE 5.

I.	**Total Provincial Area**	...	100
II.	**Cultivable land**	...	70 **of I.**
III.	**Cultivated land**	...	53 **of II.**
IV.	**Irrigated land**	...	28 **of III.**
V.	,,	...	14·84 **of the cultivable land.**

Now the exact extent of the mighty changes in the distribtion of the occupations is revealed in the succeeding table:—

---

* U. P. Census Report, 1911, Part I, P. 33.

TABLE 6.

VARIATION BETWEEN 1901 AND 1911.

No.	Occupation.	Actual Increase during the decade.	Per cent. Increase on 1901.
1	Exploitation of the surface of the earth.	2,958,015	9·2
2	Pasture and Agriculture.	2,962,274	9·2
3	Ordinary cultivation.	2,712,334	8·6
4	Forestry ...	10,218	21·1
5	Raising of farm stock.	307,616	1·6
6	Building Industries ...	13,144	10·3
7	Transport by rail ...	53,403	70·7
8	Post office, Telegraph and Telephone services.	7,503	38·7
9	Trade in fuel ...	87,417	1553·5
10	Medicine ...	9,097	17·2
11	Instruction ...	8,758	14·8

In a word, the net result of the above figures is that

3,045,432 persons have gone to agriculture and the sale of fuel,

U P. Census Rep. 1911 pp. 426-7.

while 399,521 persons alone or 13 per cent. of the former have been added to highly paid professions.

STRIKING ADMISSION.

"In a word agriculture shows increased figures (1) because it was, and had been for some time so extremely valuable that it had become temporarily more lucrative than their labour to the artizans and agricultural labourers who had a few fields of their own and (2) because agricultural wages had ruled high, which had both turned labourers into tenants and *general labourers into agricultural labourers*; whilst (3) the increase in landlords is due to the change in the method of classification"—such is the true explanation of the causes of the urban exodus by the writer of the Census Report.

DISASTROUS DECLINE OF INDUSTRIES.

Having viewed this vast migration to the primitive extractive industries connected with land, we turn our attention to a few details of the declining industries. The succeeding table presents the net and per cent. decrease of each important industry.

Even a cursory reading would show that all the highly paid, skilled, and socially better occupations have been deserted by the people. The manifold industries relating to mining, cotton manufactures, woollen manufactures, metal work, production of chemicals and articles of dress and toilet, construction of the means of transport, manufacture and sale of sugar, mollasses and *gur*, even various trades.

have greatly suffered during this decade. The sufferings of the people do not end here. There has been a considerable exodus even from public administration and professions and liberal arts. There has been such a mighty revolution that as many as 19,676 have decreased even in the class of individuals who lived on their own incomes.

TABLE 7.

Occupation.	Actual decrease.	Per cent decrease. on 1901.
1 Growers of special products ...	–68,647	–54·9
2 Extraction of minerals...	–9,290	–51·3
3 Industry :— ...	–406,801	–6·5
1. Textiles ...	–245,786	–17·4
2. Wool carders, spinners and weavers ...	–5,795	–12·6
3. Cotton spinning ...	–301,573	–23·5
4. Hides, skins, etc. ...	–69,984	–34·7
5. Metal ...	–91,370	–24·2
6. Chemical products...	–44,763	–9·5
7. Industries of dress and toilet ...	–206,974	–13·3
8. Construction of means of transport ...	–973	–20·2
9. Makers and sellers of sugar, mollasses and *gur* ...	–66,034	–38·0
4. Transport ...	–54,616	–11·0

Occupation.	Actual decrease.	Per cent decrease on 1901.
5. **Trade** ...	**−289,745**	−11·9
Boat owners, boatmen.	−16,316	−39·6
Trade in chemical products ...	−38,203	−65·2
Trade in pottery ...	−55,503	−1641·1
Trade in furniture ...	−64,886	−79·8
Trade in building materials ...	−1,339	−25·4
Trade in means of transport ...	−14,241	−23·5
Trade in articles of luxury ...	−10,083	−16·1
6. Public administration.	−45,496	−14·4
7. Professions and liberal arts ...	−90,829	−14·5
Religion ...	−98,590	−26·7
Letters and arts and sciences ...	−9367	−8·9
8. **Labourers and workmen otherwise unspecified** ...	**−1,534,622**	...
9. **Persons living on their incomes** ...	−19,676	−22

THE URBAN EXODUS.

The abnormal additions of the last decennium to the rural population can be corroborated by the vast migration of the urban population to rural areas.

While the total population has decreased by one per cent. the percentage of the decrease in urban population varies from 3·58 to 10·98 as detailed below in column II.

TABLE 8.

	Towns I	II per cent. decrease 1872-1911	III Per cent. Increase during 1872—11	IV Population of each class to total Ur. Pop.
I	100000 and over	—3·58	26·24	25·41
II	50000—100000	—8·61	11·61	13·35
III	20000—50000	—9·81	3·88	10·94
IV	10000—20000	—8·08	17·14	18·60
V	5000—10000	—10·98	·29	19·40
VI	under 5000	—4·15	60·42	12·30

Thus there has been an all round woeful decrease in the urban population during the last censual decade, but that is, no doubt, to be attributed to the abnormal economic conditions of the time ! Looking over a long period of forty years, we find quite different results.

The 3rd column shows the percentile increases in the total population of each class of town at the

U. P. Census Rep., 1911, P. 36.

time of the census of 1911 as compared with that of 1872. It *appears* to be a strong proof of the increase of urban population during the last 39 years under reveiw and the fourth column shows the proportion which the inhabitants of the various classes of cities bear to the total urban population. It is obvious that places containing less than 5,000 persons have also been classed as towns. This point would be important in instituting comparisons with other countries. But the truth of our remark that the increase of urban population is only apparent would be amply evidenced by the following figures quoted from the Census Report 1911, Page 23, Para. 13 :—

TABLE 9.

Years	No. of villages	No. of towns
1911 ...	106,020	435
1901 ...	105,068	453
1891 ...	5,716	484

Thus within 20 years, 49 places have fallen out of the category of towns, while the number of villages has marvellously increased.

In one decade alone 952 villages have been newly inhabited. The figures for 1891 seem to be absolutely wrong, absurd and inconsistent; but if they are really accurate, then the tremendous ruralization of the province is more than corroborated. We need no more proof for our assertion.

FORTY YEARS' REVIEW OF URBANIZATION.

Table 8 gives a bird's-eye view of the actual growth of urbanization in those provinces. Against 11 per cent. increase in total population, the second, third and fifth classes of towns increased by 11½, 4 and ·29 per cent., the growth of the other classes containing 56 per cent. of the total urban population was satisfactory. But the following remarks from the Census Report would summarise the whole situation :—

Class I.—"This class of city (7 in all) has increased considerably in 40 years.

Class II.—At the beginning of Census history there were increases, but by 1891 decay had begun. The loss was small in the succeeding decade but considerable in the next. The class *contains too great a number of the unprogressive or actually decaying large towns for the figures to be favourable.*

Class III.—It has lost very heavily indeed. The class as a whole has scarcely increased at all since 1872.

Class IV.—It possesses a very large proportion of the country towns *which have lost severely in the last decede. But generally speaking this class of town is flourishing.* Such towns collect and distribute the produce of the country round, provide the rural population with all necessaries outside their actual food, from cloth and brass vessels to legal and medical advice, and while not possessed of any great wealth in such commodities, still have sufficient quantity of them to meet the simple needs of the peasantry whom they serve.

Classes V and VI. consist of deceying towns of the same kind and overgrown villages. *They are not a flourishing* class simply because they are less absolutely necessary in the presence of better communications." P. 26,

This survey has clearly pointed out that only those towns can prosper in these days which are Government headquarters, or centres of religious activity or which serve to distribute foreign commodities in the country around and to collect the produce of the fields in return. All other towns which were once centres of trade and industrial enterprise are decaying because they are out of harmony with the present economy of the country.

RURALIZATION DURING 1891-1901.

But are the tendencies pointed out by Tables 6 and 7 only transitory? Have they been limited to the first decade of the twentieth century alone? No, not at all. The other decades show similar migration from skilled industries and highly paid occupations to the production of raw materials. Hundreds of thousands of men and women have been thrown out of employment by reason of the continuous decadence of our indigenous industries. Without going into details similar to those of the last decade, we will present to the reader one table which will suffice to evince all the tendencies of the modern economic forces operating in India during the last decade of the 20th century.

THE HEWERS OF WOOD AND DRAWERS OF WATER.

It swarms with incontrovertible evidences of the fast decline of sugar, oil, paper, textile, metal and leather industries and emphatically points out the inevitable increase of shepherds, herdsmen, cattle-breeders and cultivators. of

TABLE 10.

Occupation	Population supported in 1901	Population supported in 1891	Percentage of variation (+)or —)
1	2	3	4
Cattle breeders, dealers and Commissariat farm establishment.	56,576	46.286	22·2
Herdsmen ...	315,431	234,490	34·5
Sheep and goat breeders and dealers.	19,990	78,319	53·8
Shepherds and goat herds	100,495		
Fruit and vegetable growers.	114,716	40,286	184·7
Cow and buffalo keepers and milk and butter sellers.	103,160	94,496	9·1
Ghi preparers and sellers	11,328	25,811	—56·1
Sugar factories owners, managers and superior staff.			
Sugar factories; operatives and other subordinates.	67,325	78,124	—13·8
Makers of sugar, molasses and *gur* by hand			

Occupation	Population supported in 1901	Population supported in 1891	Percentage of variation (+)or(—)
1	2	3	4
Grain and pulse dealers	662,653	721,811	—8·2
Grain parchers ...	315,053	341,388	—7.7
Oil pressers ...	...	...	—20·9
Oil sellers ... / Pressers of vegetable oil for lighting ... / Sellers of vegetable oil for lighting ...	549,115	568,443	—3·4
Masons and builders ...	88,225	93,834	—5·09
Paper makers and sellers and palm leaf binders.	1,112	2,000	—43·9
Plough and agricultural implement makers.	17,730	57,025	—68·9
Sugar press makers ...	1,162	1,149	1·1
Persons occupied with blankets, woollen cloth and yarn, fur, feathers and natural wool.	40,223	79,115	—49·1
Cotton ginning, cleaning and pressing mills owner managers and superior staff ... / Cotton ginning, cleaning and pressing mills operatives and other subordinates ... / Cotton cleaners, pressers and ginners ...	149,610	256,675	—41·7

Occupation	Population supported in 1901	Population supported in 1981	Percentage of variation (+)or(—)
1	2	3	4
Cotton spinning, weaving and other mills; owners, managers and superior staff ... Cotton spinning weaving and other mills; operatives and other subordinates ... Cotton weavers; hand industry ... Cotton spinners ...	1,088,355	1,176,926	—7·5
Tailors, milliners, dressmakers and darners.	318,984	349,960	—8·8 —6·7
Gold and silver wire drawers and braid makers.	11,141	21,294	—47·6
Workers in gold, silver and precious stones.	234,211	218,700	+7·09
Dealers in gold, silver and precious stones.	2,531	3,357	—24·6
Brass, copper and bell metal workers.	42,238	56,210	—24·8
Workers in iron and hardware.	298,069	328,939	—9·3
Potters and pot and pipe-bowl makers.	369,723	466,390	—20·7
Carpenters ...	381,882	391,765	—2·5
Baskets, mats, fans, screens, brooms, &c. makers and sellers.	115,583	158,570	—27·1
Persons occupied with dyes.	47,527	791	5908·4

Occupation	Population supported in 1901	Population supported in 1981	Percentage of variation (+) or (—)
1	2	3	4
Tanneries and leather factories; owners, managers and superior staff ... Tanneries and leather factories; operatives and other subordinates ... Leather dyers ... Shoe, boot and sandal makers ... Tanners and curriers ...	328,570	356,152	—7·7
Bankers, money lenders, &c.	118,753	203,189	—41·5

Census of India, U. P. 1901, Selected occupations.

FUNCTIONAL DISTRIBUTION IN 1891.

No comparative occupational figures are available for the preceding decades, hence we have to satisfy ourselves with separate Census Statistics. During these twenty years we find the same tendency of a progressive ruralization written in letters bold and black. The Census Report of 1891, Part I, p. 330 gives the actual number of persons supported by various occupations and their percentages as below :—

TABLE 11.

OCCUPATIONAL DISTRIBUTION IN 1891.

	Actual No.	Percentage.
Agriculture and Pasture	28,912,897	61·65
Cultivation as subsidiary occupation.	3,910,470	...
Manufacturers	5,344,684	11·4
General Labourers	3,455,383	...
Commerce	...	7·9

STRENGTH OF THE VARIOUS CLASSES OF MANUFACTURERS.

Of the 5,344,684, persons above noted as manufacturers or producers, the circumstances are very different. They form 11·4 per cent. of the total population. The groups which are most important in point of numbers are detailed below that they may be compared with the corresponding groups of the preceding and the following censuses:—

TABLE 12.

Oil pressers	568,443
Makers of bangles, necklaces, etc.	190,617
Workers in cotton ...	1,524,739
Tailors	349,935
Workers in gold, silver etc. ...	248,686
Carpenters	391,765
Black-smiths	319,540
Potters	466,390
Cane-workers	205,405
Workers in leather... ...	361,783

DECLINE OF INDUSTRIES AND THE SUFFERING OF THE PEOPLE.

The writer of the Census Report has fully recognized and emphatically expressed the causes of the decline of Indian manufactures and industries. His remarks are an eloquent testimony of the miseries of the people who were being forced to give up their employments under the stress of competition.

"Of these the two most important groups, the oil-pressers and workers in cotton, have felt the competition of European goods severely. The native cotton manufactures of the country are being undersold by manufacture in Europe or on European methods and the large class which has so far hereditarily depended on these manufactures is now in process of finding some other occupation and, as already remarked in connection with the movement of the population in towns, suffering severely whilst undergoing it."

Census Report of U. P., 1891, Page 333.

TABLE 13.

THE OCCUPATIONAL SURVEY OF 1881.

		Females.	Males.
Agriculture	...	59·27	68·97
Industry	...	26·07	15·83
Commerce	...	·22	2·49
Profession	...	·85	2·49
Domestic service	...	·82	·69
Indefinite	...	12·77	9·55
Total	...	100	100

Such was the proportion of the actual workers who were two-thirds of the total male population, that is, one-third of the male population was dependent exclusively on the remaining two-thirds for a living. For our present purposes an examination of the industrial and agricultural classes, is more than sufficient. The industrials were 15·8 per cent. of the occupied males and included the following six orders:

Order X—Persons engaged in art and mechanic productions in which makers of various kinds are employed in combination. ...	155,525
,, XI—Persons working and dealing in the textile fabrics and in dress	985,226
,, XII—Persons working and dealing in food and drinks ...	521,796
,, XIII—Persons working and dealing in animal substances ...	45,450
,, XIV—Persons working and dealing in vegetable substances ...	215,132
,, XV—Persons working and dealing in minerals	506,659
Total ...	2,429,788

It would have been seen from the above that the most numerous order is the one including *workers in textile fabrics*, the weavers, cloth-dealers and tailors. The following statement gives the actual strength of each group:

Census Report of United Provinces, 1881, P. 108.

TABLE 14.

TEXTILE WORKERS IN 1881.

1.	Workers in	wool	... 14,607
2.	„	silk	... 2,823
3.	„	cotton	... 510,687
4.	„	mixed materials	... 12,958
5.	„	dress	... 433,815
6.	„	hemp, etc.	... 10,336
		Total	... 985,226

'The workers in wool consist principally of 13,570 blanket-weavers. This is perhaps an under-statement of their number. The blanket-weavers are mostly sheep-breeders (Gadies), of whom 25,079 are included in Order IX, under the head of cattle, sheep, pig dealer. Very many of these sheep-dealers are also blanket-weavers.'

The above figures relate to male workers alone, but in addition to them there were 20,00,068 women who were exclusively employed in industrial occupations. Among these the most numerously pursued occupation was that of spinning cotton, in which were engaged the 7,00,963 women shown under the head of cotton manufacture. The number of females employed in oil-pressing was 109,408 as against 116,360 men in that occupation. But it should be remembered that the above returns related to principal occupations alone. No statistics were taken of domestic and subsidiary occupations,

Census Report of United Provinces, 1881, p. 103.

for instance, 63·81 per cent. of the females were returned as of no occupation, although most of them must have been engaged in some sort of productive work. With the growth of foreign trade and the on-rush of cheap foreign goods, domestic industry has been dwindling in importance, women have no doubt become more and more dependent on men and the family incomes have necessarily decreased. However, a table has been added of the secondary occupations of tenants which gives 48,658 persons more employed in cotton manufacture. In this way the rough total of the cotton *workers* comes up to :—

Men	...	510,687	
Women	...	700,963	= 1,260,398.
Tenants	...	48,658	

This is a very important figure as a base for further comparisons.

STARTLING FACTS.

Let us now go to the first systematic and somewhat reliable census of 1872. The occupational distribution of the population of the North Western Provinces in that Census Report is given in three main classes whose strength is reported on Pp. IV and V as follows :—

TABLE. 15.

DISTRIBUTION OF POPULATION IN 1872.

	Actual population.	Percentage.
Agriculturists ...	15,330,027	50
Landowners ...	2,046,940	7
Non-agriculturists.	13,387,580	43
Total	30,764,547	100

No other information regarding the non-agricultural population is available, but it is clear that the agriculturists were only 50 per cent. of the total population and the persons pursuing occupations other than husbandry were 43 per cent.

Thus it is clear as day-light that since then there have been immense variations in the shifting of population, because while 40 years before agriculture claimed half the population or even including landowners 57 per cent. in 1911 the proportion of agricultural population rose to 71.79 per cent.

INCREASING PRESSURE ON LAND.

The density of the *rural population* in England and Wales was only 160 per square mile all over in 1881, but in the N. W. Provinces and Oudh, the *rural* density was 386 all over; in Oudh alone it was 483 and in Gorakhpur Division, 655; while in some districts it reached the terrible amount of 762, and in several parganas it was 1083!

This already heavy pressure has gone on increasing since density-figures are available. Excluding the largest towns of the Provinces, which are generally centres of trade, commerce and manufactures, we can measure the variation that has occurred in the actual pressure on land in rural areas. We will thus arrive at a most extraordinary result of a sustained and rapid advance in the density of provincial population.

TABLE 16.

INCREASING DENSITY.

Year.			Density per sq. mile.
1872	...	...	373
1881	...	...	397
1891	...	...	420
1901	...	...	427
1911	...	...	440

The increasing density of the population is justly looked upon as the surest index of the growth of the inhabitants and perhaps of the material civilization and development of a country, but the important question to be asked is whether the growing population can get sufficient means of subsistence from the land in an old country like India where no improvements worth the name have been introduced in the agricultural occupation, where the land has long been subject to the Law of Decreasing Returns, where the people deserting their unremunerative industrial occupations have been shifting to agriculture wherein is already engaged an extremely large proportion of the population, amounting to 90 per cent. in certain districts. Under these circumstances no one can hail with pleasure this growing density because it augurs a greater poverty, suffering and misery for countless people.

CONDITION OF AGRICULTURISTS.

With the lowest output of every crop per acre in the world, with no means for raising double or treble crops, but content for the most part with producing a single crop on his land, with no knowledge of improving the quality of his produce and with a heart-breaking absence of any organisations of marketing his agricultural produce and securing the highest prices for his stock, with capital got at usurous rates of interest, with the usual failure of crops from drought, with the cruel exactions and extortions of a low-paid corps of Government servants, with these and many more adverse circumstances to face, the Indian Ryot in the U. P. has to eke out his subsistence from three-fourths of an acre of land alone.

TABLE 17.

*DECREASING SHARE OF CULTIVATED LAND PER INHABITANT IN ACRES.

1872	... ·84	1901	... ·73
1881	... ·81	1911	... ·75
1891	... ·75		

If all the other facts of the lowest economic status of the Indian agriculturist were blotted out, this fact alone is most eloquent in telling volumes on the abject misery and economic slavery of the people.

When more than 70 per cent. of the people have to depend upon primitive agriculture as their sole means of subsistence and the condition of that occupation be as we have detailed above, when only

* Figures for 1872 have been calculated from the statistics given in the M. and M. Progress Report during the year 1872-78. For the rest see P. 119 *supra*.

three-fourths of an acre of land falls to the lot of each agriculturist, can there be any more atrocious fallacy than that of the hoarded and untold wealth or of the growing prosperity of India? The writer of the Census Report of 1891, has justly remarked

"How a cultivator in Azamgarh manages to subsist on half an acre, while in Saharanpur an acre and a half is required, is a question on which much might be written. P. 332.

Once again he says that the pressure of population and subdivision of land is injuriously affecting the circumstances of landholders and cultivators. There can be no hesitation in believing that the trader is in the provinces yearly advancing in wealth and importance. P. 333.

DESTRUCTION OF DOMESTIC INDUSTRIES.

As remarked above, no statistics were collected in 1881 of the domestic occupations which, however, were the principal trades that suffered most from foreign competition. Men and women in particular were largely employed in chikan and other embroidery, net work, basket making, fan-making, sewing, stocking-knitting, vermicelli-making, spinning and cleaning cotton and thread making. 64 per cent. of the females were returned as following no occupation, but we know that in every family, however rich or poor, girls and women must have occupied themselves with a few of the trades detailed above. Now these occupations have been wrested from them by the cheap mill productions of the West and East.

We have already quoted the words of the census writer about the sufferings of the poor people, but the following passages on the condition of labourers are of extraordinary interest.

We are told that the labouring classes constituting 18 per cent. of the total male population in 1881 were living on the very verge of starvation.

THE SUFFERING HUMANITY OF THE GARDEN OF INDIA.

Mr. Irwin in his 'Garden of India,' speaking of Oudh—the ancient land of Ayodhya and the most fertile garden of India reveals the hard lot of the labouring class in words like these:

"Everywhere in every hamlet, there is a residuum of half-clad starvelings, who have no cattle and no means of livelihood, save, perhaps, a tiny patch of spade tilled land, and their labour, remunerated at the rate of 4 lb. of coarse grain or of three halfpence, or at most, two pence per day. And even this wretched employment is not to be procurable all the year round. How underfed and almost unclothed as they are, they contrive to live through the cold nights of winter, which they often spend in field watching to keep off thieves, human and others, is a standing wonder".

EVIDENCE OF THE WRITER OF THE CENSUS REPORT ON STARVING LABOURERS.

'General labourers are persons returned simply as mazdur, mihnati, exclusive of the 15,773,321 returned as agricultural labourers (Khet-ke mazdur). Adding these latter we have 2,784,124 labourers among 15,352,204 males of all occupations. *Thus the labourers constitute no less than 18 per cent. of the males* who earn their own living.

They live merely from day to day, have no property beyond a few cooking-pots, and are reduced to the verge of starvation by failure to find employment for a short period."

'The next decennium has seen no improvement in their condition. It appears that they have been reduced to still greater straits. Economically and hence socially and morally they were hurled into a lower stratum. The remarks of the Census Report of 1891 abound in pathetic ravelations.

Seven Million Men Do not Enjoy Two Full Meals a Day.

"There remains for mention under class G only the important group of unskilled labourers, on whom 3,959,896 persons are shown as dependent. They are mostly, as already stated, employed on agricultural labour and, with the 3,006,785 persons shown as exclusively agricultural labourers, form the very poorest class of population. **For many of them it appears certain that two full meals a day is a luxury enjoyed only in years of prosperity.**

They are those who most promptly become dependent on Government for a bare livelihood in times of famine.

---

1. Census R U. P., 1881, P. 111.

C. R., U. P. 1891. P. 334.

SUMMARY OF OUR SURVEY.

Now we are able to sum up the results of the various enquiries detailed in the preceding pages. The upshot of the whole argument is that since *1872* (1) There has been a constant decline of the long-established Indian handicrafts on account of the comparatively cheap foreign goods, (2) There has been an unprecedented migration from industries to agriculture (3) This vast influx of industrial population in villages has added thousands of villages more to the rural area, (4) This movement is nothing less man a mighty revolution. It has shaken the very foundations of the Indian society, and has converted millions of socially, morally and economically better men and women into landless, joyless, helpless, hopeless beings, who are thoroughly steeped in ignorance, destitution and despair, and ever live on the very verge of poverty! (5) The masses of the people are in a much lower position than before, because they are depending more and more on agriculture. (6) New mill industries are extremely slow to grow up on account of the killing foreign competition. This extraordinary revolution accomplished at such an exhorbitant and undreamt-of cost is being denied by many, because India is inhabited by ignorant, silent and voiceless masses. But let us not forget the exact extent and nature of the economic transition which has changed the very structure of Indian society.

Below we reproduce some of the preceding results in a compendious form for presenting the ruralization of the U. P. during the 39 years from 1872 to 1911.

TABLE 18.

COMPARATIVE STATEMENTS.

Year.		2 Total population.	3 Agriculture and pasture.	4 Percentage of 3 to 2.
		(*in thousands.*)		
1872	...	30,764	(N.W.P.)15,330	50·0
1881	...	44,150	...	...
1891	...	46,903	28,913	61·65
1901	...	47,691	31,614	65·4
1911	...	47,182	34,384	71·6

TABLE 19.

			Actual workers.	Dependents.
*In 1901.**				
Agricultural population	...	65·4	48·5	51·5
Industrial population	...	14·9	47·3	52·7
Commercial population	...	·7	36	64
Professional population	...	1·3	40·6	59·4
In 1911.†				
1	...	71·6	50	50
2	...	12·2	53	47
3	...	5·39 (1)	47	53
4	...	1·1	45	55

* Census Report 1901, Pp. 271—275.
† Census Report 1911, Pp. 420.
(*a*) The report gives 539 per 1000 of the total population.

In 1901 agriculture had the following sub-orders :—

Land holders and tenants, agricultural labourers, growers of special products, agricultural training, and supervision and forest. All these orders claimed 65·3 per cent. of the total population. (P. 269).

Taking identical occupations *a*, *b*, *c*, of the order I we have 21·74 per cent. of the total population engaged in cultivation in 1911. Then in 1911 under commerce were included only "money and securities, general merchandise, dealing unspecified and middlemen, brokers and agents." But in 1911 trade covered a multitude of orders from 24 to 41. According to p. 417 of the Census Report trade claims 4·48 per cent. of the population, but on p. 420, 5·39 per cent. of the population are accorded to commerce. Thus the figures for industry and commerce are not reliable—the same words mean different things in the two decades. It is a pity that reliable statistics should not be available even in this 20th century regarding the main occupations of the people! But so for as the orders covered by agriculture are concerned, there can be no doubt of the real increase of the rural or agricultural population.

Views of Mr. Blunt on how industries and Commerce are passing out of the hands of Indians.

"Firstly, factories and mills have ended in the killing of hand-labour. Home industries have suffered considerably. The opening of western markets has done much harm to Indian industry or its artistic side. With the spread of a pseudo western culture, the Indian gentlman prefers to live in what he considers to be European style. The votaries of this style ignore the highly artistic industries of India and show a marked weakness for all that would be considered intensely vulgar by the very persons whom they are so anxious to imitate.

Modern mills are driving out the home industries and machinery is succeeding men. Lastly, Indian commercial methods are not suited to modern conditions. The result is that an Indian firm finds itself at a disadvantage when it has to compete with European firms in its own industry. Matters are improving, the Indian is learning the tricks of western trade and with his adaptability and capacity for limitation will ere long be able to take an equal hand in the game of commercial competition", but so far he is a mere beginner at it.

FURTHER EVIDENCE OF THE CENSUS REPORT

ON THE CAUSES OF INDUSTRIAL DECLINE.

"There is a very considerable decrease in the number of persons employed in the cotton industries, whilst the industries connected with jute, rope, silk

U P. Census Report, 1911 (Pp. 403—6).

and other fibres as well as other textiles, such as lace and embroidery, have increased. *The cotton industry is perhaps the chief industry of the province*, just as cotton is its chief non-food staple, and it is necessary *to examine the reasons for this decrease.* This, I think, is due to the well-known economic factor that machinery ousts men. The industry, as regards the majority of the persons that follow it is even still a hand industry: cotton is ginned, spun and woven with rude appliances all over the province

But hand ginning, spinning and weaving have long been known to be suffering from the competition of the mills, though the rate of decline was said to have lessened during the two decades up to 1911.

In 1901 there were 71 mills and factories for ginning, cleaning, pressing, spinning and weaving cotton: since that date there have been not less than 90 new ventures of the same kind. This must certainly have affected the hand industry and indeed it is known that many of the Julahas, hereditary weavers of Jaunpur and elsewhere are in the habit of migrating to the mills and factories of Cawnpore and other places." P. 388

CONFESSION OF THE GOVERNMENT THAT FOREIGN COMPETITION IS KILLING HOME INDUSTRIES.

Sugar.

"There has been some decrease in the area under sugarcane, and there has been a tendency towards adopting better machinery; whilst doubtless *foreign sugar has to some extent driven* Indian sugar out of the market." (Page 390, C. R. 1911).

Tabacco.

An effective cause for the *very great decrease in the number of manufacturers* of tobacco is the growing taste for tobacco manufactured in the European method (especially cigarettes). *Ibid.*, Page 390.

Indigo.

The writer of the Census Report, 1911 remarks that "the outstanding feature of the decade has been the rapid decline of Indigo. *Well over 600 indigo concerns have ceased to exist.*" (P. 42.)

With this official evidence before us let us read the words of the preceding Census Report:—"The decline in the cultivation of Indigo already noticed has involved the *closing of nearly 700 indigo factories out of 1400 in existence at the beginning of the decade.*

This decline, so disastrous to growers and manufacturers has produced wonderfully little effect on the labour market.

(Very strange indeed ! What a short shrift for growers and manufacturers ! *Author*). The work in the factories is not highly specialized ; the demand arises at a busy time of year, and lasts for a short time among the agricultural labourers in the vicinity Consequently, when factories are closed, the workmen do not loose their means of subsistence.

(Wonderful indeed! *Author*), but are absorbed *without difficulty* in the ranks of agricultural labourers."

Murder of Economics.

The last words of this official apologist must cause no slight surprise in the ranks of economists. They are full of strange logic. People are thrown out of employment and yet they do not lose their means of subsistence! They swell the numbers of ordinary unskilled labourers and with all this great increase in the supply of labour, their wages do not suffer a decrease and the readjustment of the labour market is secured without any difficulty in this land of immobile men and women! What an uneconomic logic this?

VIEWS OF THE DIRECTOR OF STATISTICS ON THE DECLINE OF INDIGO INDUSTRY.

The Hon'ble G. Findlay Shirras, Director of Statistics recognizes that the cause of the decline of Indigo industry is the keen competition of cheap synthetic dyes. His words should be carefully read.

"The *removal of the competition of synthetic dyes*, owing to the cessation of trade with Germany, has given considerable stimulus to the trade in natural indigo."

Unfair competition of cheap foreign goods with native industries which are not firmly established is for their certain destruction, but the removal of such a killing competition by artificial

Review of the Trade of India, 1915-16. P. 38.

high tariff walls or natural barriers stimulates, fosters and encourages the native industries—these points seem to have been accepted by the Director of Statistics. He has given expression to this opinion again in commenting upon the production of paper :—

The war has been a great advantage to Indian paper mills as it has resulted in curtailing the competition from abroad, and Indian mills have accordingly been able, with the decreased supply for consumption, to raise their prices. *Ibid*, P. 28

*That the native indigo industry has received a great impetus by reason of the forced cessation of the supplies of synthetic indigo on account of the war, goes without saying. In order to capture the German trade, the Government has now begun to make vigorous efforts to improve the yield and quality of native indigo. "An Indigo Conference was held at Delhi in February 8915 in which the possibility of assisting the industry was considered from three points of view—agricultural, research and commercial."

Valuable work has been already done in seed selection and the prevention of disease, experiments in manuring and improved methods of culture have given promising results. Experts are engaged on the equally important problems of extraction and preparation for the market ; and their labours are

---

Review of the Trade of India, 1914-15, P. 41,

already bearing fruit. During the past two years several discoveries have been made which may well have an important influence on the future of the industry.

If these things should have been done in 1897 or immediately after and also high import duties should have been levied on synthetic indigo, this Anglo-Indian industry must have been saved from decadence and death.

CHAPTER IX.

BENGAL RURALIZED.

In 1872 Bengal comprised five great provinces, differing from each other, more or less, not only in their physical characteristics, but in the language, race, creed, and institutions of their inhabitants. These five provinces were Bengal Proper, Behar, Orissa, Chota Nagpur, and Assam, their aggregate area including Tributary States being reckoned at 248,231 square miles, supporting a total population of 66,856,859 souls. It would be a matter of great surprise that this area of the Lieutenant-Governorship of Bengal exceeded the aggregate area of Denmark, Belgium, Netherlands and France. It was more than four times that of the United Kingdom and more than thrice that of Japan. In fact, this Governorship was far more than the German Empire and a little less than Austria-Hungary combined.

Is it a matter of little astonishment that the Governor of Bengal *is* a ruler of a State which is four times as large as the country that is directly governed by his own king whose hands he kisses at his appointment ? But what is wonderful still is that the population of this territory in 1872 exceeded that of countries which are usually acknowledged to be of the first class in the hierarchy of nations! In 1872 it was more than double the population of the United Kingdom; it exceeded by 62 per cent. that of the New German Empire and was 26 millions more than that of the most prosperous United States!

Thus the Governor of Bengal is a potentate more potent than the powerful president of the American Republic, he is mightier than the mightiest Kaiser of the most aggressive German Empire; nay, his sway extends over regions more extensive than those which all the crowned Kings of Denmark, Belgium, Netherlands and of spain can ever enjoy. This satrap rules over an ancient and *once* highly civilized, industrially supreme and most astute, sagacious and intelligent race, a race of peaceful and laborious workers, but now a race that has lost its ancient brilliance with the loss of her economic and political supremacy. He rules over a country which is one of the most charming regions of the Indian continent. Bengal with its Ganges, the Brahmaputra, the Son, the Godavari and thousand other streams and streamlets proudly prancing upon her broad bosom is physically the richest country. It is nature's most magnificent boon. Bengal with her huge rice fields, is verily, the loveliest and most romantic garden on earth.

But while the short period of 40 years from 1871 to 1911 is full of surprises in the countries of the West and in the near East in the Land of the Rising Sun, this richest region, this loveliest garden of nature and humanity has been withering and losing its prestine freshness, beauty, bloom and vigour. Retrogressive Bengal with its seered and withered, dead and dying indigenous industries, with its people steeped deep in poverty on account of being more and more dependent upon one precarious industry of poor and primitive agriculture, presents a marvellous contrast with those remarkably progressive countries. Its coal mining and jute industries have, no doubt, made rapid strides, yet these industries being for a great part controlled, managed, and financed by foreigners do not go to enhance the wealth, intelligence, enterprise and skill of the sons of the soil. Hence Bengal is economically retrogressive or at the best stationary; the condition of the masses has undergone but little change and the face of the country is no more cheering. While the New World, the Antipodes and the countries of the European continent, the celestial Republic of China and the Sunny Empire of Japan have ousted foreign made articles, have preserved the home market more and more from foreign invasion, have made themselves more and more self-contained and self-sufficient, the sacred, and inviolable self-sufficiency of Bengal has been violated, her home market being greedily grasped and swallowed up, groans under the oppressive aggression of all the progressive nations, in fact Bengal is writhing under the oppressive scourge of foreign goods. The icy cold air of decay has chilled its once most prosperous and flourishing industries. Disheartening and darkening prospects these due to the policies of Free Trade and masterly inactivity of the State! But let us have done with these thoughts for the time being and review some of the main factors of the economic situation.

A statement of the area, population and density of these several Provinces would be interesting as a base for further comparisons .—

	Area. sq. miles.	Total population.	Density. sq. miles.
Bengal Territory...	248,231	66,856,859	269
Bengal ...	94,539	36,769,735	389
Behar ...	42,417	19,736,101	465
Orissa ...	23,901	4,317,999	181
Chota Nagpur ...	43,901	3,825,571	87
Assam ...	43,473	2,207,453	51

(Census of Bengal, 1872, P. i. Stat. Results.)

POPULATION THICKEST IN BEHAR.

Then, it is obvious from the preceding statement that Behar is the most densely populated province. It is an exclusively agricultural land and yet has to support 465 persons per square mile ! But this density varies considerably in different parts of the province. The Sarun, Patna and Tirhoot Districts are most densely populated, there being *778,742,691 persons to the square mile.* Such an abnormal pressure upon the soil is nowhere to be seen throughout the world.

DENSITY IN BENGAL.

Bengal Proper comes next to Behar in its density of population. In the agricultural districts nowhere the pressure rises to that in Behar, even then it is exceedingly abnormal. Some of the densely populated districts with an average number of inhabitants exceeding 500 are :—

Fureedpore	... 677	Jessore	... 567
Dacca	... 640	Tipperah	... 578
Rangpore	... 619	Nuddea	... 530
Pubna	... 616	Moorshedabad	... 525
Rajshahye	... 587		

LESS PRESSURE IN ORISSA.

Coming to Orisa, Chota Nagpur and Assam we find that taking districts as a whole, the population per square mile does not exceed 470 (Cuttack), 203 (Manubhoom), 155 (Kamroop), respectively in these provinces.

It ought not to be ignored that the above figures respresent *averages* for whole districts, hence it is more than clear that in each district there must be some tracts where the pressure would far exceed the general average.

DENSITY IN BENGAL AND THE U. KINGDOM.

While the density of the population in the industrially supreme United Kingdom was represented by an average of 263 persons to the square mile, in agricultural Bengal the average was 269.

BENGAL IS PREDOMINENTLY RURAL.

Mr. H. Beverley remarks that *Bengal is not a country of towns*, and cannot be compared with England or other European countries in this respect. (P. 209).

Nine years after in 1881 the distinguished statistician Mr. J. A. Bourdillon wrote: 'The actual town population of Bengal appears to be 3,664,229 or about 5·26 per cent. of the whole population of the province. *This total is considerably less than that for London alone. In the smallness of its urban population indeed, as in the number of its towns, Bengal stands last among all the great provinces of India ?*

URBAN COMPARISONS WITH INDIAN PROVINCES AND WESTERN COUNTRIES.

This statement can be confirmed by the following figures of urbanization :—

Bengal ...	**5·26**	Bombay	...	17·7
Central Provinces	6·04	U. S. A.	...	22·5
N.W.P. & Oudh	9·70	France	...	31·06
Madras ...	9·71	U. Kingdom	...	66·6
Punjab ...	11·07			

URBAN POPULATION IN 1872 AND 1881.

Much reliance cannot be placed on the comparative figures of 1872 and 1881, yet there has apparently been a very slight growth in urbanization. In 1872 the number of *towns*, was 140, with a total urban population of 3,110,231 persons or 4·96 per cent. of the whole. During the last nine years there has consequently been ·3 per cent. advance in urbanization. That even this slight growth is fictitious has been emphatically pointed out in the next Census Report (see P. 253). What a remarkable contrast between the most insignificant and stationary urban population of Bengal and the rapid advance made by England and Germany where urban growth has been 6 and 5 per cent. during one decade !

(Bengal Census, 1881, P. 33—34.)

AREA AND POPULATION IN 1881.

At this enumeration Assam was excluded from the territory which constituted the Lieutenant-Governorship of Bengal and numerous other changes of boundary were carried out within those nine years. The result was that the area and population of the territory were respectively 193,198 square miles and 69,536,861 souls, Comparisons cannot obviously be instituted between these two enumerations. However after an elaborate manipulation Mr. Bourdillon arrives at the conclusion that there has been an increase of 10·89 per cent. in the provincial population during the nine years under review. These figures yield an average increase of 1·21 per cent. for both sexes. Excluding the Feudatory States there has been an increase of 10·26 per cent. in the British Territorry. The density must have naturally increased with the growth of population.

Several instances from Bengal would be highly interesting and useful.

GROWTH OF DENSITY IN BENGAL.

Districts			Density	
			1872	1881
Freedpore	...	...	677	720
Dacca	...	...	640	757
Pubna	...	...	616	710
Jessore	...	...	578	693
Tipperah	...	...	591	610
Nuddea	...	...	530	593
Moorshedabad	...	...	525	572

DENSITY IN BEHAR.

The growth of density in the Behar districts is no less wonderful. The inhabitants supported on every square mile in the districts of Sarun and Patna have risen to 870 and 845 from 778 and 742, while Mozufferpore and Durbhanga were newly included in Behar having the abnormal density of 860 and 790 persons. Similarly marked changes have occurred in the densities of a few districts of Orissa, as

			1872	1811
Cuttack	...	...	470	494
Pooree	...	...	311	359
Balasore	...	...	373	458
Angul	...	...	79	116

POVERTY INCARNATED.

This summary survey of district density has emphatically brought to view the growing danger of an economic bankruptcy. The pressure on land, already the heaviest in the world, was growing to a breaking point. Rural Bengal was verily the most thickly inhabited country in the world.

While on one side in the U. States of America 18 to 45 persons inhabited one square mile, British Bengal supported 442 souls on the same area, that is, about ten times as great as that of the *best* cultivated parts of the American continent.

Belgium with 486 and England with 445 took the palm in density, but it should be remembered that Bengal with an insignificant urban population cannot be compared with these which have a sufficient preponderance of urbanization. Large cities in a country unduly raise the mean density of the whole; hence the pressure of the population of the land in Bengal which has hardly any towns can be more easily realized. When we come to know that the density of countries like Norway, Sweden, Russia (in Europe), Greece, Spain, Hungary, Switzerland, Austria, France, Russia was respectively 14, 26, 34, 73, 92, 124, 171, 175, 180, 187 per square mile, in 1881 we cannot but be startled at the low economic condition of the people of the exclusively agricultural Bengal, who had to eke out their subsistence from a small piece of land by primitive and crude methods of agriculture!

Bengal Census Report, 1881, pp. 28, 29.

VOCATIONAL DISTRIBUTION IN 1881.

The Occupation Tables inspite of the elaborate classification and voluminous compilation 'are but a sorry equivalent for the immense labour and expense which this preparation involves.' It is also painful to learn that information concerning the occupations of the people is one of the least satisfactory features of the census of 1881. "The importance of the subject in all its bearings on the social condition and physical and moral progress of the people can hardly be overrated ; yet it would scarcely be too much to say that the statistics compiled in 1881 have not made any addition to the knowledge obtained in 1872."

The following table, however, shows the per cent. distribution of the population of all ages :—

	Percentage.		
	Males	Females	Total
Professional ...	1·80	·16	·98
Domestic ...	2·73	·70	1·71
Commercial ...	3·29	·56	1·92
Agricultural ...	38·62	5·62	22·05
Industrial ...	7·68	5·45	6·56
Indefinite and Non-productive	45·86	87·49	66·76

(Bengal C. R., 1881, P. 171.)

EXODUS TO AGRICULTURE.

We will now consider the comparative occupation statistics of 1872 and 1881. 'The principle of classification and the method of collecting information as to occupations,' writes Mr. Bourdillon, 'differed so much in 1872 and in 1881 that it is quite useless to attempt any detailed comparison of the results of the two censuses. The figures for each class are compared in the margin for what they are worth. Taken literally, they would seem to show that among the women there has been an increase of 10 per cent. in the number of workers and an advance of 11 per cent. in the number of employed men ; that among the women this increase has been about equal in the direction of agriculture and industrial pursuits, while among the men it has taken the form of increased application to agriculture, with the decrease in all the other classes, except that of the industry and manufactures. The figures are, however, given more to show a general coincidence than as affording *grounds for serious conclutions*'.

While his statistical investigation distinctly points out large increases in agricultural workers, being an official apologist he is trying to twist and turn his figures. The reader would do well to fix his attention on Class IV

	Males.		Females.	
	1872	1881	1872	1881
Class I Professional class—	1'89	1'80	'06	'16
,, II Domestic ,,	3'35	2'73	'43	'70
,, III Commercial ,,	3'68	3'29	'13	'56
,, IV Agricultural ,,	36'68	38'62	'65	5'62
,, V Manufacturing and industrial ,,	7'03	7'68	'97	5'45
,, VI Indefinite and non-productive ,,	47'34	45'86	97'72	87'49
All occupations	100	100	100	100

THE CENSUS OF 1891.

At the third Census Enumeration the Lieutenant-Governorship of Bengal was called the Lower Provinces of Bengal. It comprised the same provinces, but the area was reduced to 187,336 square miles. The population inhabiting this area consisted of 37,236,485 males and 37,406,881 females. It means that the total increase during the decade was 7·3 per cent. 'but if we exclude that part of it due to more accurate enumeration, it probably does not exceed 6 per cent., and may be less' (P. 50).

The following statement gives in a summary form the area, population and mean density of the several provinces included in the Lieutenant-Governorship of Bengal :—

Province.	Area.	Population.	Density.
Begal Proper...	79,098	40,398,265	510
Bihar ...	35,539	21,265,150	598
Orissa ...	24,240	5,744,062	410 B 118 F
Chota Nagpur	43,020	5,512,151	171 B 55 F

(Bengal C. R., 1891, P. 37.)

DECLINING URBANIZATION IN 1881-1891.

The year 1891 brought about a decrease of ·4 per cent. in the already least urban Bengal. The percentage of urban to total population fell off from 5·26 in 1881 to 4·8 in 1891, but we are told by the writer of the Census Report (p. 136) that the decrease was not real and he goes on to show that the increase of 1881 in urban population was unreal :—

"In the tables of 1881 a number of villages, with no true urban characteristics, were included. In 1891, only such groups of inhabitants, as, after full consideration of the local circumstances, Government has seen fit to extend the provincial legislation to, have been treated as urban and classed in the category of towns." (p. 136).

It must have been clear that the insignificant urban growth of the last decade was fictitious while in this decade there has been some decrease. The increase of ruralization is proved from the following irrefutable evidence of the Census Report (p. 138.)

"Although there is little tendency in Bengal to congregate in large towns, the growth of villages is proved by the following table, in which a comparison with the figures of 1872 shows a decided increase in villages with more than 200 inhabitants. The number of this class of hamlet was exaggerated in 1881 by very many petty groups of houses having been treated as separate villages, when they really were suburbs of large villages." p. 138.

No. of Towns and Villages in

1872 ...	190	223
1891 ...	244	667
Increase is ...	54	444

The result of 19 years' urban growth is that

(*a*) the percentage of the urban to total population in 1872 was 4·96 against 4·8 in 1891!

(*b*) the per cent. growth in urban population during these 19 years was 7 against 15 per cent. increase in the total population! Such is the Ruralization of Bengal!

The Census enumeration of 1891 is hopelessly barren in comparative occupational results. While in 1881, only the occupations of actual workers were recorded in 1891 the number of persons dependent on each industry was ascertained, hence the growth and strength of the agricultural population cannot be given here. We will therefore pass on to discuss the results of the next enumeration.

AREA AND POPULATION IN 1901.

At the Census of 1901 the Lieutenant-Governorship of Bengal (excluding Sambalpur and five Feudatory States) extended over 166,408 square miles and contained a population of 78,493,410 persons. It meant an increase of 4·9 per cent. over the period of ten years against 7·5 and 11·9 per cent. increase during the preceding decades. This small decrease was owing to the severe famine that ranged over the greater part of the country for a few years.

GROWTH OF URBANIZATION DURING 1891—1901.

The following statement of the comparative growths of the total and urban populations in the various Census Divisions would reveal that four divisions increased more and the same number decreased more in urban than in the total population.

	Percentage increase in total population.	Percent. increase in urban population.
West Bengal ...	7·1	12·5
Central „ ...	5·1	12·6
North „ ...	5·9	4·4
East „ ...	10·4	13·7
South Bihar ...	3·6	16·0
North „ ...	·1	4·9
Orissa ...	7·06	17·9
Chota Nagpur ...	7·8	5·1
Bengal ...	5·1	5·4

(C. R. Pp. 124 and 33.)

THE INCRESE IS ONLY APPARENT.

Bihar, Chota Nagpur and the northern part of Bengal have suffered a decline in urbanization, while other parts of Bengal show an appreciable advance. *However the province as a whole* shows an extremely *slight increase.* The causes of this upward movement and the position of the declining towns have been ably discussed by Mr. Gait in the Bengal Census Report. His words are :—

"If places now treated as towns for the first time be left out of account the urban population at the present census shows an increase of 5·4 per cent. over that recorded in 1891. The apparent rate of progress is greatest in Orissa, where however it is to a great extent fictitious, being mainly due to the crowd of pilgrims collected at Puri in connection with a religious festival. In East Bengal which comes next, most of the towns are growing. The country is prosperous and trade is increasing, and the most progressive towns are those connected wfth the export trade in jute. The high rate of increase in Central Bengal is due to the expansion of Calcutta and the modern industrial towns on the banks *of the Hughly. In other parts of this tract the old native industries have ceased to be profitable and the urban population is declining* ''

West Bengal also owes its high position to the rapid expansion of new industries fostered by European capital in Howra and its environs, and at Raniganj and Asansol. *The older towns show no tendency to grow.* The progress of the population in North Bengal and Chota Nagpur is normal, and presents no points of interest. Throughout Bihar the urban population is stationary or decadent, save only in Bhagulpur and one or two smaller towns that owe their prosperity to the construction of new lines of railway. Few of the other towns contain any of the elements that make for progress, and

many of them have suffered by the diversion of the traffic from the rivers to the railways." *(Pp. 33-34)*.

The retalively higher rate of increase in urbanizatiou cannot but influence the relative proportion of the urban and rural population. Hence in 1901 these proportions did undergo a slight change. Exactly 5 per cent. of the population lived in towns, while the other 95 per cent. were inhabitants of villages *(P. 37, Table II)*. However there was no increase but a positive decrease when compared witth the 5·26 per cent. urbanization of the year 1881.

The following table will more than visualize the growth of ruralization from 1872 to 1891 :—

Places.		Increase or decrease from 1872 to 1891.
With less than	3000	+ 54,536
3,000	5,000	—44
5,000	10,000	—58
10,000	15,000	— 4
15,000	20,000	+ 10
20,000	50,000	+ 5
More than	50,000	— 1

It is quite plain that there has been a galloping rush for inhabiting new villages which increased by more than 54½ thousands, but there was a fast decline in big villages and in places containing persons from 5000 to 15,000. The next two classes of towns show an increase of 15 places, but the cities with more than 50,000 inhabitants exhibit a decrease of one. This important statement needs no further comment, because it is more than eloquent in pointing out a persistent tendency of the people in residing in pettiest hamlets.

PORTENTOUS INCREASE IN AGRICULTURAL CLASSES.

As noticed above, the inhabitants of Bengal are more than those of any other part of India or of the world even, agricultural.

But the Agricultural rate of increase is more like a mushroom growth. The rual and agricultural classes increased from 47,754,686, to 56, 860, 469

by 9,105,783 persons, or 19 per cent. against the 5·1 per cent. of the total population. The total increase since 1891 was 3,819,612 persons, but the difference in the agricultural classes comes up to 9,105,783 souls, that is, the latter increase was 2½ times of the former.

In other words, more than nine million persons were thrown out of non-agricultural employments and were forced to labour on the land. More briefly the position of the two classes can be expressed thus:

	Agricultural per cent.	Non-agricultural.
1891	... 64·2	35·8
1901	... 72·44	27·56

(Tables I and III, Pp. 418—492.)

The reasons for such an abnormal increase are, according to Mr. Gait, to be found in the different systems of Census Classification and the greater care taken at the present census to secure entries in the schedules. But the agricultural and non-agricultural occupations are so very different that it is impossible to take the one class, for the other. There is a great probability of false entries in the minute groups of an occupational class, but in the main four classes, it is next to impossible. When the indigenous industries are continuously declining and the new industries are not absorbing all the persons thrown out of their employments as well as the persons who are every year being added to the population, it is but natural that the rural population should go on increasiug faster than the national population. In short, more than nine million persons were added to the ranks of low-paid, ignorant, illiterate, unskilled, poverty-stricken agriculturists.

The results of the next census are scarcely inspiriting.

URBANIZATION DURING 1901—1911.

The urban variation during the ten years' period 1901-1911 has been summed up in the Census Report (p. 23) in these words :—

'*In neither Province have the people shown any appreciable tendency to desert the villages for the towns. In Bengal the urban population has increased by 13·2 per cent. since 1901, its growth being more rapid than that of the general population, but only 64 out of every thousand persons live in towns. In Bihar and Orissa, on the other hand, an increase in the general population has been accompanied by a decrease of 2·8 per cent. in the number of persons living in towns, who now constitute only 34 per mille of the total population. This decline is as will be shown later, due mainly to the continued presence of plague in Bihar, which has not only caused a grievous mortality, but disorganized the industries and trade of the towns it afflicted. Prima facie the Bengalis appear to have a greater predilection for town life than the inhabitants of Bihar and Orissa.*'

However if Greater Calcutta including Howrah, Maniktollah, Cassipur-Chitpur and Garden Reach which contain two-fifths of the urban population of Bengal be left out of account, the urban population falls to 3·8 per cent. or a little more than in Bihar and Orissa. The urban population and growth remains much inflated only on account of the rapid growth of the metropolitan town of Calcutta which is also the only principal centre for foreign trade in Northern India.

Bihar and Orissa have continually been suffering from urban decay, but in Bengal also many old towns have declined. The causes of the unusual urban decrease in these provinces have been detailed by the writer as changes in the course of a river, removal of the court, loss of trade and the prevalance of endemic and epidemic diseases. It is exceedingly painful to learn that 26 towns show a decrease of 80,373 inhabitants during 1901—11, only on account of the last cause. However, 'after the somewhat dreary sketch of urban decay, stagnation or decimation by disease, it is refreshing to turn to the number of towns, some old, some young and nascent, which are fast developing owing to the expansion of trade or industrial enterprise, often introduced or directed by Europeans?'

The passage is remarkable for the candid admission of the writer that indigenous industries are not growing in the country, a few towns are, indeed developing because they are centres of European enterprise and serve as depots for the collection of raw material from villages for shipment to foreign lands and the distribution of foreign goods in the country around. Thus on one side is visible the rapid decline of old industrial and commercial towns involving an immeasurable loss of capital to the children of this country, and on the other is to be seen the rise of new towns-centres of European industry and commerce which go a very small way to vitalize, fertilize and fructify the indigenous industries or to enhance the capital, the wealth, the skill or enterprise of the sons of the soil. A little reflection would show that the wastage of capital is continually growing in the declining and decadent towns, the dislocation and the readjustments effected by the present economic conditions at work in India and the loss of human skill, social grade, enterprising and hopeful spirit all go a long way to increase the sufferings of the already depressed masses. The figures of urbanization do not reveal any tendency for upward movement, indeed they show a stationary situation. But underneath those figures lies burried deep an appalling mass of the debries of hundreds and thousands of buildings, ruins of once-flourishing commercial houses and the remains of crippled and crushed industries; they do conceal the indescribable miseries, sufferings, agonies, of the unemployed millions who were forced to migrate from their ancenstral homes and hearths to starve, die or work as houseless and landless labourers.

INCREASING PRESSURE ON LAND.

Now a few points regarding the growing density of population will be highly important as they will throw a flood of light on the problem of Indian poverty. With the growth of provincial population, its density in an old and conservative country like India can not but grow. The pressure on land whose productive capacity is being slowly lessened, is fast growing for the deepening of the misery and poverty of the agricultural classes. In Bengal alone the increase of pressure in some of the thickly populated districts during twenty years from 1891 to 1911 can be seen in the table below :—*

Districts	1891	1901	1911
Feridpur	714	758	824
Dacca	861	952	1066
Pubna	736	768	772
Jessore	646	620	601
Tipperah	713	848	972
Nudden	586	594	580
Murshidabad	584	622	640
Bogra	562	628	724

GROWTH OF DENSITY IN BIHAR.

Saran	919	898	853
Patna	857	785	778
Muzaffarpur	894	908	937
Darbhanga	837	870	875

RISING PRESSURE IN ORISSA.

Cuttack ...	530	564	577
Pari ...	378	407	410
Balasore ...	478	515	506

These instances of the most populous districts can be multiplied, but they do suffice to show the ever increasing pressure in rural Bengal. Some of the districts exhibit extraordinary variations, but these changes grow doubly extraordinary and

* Bengal Census Report, 1911, P. 161.

remarkable when we compare the mean density of these places in 1911 with that in 1872. The succeeding table of the forty years' growth of density sufficiently shows the evil effects the development of population must have had on the economic condition of the masses:—

FORTY YEARS' NET INCREASE IN DENSITY.

Tipperah	... 410		
Dacca	... 409	Balasore	... 126
Bogra	... 252	Pubna	... 117
Darbhanga	... 237	Jessore	... 105
Faridpur	... 226	Puri	... 102
Muzaffarpur	... 197	Saran	... 79
Cuttack	... 155	Murshidabad	... 73

While in the European countries with highest yields of grain crops and with subsidiary industries to add to the family incomes of the agricultural classes, it is considered impossible that more than 200 to 250 inhabitants can ever have a healthy existence on agricultural and pastoral industries, in Bengal where the pressure on land was already the heaviest in the world, it has tremendously increased in some of the most populous districts. Within 39 years those districts have had to support from 200 to 410 *additional inhabitants* per square mile. We have dilated upon the incarnated poverty of Bengal in the preceding pages, at this occasion we can only add that the ghastly picture of poverty and penury has become still more horrible. Cultivation has indeed extended, but it has not kept pace even with the slow increase of the provincial population. The result of this phenomenon cannot but be the growth of impoverishment and pauperization. The cultivated area per head has terribly declined. While in 1881 each man could claim 1·5 acres, in 1901-2 he could only live on the reduced produce of 1·12 acres, but ten years after the share was still more lessened to about an acre. Is it not miraculous that the industrially supreme countries like the United Kingdom, Germany and France, although densely populated, contain * 460, 311 and 189 inhabitants per square mile against 551 in industrially backward and rural Bengal?

From this it is at once apparent that the economic condition of the exclusively agricultural provinces of Bengal, Bihar, Orissa, and Chota Nagpur must be absolutely and relatively the lowest imaginable, that the eighty-five millions of human beings must be toiling and suffering in a way that is inconceivable by a Globe-trotter who like a butterfly pays flying visits to a few old and metropolitan cities. In this seemingly prosperous Bengal myriads of tenants and peasants wrung and screwed by landlords and having to subsist on the minutely subdivided holdings and vegetating on the poisonous verdure of their rice and jute fields have patiently to starve and starve and die a miserable death.

The extreme depression and distress, penury and misery of the singularly thrifty peasants of Behar and Bengal has been well described by some of the highest officials in indignant words. Below we quote only a few instances.

* Bengal Census Rep., 1911, P. 2.

Sir Richard Temple wrote in 1875 :—

"Undoubtedly the condition of the peasantry is low in Behar—lower than in that of any other peasantry, with equal natural advantages."

Sir Ashley Eden in 1877 described the tenantry of Behar as "poor, helpless, discontented men, driven about from village to village by the extortion of underlings or the exactions of irresponsible under-farmers—tenants who never know whether they will possess next year the land they occupy, and who feel that any attempt to grow more profitable crops will only end in increased demands."

In 1893 Mr. G. A. Grierson, C. I. E., probably the best authority in connection with everything relating to the Behar Province, published "Notes on the District of Gaya," one of the largest district of Behar.

After discussing the arguments set out in this work the *Pioneer* concluded thus: "If we sum up the facts Mr. Grierson thus puts before us regarding the various sections of the District population, the conclusion we arrive at is certainly not encouraging. Briefly, it is that all the persons of the labouring classes, and 10 per cent. of the cultivating and artisan classes, or 45 per cent. of the total population, are insufficiently clothed or insufficiently fed, or both. In Gaya District this would give about a million persons without sufficient means of support. If we assume that the circumstances of Gaya are not exceptional—and there is no reason for thinking otherwise—it follows that nearly one hundred millions of people in British India are living in extreme poverty."

One Meal a day the Normal Diet.

The Chief Magistrate of Patna, another Behar District (Mr. G. Toynbee, C.S,I.), afterwards senior member of the Board of Revenue and a member of the Viceroy's Council, stated a few years before that "the conclusion to be drawn is that of the agricultural population a large proportion, say 40 per cent., are insufficiently fed to say nothing of clothing and housing. They have enough food to support life and to enable them to work, but they have to undergo long fasts, having for a considerable part of the year to satisfy themselves with one full meal in the day." Sir Alfred Lethbridge, K.C.S.I., declared that "in Behar the Districts of Muzafarpur and Saran and parts of the Durbhunga and Chumparan are the worst, and there is an almost constant insufficiency of food."

The status of the Bengal ryots was no better. The same Sir Ashley Eden writes:—"The ryots of the richest province of Bengal are the poorest and most wretched class we find in the country."

Failure of Lord Curzon, P. 35.

GRIEVOUS RURALIZATION DURING 1901-1911.

The succeeding statement gives actual and proportional figures for the four main classes of occupations in the two provinces. In both the great majority of the people were already largely dependent on agriculture and cognate pursuits, but the present decade has added a great bulk of the unemployed to swell their ranks.

GENERAL DISTRIBUTION OF OCCUPATIONS.

Class	Bengal		Bihar and Orissa	
		Per centage		Per centage
Production of raw materials	36,078,000	78	31,115,000	81
Preparation and supply ...	6,724,000	14½	4,808,000	12½
Public Administration and liberal arts	1,182,000	2½	652,000	2
Miscellaneous	2,322,000	5	1,860,000	5

DISLOCATION MIRRORIZED.

The dislocation of industry within this one decade can best be visualized in the following statement of the vocational shifting of population.

(Bengal C. R. 1911, Pp. 567-70.)

	Population supported in 1911.	Population supported in 1911.	Percentage of Variation.
Exploitation of the surface of the Earth	66,326,209	57,588,534	+15
Extraction of minerals ...	279,616	110,05	+154
Preparation and supply of material substances ...	11,419,200	11,351,179	+1
Industry	6,152,078	5,958,411	+3
Textiles	1,317,181	1,378,590	—4
Industries of dress and toilet	1,098,421	1,150,021	—4
Metals	385,786	392,573	—2
Transport	1,316,040	1,008.534	+30
Trade	3,951,082	438,234	—10
Public administration and liberal arts	1,199,050	1,994,585	7
Persons living on their incomes	61,788	78,757	—22
Micellaneous	4,162,314	7,522,373	—45

AGRICULTURAL AND NON-AGRICULTURAL CLASSES.

Making two broad divisions of agricultural and non-agricultural classes we find that there has been an extraordinary increase of 9,531,197 in pasture and agriculture, but the variation of the non-agricultural occupations is represented thus:—

Extraction of Minerals	+169,521
Industry	+193,667
Transport and Trade	—125,6S6
Public Administration and Liberal Arts	—131,826
Miscellaneous Occupations	—3,360,059
The Net Decrease in Non-Agricultural Occupations	**—3,264,343**

15 PERCENT. DECLINE IN THE NUMBER OF INDUSTRIALS.

In other words, the non-agricultural occupations instead of showing an absolute and a relative increase of at least 6·9 per cent. at which rate the general population made an advance during this decade exhibited an absolute or actual decrease of 3·26 million persons, or a decline of more than 15 per cent.

ACTUAL DECLINE 27 PER CENT.

Had these classes, amounting to about 22,312,204 persons in 1901 kept pace with the growth of the pro vincial population, they would have numbered 23·85 millions in 1911, but what a reversal of industrial, commercial, educational progress was this that the year 1911 found 18·49 million persons alone in the fold of the non-agricultural classes ; *i.e.*, there was a net loss of 5·36 millions or 27 per cent. in those pursuits. But these economically depressed millions could not grow at the national rate, they had to bid farewell to their long-established, heriditary, socially and economically higher occupation in order that they might earn a scanty and precarious living on land as landless labourers !

The result of this enquiry can be summarized as below :—

		Persons
Added to Pasture and Agriculture	...	9,531,147
Pushed out of Non-Agricultural Occupations	...	3,264,343
Growth of Population	...	5,499,785
Available population	...	8,764,122
Calculated Loss of the Non-Agricultural classes		5,367,194

URBAN EXODUS.

The preceding investigation clearly points out that within one decade more than 9·5 million souls had to migrate from the non-agricultural pursuits to the primitive agrestic occupations ! Such is the very striking transition going on most silently under our very eyes, but the ignorant and illiterate, helpless and hopeless, sad and suffering, depressed and disheartened, the dumb and deluded millions, going down and down in the scale of humanity and civilization know not how to grumble. Every year hordes of the unemployed annually amounting to about a million, go to seek employment upon the land and thus help to keep down the wages of the agricultural labourer. Every year this incessant stream of the unemployed flows upon the land like the waters of Marah not to fertilize and fructify but to entirely dry up the agricultural industry. These shoals of the illiterate and the unemployed, choking up all the sources of wealth are becoming more and more pauperized. The national industries instead of being amplified and diversified, are continuously being simplified, reduced in number and crippled and crushed. Such in fact is the real condition of Bengal-the home of the jute industry and coal mining.

RISE IN AGRICULTURAL PERCENTAGE.

While the general average for the whole Lieutenant-Governorship was 72·44 in 1901, the proportional strength of the agricultural classes in 1911 (1) rose to 76·26, but 75·4 in Bengal and 78·3 in Bihar, 73·8 in Orissa and 75 in Chota Nagpur. Such is the wild rush after primitive agriculture, such the headlong decline in Bengal industries.'

RATES OF THE GROWTH OF AGRICULTURAL AND NATIONAL POPULATIONS.

While the national population of the two provinces increased at the rates of 6·7 and 5·1 per cent.* the actual increase amounting to 5,301,802 souls in both, the agricultural community increased at the rate of 15 per cent., the actual addition within the decade being 8,755,675 persons.

Addition to total pop. =5·3 millions.

Addition to Agricultural pop. =8·7 millions.

MARKED TENDENCIES OF THE TIME.

On analysing this increase in agriculture we find three very remarkable tendencies:

Ordinary cultivators have increased by 5 %, *rent-receivers* by 19 per cent., and *agricultural labourers* have increased by 110 %.

(a) Labourer-peasants on the Increase.

It is obvious therefore that land is going out of the hands of the cultivating classes, it is being acquired by pleaders, traders and other non-agricultural classes. Thus the element of personal interest and affection which landed property always naturally inspires, in the tillers of the soil is being steadily destroyed. Thus the great danger of landlessness is growing apace. It was indeed 'that wise and honest traveller,' Arthur Young, that Prince of Paradoxes who wrote a century ago

'The magic of property turns sand into gold. Give a man secure possession of a bleak rock, and he will turn it into a garden.'

However the present day tendencies in Bengal as in the other Indian provinces, are loosening the fast bonds of affection and self-interest, industry and intelligence, enterprise and success that result from ownership in the land.

(b) Landless Labourers Growing Apace—110 per cent. Increase.

When peasant-proprietors are being turned by stress of circumstances into labourer-peasants, it is but natural that any new additions to agriculture from the ranks of the unemployed non-agricultural classes must *pari passu* be landless labourers.

THE FLOATING POPULATION.

The labouring class, both agricultural or non-agricultural, amounting to

10,866,545 in 1901 and

12,513,013 in 1911

forms a floating part of the general population. They migrate from the country to the town or from rural industries to the urban ones and *vice versa* according to the needs of the seasons.

During this decade the number of persons allocated to the head "Labourers and workmen otherwise unspecified" fell from 5·87 to 2·01 millions, that is, on account of the greater attractiveness of agriculture, four and-a-half million persons (allowing for their natural increase) left non-agricultural occupations. But that was not all. The landless labouring class working on the land **numbered 4,991,264 souls in 1901, and grew to be 10,503,591 souls in 1911.**

Even making an allowance of 41 millions who migrated from urban industries as labourers and workmen, we have to account for 1⅓ million persons more. It is therefore certain that the ranks of landless labourers have been swollen by the

(1) Bengal Census Report. p. p. 557—562.
* Bengal Census Report, p p. 63.64.
† Bengal Census Report, p. 62.
Bengal Census Report, p. 567.

accretion of about one million from cultivators who had lost their land and from artisans who could no longer support themselves by the earnings of their ancient occupations. Thus persons who have no stake in the country, who being unemployed for the greater part of the year on account of the desultory character of the work of agriculture are sunk in poverty and suffering, are ever on the increase. They are swelling the ranks of labour and thus tend to keep down wages in these times of rising prices. They already live from hand to mouth on the coarsest food, and thousands have to be satisfied with one meal a day, yet their misery is being constantly deepened.

Thus a vast number of people amounting to 12½ millions in Bengal, Bihar, and Orissa alone,

Strangers to the bare necessities of human existence,
Strangers to education, culture and refinement,
Unknown to any comforts and luxuries, health and happiness,
Ever striving and struggling against
Starvation steadily staring them in the face,
Being more and more involved in
Mental, moral and physical prostitution,
Incapable of extricating themselves
from the Meshes of Misery,
Are sunk in the slough of slavery, suffering and sorrow, deepening dejection and degradation.

Is there any way out of this hellish helotism?

No, none, so long as Free Trade is the ruling policy of the State. The misery of these millions of unfed, unclothed, unhoused, and unlettered men, women and children would ever be on the increase as long as we allow the foreigner to crush and murder our home industries by his bounty-fed, kartell-produced, subsidized cheap products.

Let it not be forgotten that even the writer of the Bengal Census Report, 1911 has drawn the attention of his readers to this point.

" This decrease is not to be wondered at, for, as is well-known, the indigo industry is declining owing to the competition of the synthetic dye and the falling of the price of the natural dye."

COTTON INDUSTRY DECLINING.

" In spite of the stimulus given to this industry by the *swadeshi* movement and by the efforts of Government to introduce improved and more profitable methods of work, *there has been a serious decline* in the number who subsist by the produce of their looms : the actual decrease in both provinces is a quarter of a million or 23 per cent."

Similarly *metal* industry shows a decline from 392,753 to 385,786 = 2 per cent., *trade* from 4,384,234 to 3,951,082 = 10 percent., *public administration* from 244,709 to 196,737 and *persons living on their income* from 78,757 to 61778 = 22 per cent. Such are the results of the working of Free Trade in one decade alone !

Then in the Census Report of 1891 the same sorry tale of decline has already been told. "It is sufficient to notice here the great prominence of cotton weaving, *which although in a state of decline* gives employment to a large number of persons, 1,092,577, than any other industrial occupation does." p. 284.

"Much as the weaving industry has suffered from the competition of Lancashire,"*

yet nothing has been done to revive that industry or to replace it by other industries through protective tariffs and active state aid.

CAUSES OF THE DESTRUCTION OF NADIA INDUSTRIES.

The District Magistrate, Mr. K. G. Gupta, now Sir K. G. Gupta, an ex-member of the India Council, observed that besides malaria and floods economic causes were at work for the diminution of population in Nadia.

"Foreign competition" he writes, "has gradually displaced local industries, such as the cotton fabrics of Santipur and Kumarkhali and the cutlery of Haringhata, and greatly impoverished the weavers and artisans engaged in them. The decline of indigo manufacture has been by no means an unmixed good. The factories gave employment to a large number of the respectable classes, imported labourers from the west, and spent a large amount of capital in the district. Their closure has certainly had a prejudicial effect on the growth of population. The impoverishment of the older families, especially of the Nadia Raj, and the transfer of their possessions to absentee proprietors, have greatly affected the Brahman communities, which were mainly supported by their liberality and piety, and also the numerous dependents and retainers whom their bounty maintained. Almost all the older settlements bear unmistakeable signs of decay—rank vegetation, ruined

* Census Report, 1891, 278.

houses, dried-up tanks, and abandoned homesteads. Want of occupation and the growing unhealthiness of the district have induced many of those who could afford to go and settle in Calcutta, and the healthier places of the West." (Bengal C. R., 1891, P. 90.)

THE GLORY OF MOORSHADABAD.

Another District Magistrate confirms the opinions of Mr. K. G. Gupta regarding the once world-famous Industries of Moorshadabad. The silk industry, the glory of Moorshadabad has now dwindled to nothing. But this old capital of Bengal was described by Lord Clive in these words .—

"This city is as extensive, populous, and rich as the city of London, with this difference, that there are individuals in the first possessing infinitely greater property than in the last city."

"The causes of the unprogressive condition of the district of Moorshadabad must be sought for within itself, and they are no doubt the decay of the silk and indigo industries, and in a larger degree the prevalance of fever similar to that which has been so fatal in neighbouring districts." Bengal C. R., 1891, P. 91.

THE MANCHESTER OF INDIA.

Then the weaving industry, the glory of Dacca has long been extinguished. "The Bengal silks, cloths, etc." writes Mr. Verelst, who was Governor of Bengal before Hastings, "were dispersed to a vast amount to the west and north, inland as far as Guzerat, Lahore, and even Ispahan."

The Whig Chancellor of the Exchequer, Mr. Labouchere, said in a speech on 12th February,

1841, that the British had utterly destroyed the manufactures of India by their manufactures, and that the district of Dacca, the Manchester of India, had dwindled into insignificance before the strides which British goods had made.

Dr. Lushington, in the same debate, referring to the evidence taken on the subject by a Committee in 1832, showing the "destruction of the manufactures and decline of the produce of Dacca," said that no one could read this " without the strongest feelings of sympathy and pain."

Sir Robert Peel (18th May, 1841) thus nobly expressed himself on the ruin of India's and especially of Dacca's Manufactures :—

"Can I forget the accounts of Dacca, once a great and flourishing city, the seat of prosperous manufactures, containing a population of 150,000 inhabitants, now reduced to 20,000 or 30,000, with malaria and fever extending their ravages and threatening to turn it into a desert ? Have the people of that country, ruined by our manufactures and subject to heavy fiscal demands, to be met only by the produce of Agricultural labour, have they no paramount claim on us ?"

RUIN OF INDUSTRIAL DACCA.

In the course of his speech at the opening ceremony of an Arts and Industries Exhibition at Dacca in 1916 the ex-Governor of Bengal, Lord Carmichael drew a picture of industrial Dacca in

---

The Fall of Protection by Bernard Holland, London, 1913, P. 91.

pre-British days and described how its downfall came about. Said His Excellency:—

"The name of Dacca is associated all the world over with the production of the finest muslin fabrics which the hand of the weaver has ever wrought and many are the stories told of these muslins which are remembered under such picturesque names as "morning dew" and "running water", to quote but two of them. Travellers have left their record of the glories of Dacca in the old days and of the embroideries and silver work produced by the inhabitants. But from the day when Alivardi Khan left here and took up his residence at Murshidabad the glories of Dacca began to decline.

The court rapidly decreased and much of the market for beautiful things consequently was lost. To add to this disaster the English merchants whose influence became paramount were more interested in making fortunes for themselves and profits for the Company which they served than in encouraging and preserving indigenous industries and *the cheaper goods of the west took away most of what market* **remained and such of the artisans** *as did not return to agriculture* **kept themselves alive by supplying the small demand from the richer families mostly**

on the Surat side of India, who refused to be satisfied with anything but the genuine article.

TABLE I

A BIRD'S-EYE VIEW OF BENGAL.

	1891	1901	1911
Agricultural Pop.	65·2	72·44	76·26
Non-Agricultural Population ...	35·8	27·56	23·74

TABLE II.

Growth of Provincial population	5·1	6·9
Growth of agricultural population	19	15

TABLE III.

MEAN DENSITY PER SQ. MILE in Bengal, Bihar and Orissa.

1872	1881	1891	1901	1911
321	359	386	405	433
IN BENGAL.				
412	440	473	510	515
IN BIHAR AND ORISSA.				
252	299	321	327	344

C. R. 1911, P. 161.

TABLE IV.

URBANIZATION.

Growth of population during 1872—1891	...=15 per cent.	
Growth of Urban Pop.	.. =7 per cent.	
Growth of T. Pop. during 1891—1911	...=13½ per cent.	
„ Urban Pop.	...= 2z „	
Growth of T. Pop. during 1871—1911	...	34·7
„ of Urban in Bengal		32 } *a*
„ in Bihar and Orissa		8 } *a*
„ in Bengal	...	61 } *b*
„ in Bihar and Orissa		21 } *b*

(*a*) Shows increase in places that were treated as towns in 1872, (*b*) includes even those places that were subsequently treated as towns.

The position of Bengal as of the whole of India is very peculiar. While in the civilized world a most remarkable development is to be seen in urban population, Bengal has practically remained stationary in this respect during this long period of 39 years. While on one side even in republican and democratic France where the growth of national population is insignificant, large cities have rapidly grown up, where 'with its sub-divided land and its much talked-of *petite culture*, a real *depopulation of the rural communes is taking place*,'* in Bengal we note the extraordinary phenomenon of a marked migration from urban districts into rural areas, of *urban* depopulation and with it the decay of urban and village industries in these already predominantly rural and agricultural provinces.

---

* Studies in Statistics by G. B. Langstaff, P. 164.

CHAPTER X.

BACKWARD BURMA.

Burma is a country of singular beauty and fascinating scenery, of gaiety and vivacity. Its people are, by nature, probably the happiest in the world. Most of the requisites of modern Utopias they already possess: leisure, independence, absolute equality, the nearest approach to a perfect distribution of wealth; in addition, a happy temper, cheerful in all adversities. They are full of laughter and fun, of lively fancy, of wit and of creative power. In short, the life of a Burmese is all vivacity, charm and fascination. His gaiety, his light-heartedness, his love of sport and amusement, his bisure and happiness are in singular contrast to the cheap, inferior and squalid life of his Indian neighbours 'of whom many millions live all their lives upon the verge of starvation. It is the Burmese idiosyncrasy that gives to Burma its fascination and its charm; that makes of it, with its colour, its luxury; its beauty, and its ease, a Silken East.' Hidden away in the folds of mountains Burma has for thousands of years, remained protected from the aggression of Indian and Chinese invaders, but 'the sea did at last open the floodgates of in-

---

This description is based on the first two chapters of the 'Silken East' by V. C. Scott O'Connor.

vasion, and under the political supremacy of England, the economic competition of inferior and cheaper races from India, and of the superior Chinese now crowding up from the Straits, *the Burmese personality runs in some peril of extinction.* There is no longer a court to form the heart of any national feeling; there is no longer, it would seem, any motive in keeping the race supreme in its own country, and there is lacking in the people that sternness which might alone, in the absence of such fostering influences, help to maintain their idiosyncrasy intact.'

Ever since British peace has been established there, the Burmese of the Silken East, no longer able to cope with their stern and vigorous competitors are in danger of being superseded, driven away and wiped out of the higher economic life. In this chapter it will be our painful duty to describe the transition that under Pax Britannica is silently going on to the permanent detriment, deterioration and degeneration of such a lively and interesting race.

VOCATIONAL DISTRIBUTION.

In 1881 the whole population—male and female—was distributed over the six classes of occupations as follows :—

TABLE 1.

Agricultural	...	31·8	Professional	...	1·4
Industrial	...	9·0	Domestic	...	·7
Commercial	...	4·2	Indefinite and non-productive		52·7

(Burma C. R., 1881, P. 95.)

But the number of persons supported by agricultural occupations was said to be 2,562,070 or 68·56 per cent.—a rough calculation indeed, as we will see afterwards.

URBAN DECLINE DURING 1872—81.

Then in 1881, the urban population formed 11·4 per cent. of the whole as compared with 13 per cent. in 1872. Thus the proportion of the urban to the total population *fell by 1·6 per cent.* during these 9 years.

INDUSTRIAL DECAY DURING 1872—1881.

Comparing the statistics of Table 1 with those of 1872 given below, the following points strike the observer. The proportion of *Agricultural workers* was 22·4 per cent. in 1872, instead of 31·8 in 1881; then industry, commerce and professions occupied 10·9, 4·1 and 2 per cent. of the population, in other words, in 1872, these three engaged 17 per cent., but in 1881 only 14·8; thirdly, the ratio of the indefinite and the unoccupied persons was less by three per cent. in 1881. All these are sure indices *of the decline of the non-agricultural classes and the rapid growth—more than 10 per cent. of the agricultural population.*

TABLE 2.

OCCUPATIONAL DISTRIBUTION IN 1871.

	Actual Nos.	%		Actual Nos.	%
Agricultural	... 615,772	22·4	Professional...	56,161	2·0
Industrial	... 299,656	10·9	Domestic ...	133,657	4·8
Commercial	... 112,612	4·	Indefinite	...1,529,290	55·7

(Burma C. R., 1881, P. 87.)

GROWTH OF POPULATION.

The total area of British Burma remained the same, 87,220 square miles in these nine years, but the population of British Burma was 2,747,148 in August 1872 and 3,736,771 in February 1881, showing an increase of 989,623 or 36·02 per cent. 1·1 per cent. of this increase, we are told, was due to deficient enumeration in the year 1872; 12·7 per cent. was due to immigration, and 22·2 per cent. to natural growth. It will also be interesting to notice how far the province made progress in other respects during the ten years from 1871 to 1881.

	1871	1881
Cultivated area in acres ...	2,090,386	3,518,585
Value of seaborne trade. Exports £ ...	3,894,894	9,478,143
Value of seaborne trade. Import £ ...	3,903,144	8,802,273
Total rice exports in tons ...	487,162	892,262
Number of boats plying on the rivers	60,329	65,000
Miles of railway open	9	38
,, canal ,, ...	0	39
Land Revenue £"	331,944	656,891

Hence it is obvious that so far as the growth of population, agriculture, foreign trade and transport by rail or canal were concerned, the province showed a most remarkable progress. (Burma C. R., P. 96.)

The cultivated area per head of the population did also increase from ·76 to ·94 per acre, but the land revenue received by the Government did also rise from 3·2 to 3·7 shillings per acre. Thus the province presented every prospect of prosperity.

GROWTH OF POPULATION, 1881—1891.

In 1885 the Kingdom of Ava with its states was annexed to the British Territory by the name of Upper Burma. This new land had an area of 83,473 square miles. The Census of 1891 showed a population of 4,658,627 souls in Lower Burma and 3,063,426 in Upper Burma. The growth of 24·67 per cent. shown by the population of Lower Burma alone was the most rapid among all the Indian provinces. It was far in excess of any of the returns of these territories of the Empire, because Madras and Bombay alone showed a decennial increase of about 16 and 14½ per cent., while none could claim to have even half the extraordinary increase of Lower Burma. In fact this very high rate of increase far exceeded the annual rate of increase of any European country and almost equalled the extraordinarily rapid growth of the United States where the population having a maximum natural increase is being annually recruited by large swarms of immigrants.

DECAY OF TOWNS FROM 1871 to 1891.

The growth of urban population which had experienced a set-back in 1881 seems to have continued to be slack even in this decade, because no more than 11·6 per cent. of the population in that year were inhabitants of towns against 13 per cent. in 1872. This tendency of declining urbanization during the last two decenniums may be observed by the fact

that while the urban population increased by 19 per cent. between 1872 and 1891, the rural increas-

ed at the rate of 38·6 per cent. Some of this disparity is certainly to be accredited to faulty enumeration of 1872, yet there can be no doubt that the rural tracts gained at the expense of the urban. This constant tendency is visible during the next decade even and has been frankly confirmed by the writer of the Burma Census Report of 1891 (P. 43). "Whether we take," says Mr. H. L. Eales, "The growth of the towns in detail or in the aggregate, we see that the population of the rural tracts is on the whole growing more quickly than that of the towns."

CAUSES OF URBAN DECAY.

'This of course is due to the fact that with exception of the timber and rice mills we have no large manufacturing industries in the province. Moreever, the Burmans find that the demand for rice has raised the price of paddy so high that the cultivator is handsomely paid for his labour.' But we might add that by reason of the settled policy of the Government, agriculture was pushed by all means, hence the **extension of cultivation during these ten years has been simply remarkable, for whereas the population grew by 24½ per cent., area under cultivation showed an increase of 49½ per cent.**

PROGRESS OF RURALIZATION IN 1881-1891.

Such an enormons growth cannot but augur an abnormal rural increase. This forecast is amply borne out by the statistics of the next decade. We will describe this growing exodus to the land in the words of the writer of the Census Report.

"So far as can be ascertained," writes Mr. Eales, "from the return of 1881, about 56·68 per cent. of the males over 14 years of age were engaged in agriculture. Taking the return for the whole of Burma, we find that out of 2,418,639 males over 14 years of age, 1,434,017 or 59·29 per cent. were employed in agricultural pursuits. We find that **this order absorbs 63·46 per cent. of the total population; in Lower Burma the percentage rises to 68·15, while in Upper Burma it sinks to 56·06** which is almost exactly the same as the return of Lower Burma in 1881. It is very certain that agriculture in Lower Burma, with its broad paddy plains, must absorb a larger proportion of population, and it is probable that a large number of farm hands were in 1881, classed as coolies, of whom there were 87,675, and who were shown in the Indefinite class. It is possible however, that the **extension of cultivation and the decay of the fisheries in more than one of the deltaic districts may account for the higher percentage of agricultural labourers shown in our Lower Burma returns. It is at least quite clear that agriculture has lost none of its attractions and still absorbs as much, if not more, of the total working population" (p. 254).**

DECLINING URBANIZATION DURING 1891-1901.

From the Census Statistics we find that of the total population of the province 9,500,686 persons, or 90·6 per cent. of the aggregate, were enumerated in rural areas and 989, 938 or 9·4 per cent. in urban.

In 1891 the urban population amounted to 946, 649 or 12·4 of the total population, that is to say, it was 3 per cent. higher than in 1901.

This fall from 12·4 to 9·4 per cent. was due to a small extent to the addition of the Shan States and the Chin Hill areas comprising a vast rural population, but apart from this,

'the urban figures for Burma show a real decline.'

Once again the writer of the Census Report acknowledges that

'The inference to be drawn from this is that in Burma the growth of the urban population does not keep step with the growth of population as a whole. (P. 14.

Thus in thirty years the proportion of urban population fell from 13 to 9·4 per cent. of the total population. Let us now look to the strength of the agricultural community.

GROWTH OF THE ARICULTURAL CLASSES.

In 1901, 6,947,945 or 67 per cent. of the total population were supported by pasture and agriculture. In 1891 the corresponding figure was 4,879,490, in other words, the Pastoral and Agricultural class then comprised 6,415 out of every 10,000 persons of both sexes. It will thus be seen that the proportion of agriculturists in the wider sense of the term rose by 285 per ten thousand during the past decade.

The opening up of the delta districts to the foreign and Upper Burma immigrant must be looked upon as part cause of this rise, but the main factor in the increase is, no doubt, the inclusion in the operations ot the political areas in which the agricultural element preponderated. (P. 138.)

PROGRESSIVE DECLINE OF URBAN POPULATION 1901—1911.

When we turn our attention to the last Census enumeration, we observe the same tendencies strengthened and intensified as have been painfully presented in the preceding pages.

It is extremely remarkable that the urban population shows again a slight decrease during the next ten years.

The percentage of the urban population of the province fell slightly from 9·4 to 9·3, whereas, for Burma Proper, an identical area for both enumerations, the percentage was similarly reduced from 10·7 to 10·6.

'The extremely slight difference' writes Mr. Morgan Webb, 'between the percentages of the urban population for 1901 and 1911, respectively suggests that the loss of population in certain towns has been compensated by its increase in other towns and by the growth of the 15 new urban centres now included for the first time. It would almost appear as if the loss in one direction had been made good in another, leaving the proportion of urban to the total population practically unaffected. Such a conclusion, though apparently justified by the figures would not be consistent with the facts. The percentage has only **been maintained by the transfer of large number of persons from one class to another, by the operation of irrelevant causes without any corresponding change in conditions'. (P. 19).**

This last part of the remark fully reveals how the superintendent of the census operations himself is dissatisfied at the irrelevancy of transferring certain villages to urban areas and how he feels that the stationary character of the urban ratio is only apparent than real, because there has actually *been an urban decline.*

The enquiry into the true causes of urban decline in India is highly interesting. It is therefore most satisfactory that Mr. Morgan Webb has thrown a searchlight upon the causes of this lamentable decadence. His remarks howsoever lengthy are instructive in many ways, hence they are reproduced here in full.

EFFECT OF AGRICULTURAL DEVELOPMENT ON URBAN POPULATION.

It is possible to give some specific, conclusive, local reason in each instance for the failure of the 26 non-progressive towns to keep pace with the general movement of the province for the past twenty years. And yet such detailed explanations would be of little value. The symptoms are too widespread to be the result of the operation of purely local causes. There must be some broad, potent influence, *operating over a wide range of space and time, to produce so extensive and so unexpected a result. An untimely* break of plague, the silting of a river channel, the deterrent effect of Municipal taxation, and similar minor causes, may be ostensible and genuine immediate factors in the diminution of the population of a town. But such factors could not simultaneously prevail over a wide area if the urban population of the province were proportionate to the economic *functions it performed. The existence of so large a proportion of non-progressive towns in a rapidly progressive province indicates some mal-adjustment of population gradually being corrected* by the transfer of the superfluous urban inhabitants to localities where their services are more urgently required. *It suggests a natural spontaneous movement back to the land. It implies an exact reversal of the economic conditions which are driving the surplus rural population of Western Europe into the towns. It is in fact due to a comprehensive instinctive effort to affect the colonization of the waste places of the province.* The movement from the towns is but one aspect of the general movement towards its available culturable areas. It is in this direction, and not in a minute examination of petty, partial and diverse local causes, that the true solution of the problems of the urban population of Burma is to be found. In the past circumstances *have permitted a larger concentration of the population in towns than modern conditions will support.*

But with the advent of peace and security *the possible area of cultivation has widely extended. High prices, a strong export demand, the certainty of a market, and land waiting to be cultivated, have combined to exert a strong economic pressure towards areas remote from the possibility of urban residence. The policy of the Government in* preventing the wholesale appropriation of available areas, and in making a plot of 15 acres the unit of distribution, has tended to effect a wide dispersal of population, and to perpetuate the conditions of dispersion. *The object of the Government, the establishment of a peasant proprietary on the land gradually coming under occupation, has stimulated the growth of an agricultural, rather than of an urban population.*" (*P. 20.*)

URBAN DECAY SUMMARIZED.

The net result of these permanent causes is a continuous urban decline in Burma. The dynamic variation can be presented in the appended table as follows :—

Percentage of Urban Population in

	1911	1901	1891	1881	1872
Lower Burma	10·6	10·7	12	11·4	13
Province	9·3	9·4	12 4	...	...

Thus over a period of 39 years, while the population of Burma has been steadily and rapidly increasing, so that it has

more than doubled, the urban population has gone on declining to such an extent that it is 2·4 per cent. less in the total population than it was in 1872.

The summarized growth of the population from 1872 to 1911 is given in the subjoined statement :

Year.		Population.	Per cent. Increase.
1872	...	2,747,148	...
1881	...	3,736,771	36
1891	...	4,658,627	25
1901	...	5,645,673	21
1911	...	6,460,687	14·5
1872—1911	...	3,713,439	135 %

Upper Burma was first brought under Census enumeration in 1891. Its population then amounted to 3,063,426 souls. In 1901 new areas were added having a population of 1,371,890, but in the next census of 1911 the increase of population due to new areas was only 43,289 souls. Thus the statistics of population for 1901 and 1911 over every portion of Burma proper for which statistics were recorded in 1891 are :—

1891	...	7,390,065	17·5 per cent. Increase.
1901	...	8,687,493	14·5 " "
1911	...	9,947,435	34·6 " "

RELATIVE STRENGTH OF EACH CLASS OF OCCUPATION IN 1911.

A general review of the proportion of the population supported by the four main classes and by the twelve chief subclasses of occupations will be highly interesting :—

Class		Subclass	
Production of Raw materials	71·75	Exploitation of the surface of the earth	71·63
		Extraction of Minerals	·13
Preparation and Supply of Material Substances	19·97	Industries	6·70
		Transport	3·27
		Trade	10·00
Public Administration and Liberal Arts	3·70	Public Force	·66
		Public Administration	·86
		Professions and Liberal Arts	2·12
		Persons living on their incomes	·06

Miscellaneous	4·57	Domestic service	·71
		Insufficiently described occupations	3·57
(Burma C. R, 1911, (Pp. 298=99)		Unproductive	·29

It is obvious that agricultural pursuits have got a decided preponderance over all the remaining occupations combined, for whereas the former support 71·63 per cent. of the total population. the latter, i.e., all the remaining industries of the province engage only 28·37 per cent. It means that

Agricultural Population = 71·63 per cent.
Non-Agricultural Population = 28·37 per cent.

But these figures do not reveal the whole truth. We learn from the writer of the Census Report that 'these proportions are based on records taken at a period when agricultural operations *are almost at their slackest for the whole year*, and consequently many persons normally engaged in agriculture are entered under other occupations. 'It is therefore probable,' says he, 'that on the whole more than 79 per cent. of the inhabitants of the province derive their means of subsistence from direct exploitation of the surface of the earth.' P. 298.

The economic dangers of such an exclusive dependence upon one occupation alone have been discussed and enlarged upon at more than one occasion in the preceding pages. Every nation has tried hard to broaden the basis of the means of livelihood, but it is a thousand pities that

Burma like all other provinces in India is being obliged by the stress of circumtances to depend more and more upon one sole means of subsistence. It is highly strange that industry, with its 14 orders of industries connected with textiles. hides and skins. wood, metals, ceramics, chemical products, food, dress and toilet, furniture, building, transport, construction, physical forces, luxury and refuse matter, *affords the means of subsistence to only 6·7 per cent. of the population against 11 per cent. in 1872.* Trade alone comes next to agriculture, supporting exactly 10 per cent. of the population. But what sorts of industry and trade are to be found in this country? The answer is best supplied in the words of the distinguished writer of the Burma Census Report ;—

> The remaining industries are almost entirely dependent on agriculture for their welfare. 'Transport' is little more than the collection of agricultural produce and the distribution of general requirements to agriculturists. 'Industry' is largely the conversion of agricultural produce for export or use, or the preparation of the requirements of the agricultural population. Similarly, 'Trade' is vitally dependent on agriculture, advancing with its advance and sharing its vicissitudes. In the undeveloped condition of the mineral resources of the province, agriculture is the only extensive primary industry, the remaining industries are subsidiary, and dependent for their existence on its general prosperity."

(B. C. Rep. 1911, P. 317).

There is already little industry, but even that little is being constantly taken away from the sons of the soil. The Burman, it is said, is not suited to town life, though he is extremely fond of the amenities of town life. It is boldly asserted that he is not born for industries but for agrestic pursuits and hence he is to patiently suffer the terrible result of being invaded and pushed aside from his ancient industries by Indian and European settlers. Is it not extremely strange that the Indian—Hindu or Moslem-whose energies remain cramped and confined to primitive agriculture and from whose hands industries are being wrested, finds a very healthy scope for his energy and art in Burma? There he has monopolized the non-agriculrural industries and is filling up the Burman towns to the detriment of the Burman himself ?

'Perhaps the best method of exhibiting the contrast between the distribution of the general population of the province and the Indian population between agricultural and non-agricultural occupations, is to be seen in the appended table. The percentages are almost reversed. While the agriculturists of the whole province are roughly in the proportion of 70 to 30, for the Hindu population the proportion is 24 to 76 and for the Mahomedans (excluding Akyab) it is 27 to 72.

AGRICULTURAL AND NON-AGRICUTURAL OCCUPATIONS.

	Province.	Hindu.	Mahomedans.
Pasture and agriculture	70·37	23·48	27·07
Remaining occupations	29·63	76·52	72·93

Then for the confirmation of the second part of our statement let us look to subsidiary Table IV on page 31 of the Burma Census Report 1911. It gives the per mille composition of the urban population of the province.

From that table we learn that over one half $\frac{532}{1000}$ of its Hindu inhabitants and over one third $\frac{352}{1000}$ of its Musalman inhabitants live in towns compared with so low a population, as 6·7 per cent. of the Budhistic community. The remarks of the Census Superintendent deserve to be carefully read by all those who are interested in the dynamics of Indian economic life. "But penetrating beneath this obscurity two definite and distinct tendencies are observed : the first is a slow but continuous transfer of a portion of the indigenous population from the towns to the available uncultivated areas of the province. The second is a complementary *invasion of the towns by the members of alien races who are quite prepared* to undertake the mechanical and industrial occupations of modern industry.

The two movements act and react upon one another. At the present time they are tending towards an equilibrium between the rural and urban populations of the province." (Page 24).

THE PAUCITY OF BURMAN INDUSTRY

Can be best exhibited by the number of industrial units which have been reported as employing 20 or more persons. On the date of the census enumeration they were 350 only giving employment to 78,677 persons, comprising 75,337 males and 3,340 females. The largest number 30,059 was occupied in food industries, 29,872 of these being employed in rice milling operations; chemical industries formed the second largest industrial group with 11,150 workers, of these 10,747 were engaged in the various operations of petroleum refining. The next largest group of industries with 9,833 persons was connected with the conversion of timber. This is closely followed by mines and petroleum wells with 9,006 workers. The rubber industry which is even now emerging from infancy claimed 4047 workers.

Thus rice milling, refinery and extraction of petroleum, conversion of timber and extraction of minerals (employing 15,293 according to the special Industrial Report) are the five principal industries of the province. Combined with all the minor industries they gave employment to not more than 80,000 persons in 1911. But the Burman is largely excluded from these, he is mainly dependent on immigrant labour for the large associated industries. Oil refinery, for instance, employed over ten thousand workers, but the indigenous Burmese formed only 15·8 per cent. of the population supported, 83·6 per cent. being Indians (*59·5 per cent*. Hindus and 24·1 per cent. Mahomedans) (Page 321.)

A VIEW OF THE LARGE INDUSTRIES OF BURMA IN 1911.

Industry.	Number of industrial units	Actual workers Total	Average number of workers per cent.
Growing of special Products.	10	4,047	404
Mines and Petroleum wells.	38	9,006	237
Quarries of hard rock	14	4,125	295
Textiles ...	6	889	148
Wood ...	82	9,833	120
Metal ...	11	2,486	226
Glass and earthenware.	2	153	76
Chemical ...	12	11,150	929
Food ...	155	30,059	194
Transport construction.	10	4,907	491
Production and transmission of physical force.	2	267	133
Printing ...	8	1,755	219
Total ...	350	78,677	225

Burma Census Rep., 1911, P. 303.

It was remarked that poor 'Industry' is severely suffering from foreign encroachment in the shape of foreign cheap goods and from internal ignorance with the consequent increase of ruralization. The most remarkable feature of the last intercensual period is the large decline in the population supported by industrial occupations from

1,028,022	in	1901	to
806,431	in	1911	

The writer of the 1911 Census Report remarks that there has been a *genuine decrease in some* of the industrial occupations, but that a large portion of the decrease is apparent only, and due to the impossibility of instituting any effective comparison between the figures for the two enumerations He advances two reasons for not separating the returns of industry from trade. The one is that the distinction between 'Industry' and 'Trade' is very largely artificial in Burma, the maker and seller of a commodity being generally the same person. The second reason is more to the point and it is that in 1901 the distinction was not even attempted in the census returns. It therefore means that instead of artificially separating the combined figures, we should take the whole main class of the Preparation and Supply of Material Substances and institute comparisons in the two census years. The results are presented in the statement below :—

	Population supported in 1901	1911	% Variation.
Industry ...	1,028,022	806,131	−22
Transport ...	259,053	393,652	52
Trade ...	1,010,081	1,203,721	19
Total ...	2,297,156	2,403,804	4·6

These three sub-classes combined exhibit a small increase of 4·6 per cent. against the 52 per cent. extraordinary growth in transport and 19 per cent. increase in trade. *Industry, however shows a very marked decline of 22 per cent.* We cannot ignore this industrial decadence and call it merely apparent, because *the whole class supported 19·97 per cent. of the inhabitants of the province in 1911 against 22·89 per cent. in 1901.* The position occupied in the general classification of occupations by this class has thus been lowered by about 3 per cent. during ten years. If there be any shred of doubt concerning the decadent condition of industry and commerce in Burma, we ought to compare their decennial progress with the growth of the total population.

While the latter has increased by 15·5 per cent., the population employed in the preparation and supply of material substances increased by 4·6 per cent. alone.

Decennial Growth of total population = 15·5 per cent.
" " " Industrial " = 4·6 per cent.

In the face of these facts, it is to be hoped, that it would be frankly recognised that *much* of the industrial decline is genuine and only a *small* part apparent. The comparative position of occupations can now be presented in the following statement:—

DISTRIBUTION OF POPULATION BY FOUR MAIN CLASSES.

Designation.	Percentage in 1901.	Percentage in 1911.
Production of Raw Materials ...	67·97	71·76
Preparation and Supply ...	22·89	19·97
Public Administration and Liberal Arts ...	5·39	3·70
Miscellaneous ...	3·75	4·57
	100.	100.

Thus the occupational distribution has undergone great variations in its percentage strength. For instance, the proportional strength of the population employed in the production of raw materials has risen by a little less than four per cent, the miscellaneous also shows some increase, but the other two classes exhibit a marked decline.

Throughout this book we have been showing how the industrial decline is interchangeably and inevitably related to agricultural growth. In

Burma, the same fact comes out with great prominence, for within ten years, there has been effected a very big change in the main classes of occupations.

But the true extent of this movement to the land, of this constant exodus to the primitive extractive industry will best be shown by the succeeding statement :—

PASTORAL AND AGRICULTURAL POPULATION.

1911	8,472,391
1901	6,950,359
Increase	1,522,032
Per cent. Increase	22

It is a pity that such a sane and liberal writer as Mr. C. Morgan Webb, should add insult to injury by remarking that the increase of 1,522,032 persons or 22 per cent. in the population dependent on Agriculture in ten years *appears to show a healthy rate of increase.* This remark more than ever acts like sprinkling salt upon deep wounds. That the primitive industry of agriculture should increase at the rate of 22 per cent. per decade against 4·6 per cent. increase in the manufacturing, commercial and tradal pursuits and against 15½ per cent. increase in the total population, that pasture and agriculture should claim 1,522,032 persons more while the gross increase in the actual population of the census enumerations be 1,624,593,* and yet this increase should

* C. R., 1911, P. 95.

be dubbed a healthy increase, is nothing but a wonder. If ever a black can become a white, then this unhealthy, injurious and uneconomic and degrading agricultural expansion can justly be termed a healthy progress. The impertinency of this remark must be apparent to every unbiased reader and to every writer free from official bias. In the light of the preceding enquiry, we are sure that the feelings of every reader must have been deeply wounded by such an ill-placed opinion. It is really very wonderful that this ordinary statement of facts should have been so distorted and disfigured by Mr. Webb.

FORTY YEARS OF BACKWARD BURMA.

COMPARISONS AS REGARDS ACTUAL WORKERS.

Below we show the percentage proportion which the actual workers in Agriculture bore at each successive census to the total population of the province :—

1872	...	22·4
1881	...	31·8
1891	...	...
1901	...	27·87 (Burma C. R., P.148).
1911	...	37·04 (C. R., P.332.)

A period of 39 years has so transformed the strength of the workers engaged in agrestic pursuits that about 15 per cent. more persons were occupied in 1911 as compared with the year 1871.

A statement can similarly be made for presenting the proportions of persons *supported* by pasture and agriculture.

GROWTH OF THE PASTORAL AND AGRICULTURAL CLASSES, 1872—1911.

Percentage of Total Population.

1872	22·4	Of actual workers in Lower Burma.
1881	31·8	Ditto.
	68·56	Supported, a rough guess of the census writer.
1891	64·15	For Upper Burma as well as Lower Burma.
1901	67·97	For the Province.
1911	71·76	Ditto.

Leaving aside the first two censuses we find that during the small period of twenty years the percentage strength of the agricultural population was enhanced by 7·61 per cent. with a *pari passu* proportional decrease in industry, transport and trade. Thus similar to other provinces, in the economic history of Burma the four inevitable facts that come to the surface are:—

2·4 per cent.	**Increase in rural proportion during**	**... 1872—.1911**
7·6 ,,	**Increase in Agricultural proportion during**	**... 1891—1911.**
4 ,,	**Decrease in Industrial proportion during**	**... 1872—1911.**
2·4 ,,	**Decline in urban proportion during**	**... 1872—1911.**

With these four incontestable facts before us can it be averred that Burma is not a retrogressive but a progressive province, *that it is not going backward* but forward?

THE DECLINE OF TEXTILE INDUSTRY.

From Table IX-A, P. 149 we learn that the textile industry supported 3·94 per cent. of the total population of whom 2·27 per cent. of the population were actual workers. Their actual number is not given in Part I of the Report, but on page 141 we are informed that in all 136,628 women and girls returned themselves as cotton weavers at the Census of 1901. The numbers engaged in the weaving industry are reduced to a sorry insignificance during the next ten years. Let us have the evidence of the writer of the Census in his own words on this vital point.

"*Textile industries*:—The decline in the number of persons supported by cotton weaving noticed in the Report for 1901 has continued with accelerated rapidity.

POPULATION SUPPORTED BY TEXTILE INDUSTRIES.

Occupation.	1911	1901
Cotton spinning, sizing and weaving ...	132,737	243,670
Silk spinners and weavers ...	18,621	34,104

Census Report, Burma, 1911 p. 322.

"The figures, however disturbed and distorted they may be by differences of record and differences of classification, are a reflection of the actual decline of the textile industries of the province. The indusries of spinning and weaving both silk and cotton, are domestic industries generally performed by the younger females of the household. The great majority of weavers and spinners are members of agricultural families, though in some localities the industries are sufficiently established to furnish full time occupation for a comparatively large proportion of the population. *The agricultural expansion of the past 30 years has tended to affect the textile industries adversely in two directions.* On the one hand the large extension of cultivation with advancing prices, has made the population as a whole much less dependent than formerly on the produce of such domestic industries. **On the other hand, in order to balance the enormous and advancing export of paddy, manufactures (largely textiles) have been imported in immense quantities. Economic forces have been tending to stimulate the agricultural industries of the province at the expense of those industries not directly connected with the disposal of agricultural produce. It is a commonplace among administrative officials of long standing that both the cotton and silk village industries are decaying. The sound of the loom that used to be heard continuously from morn till eve in almost every house in the village, is now heard neither so continuously nor so frequently as formerly."**

CHAPTER XI.

MALADIES OF MADRAS.

Now we turn our attention to the premier presidency which is still unfortunately, and perversely sometimes called the "benighted presidency." It has, no doubt been slowly and steadily making progress in many ways. Even a necessarily brief sketch of its economic conditions that is possible here, would reveal the main similarities or dissimilarities which this southern presidency bears to its northern sisters. We will consequently take up the following questions in the order as under: (*i*) the growth of its population (*ii*) the increasing pressure on land (*iii*) variations in avocational distribution (*iv*) decadence of Madras industries and (*v*) the present situation that has resulted from the dynamic changes of population and occupation.

GROWTH OF POPULATION IN MADRAS.

The population survey of the Madras Presidency presents large oscillations during the last forty years. Madras is the third largest of all the provinces of the Indian Empire including Burma, in area as well as in population. It is more than 20,000 square miles larger than the

United Kingdom and is even greater in extent than Austria and Greece together. The total population of the presidency including the feudatory states is just equal to that of the United Kingdom, but the strangest of all things is that the population of the whole presidency, though it is less by 55,434 square miles in area, exceeds that of France by more than 6·7 millions. It is, therefore, quite apparent that agricultural Madras has to support a greater number of persons per square mile than the industrially and agriculturally supreme French territory has to do. In fact the mean densities per square mile are 291 and 191 respectively. Hence it means that Madras with its primitive agriculture has to support one hundred more persons per square mile than the third richest and industrially predominant country of Europe has to do.

There has been a rapid increase in its population and hence in its mean density during the last 40 years. The total increase in population for the whole period is 10,274,782 and the ratio of increase in each decade since 1871 has been—1·24, 15·7, 7·2 and 8·3 respectively. The first *systematic* * census

---

The enumeration of 1871 has been called the first systematic census, not because previously no censuses had been taken, but only for the reason that the results of that census showed the previous enumerations of 1822, 1836, 1857, 1862, and 1867 to be worthless and hence quite unreliable.

Statement of the Moral and Mat. Progress, Rep. 1872—P. 123.

was taken in 1871, and, as the following table shows, there has been considerable variation in the intercensal growth of the population during the forty years under review.

GROWTH OF POPULATION, 1871—1911.

Census year.	Population of Madras in thousands.	Actual Intercensual increase in thousands.	Decennial increase per cent.
1871...	31,230	...	...
1881...	30,841	− 389	− 1·24
1891...	35,630	+4,789	+15·7
1901...	38,199	+2,568	+ 7·2
1911...	41,505	+3,306	+ 8·3

Thus with the exception of the first intercensual period of 1871—81 when there was an actual decrease in the population on account of the unprecedented mortality caused by the great famine of 1877, the three successive censuses have shown large increases. This presidency unlike the Punjab and the United Provinces has better chances of being compared with the progressive countries of the world, but that comparison would, at the same time, serve to show how far an Indian province can fall behind the really progressive countries in developing its numerical strength. It should however be remarked that the increase of the population in the ten years from 1881 to 1891 is simply remarkable in the light of the preceding and succeeding growths. It fully reveals the recuperative power of the people from the extremely depressing effects of a severe famine. Their rate of growth was *about* twice as great as in the two succeeding decades. But comparing this increase with the rates of the years preceding 1871, we find some different results. If the populations of 1851 and 1867 be taken as the basis of the calculation, the annual rate of increase becomes 1·186 per cent. Again, Mr. H. A. Stuart, writer of the Madras Census Report of 1891, after an elaborate calculation arrives at the result that 'in normal times, the population of the Madras Presidency will increase by about 12½ per mille per annum—and taking all circumstances into consideration, it seems to me probable that the rate of increase between 1891 and 1901 will not exceed 10 per mille per annum.'* But plague checked trade and enterprise, and there were three scarcities in 1891–92, in 1897 and in 1900, hence the prognastication of Mr. Stuart who had taken all circumstances into consideration, was falsified. Then the Superintendent of the Census of 1901 was wise enough to remark that 'the growth of the population in the next *thirty* years is *likely* to be at least as rapid as in the last thirty.' Whatever the value of this oracular prediction, it is undoubtedly a matter of great satisfaction that the net result of the last four

* Pp. 49—50.

census enumerations is an appreciable increase over the population of 1871. The following comparative statement would serve to bring out the salient feature of this growth as compared with some of the civilized countries of Europe and America :—

	Pop. in 1871	Pop. in 1911	* Increase % during 40 years
	(*In thous.*)		
United States ...	39,555	93,792	137·1
German Empire ...	41,000	66,096	61·2
England and Wales	22,712	36,075	59·0
Denmark	1,785	2,755	54·3
U. Kingdom ...	*31,629*	*45,653*	*44·3*
Sweden	4,169	5,609	34·6
Madras	*31,230*	*41,505*	*32·9*
Italy	26,801	34,687	29·4
Spain	16,799	19,944	18·7
France	37,000	39,602	7·0

It will be observed that the rates of the growth of population in Italy, Spain and France are lower than that of Madras, but those of the other six countries and especially of countries like the United States, Germany, England and Denmark are far higher than that of the Presidency. Madras and the United Kingdom had approximately the same

* Or in the latest available date. Figures for 1871 are taken from Mulhull's Dictionary, but those of 1911, from the Statistical Ab. of the U. States for 1913, p. 688.

population, but in the forty years that elapsed since 1871, the British Isles had about 4,048,000 persons more than Madras in 1911. Marvellous is the development of the population in Germany and still more dazzling is its growth in the States where it rose to respectively 161 and 237 in 1911 for every 100 in 1871.

However, the increase in Madras is relatively very high as compared with the Indian growth, because it is about 33 % against 19 per cent. of India during the forty years under review.

With the lowest productive area per head among all the provinces of India and with ever-growing exports of agricultural products, Madras cannot but be most liable to drought and famine. Combined with these maladies is the evil most admirably pointed out by the writer of the Census Report of 1871 (P. 365) in these words:—

> The actual condition of the cultivating classes is a subject of serious anxiety in a country where so many millions are dependent on the products of the soil. A single bad season is often sufficient to bring the population of extensive tracts to the verge of starvation, and to necessitate wholesale remissions of the land assessment, and national losses in many indirect ways. All this is extremely unsatisfactory, and points to the importance of directing administrative energy persistently towards agricultural improvements."

But the writer has again frankly and boldly charged the state for having done nothing to improve agriculture up to his time.

"Farming in India, like most of the industrial employments has made no practical advance under British rule. It is true that more waste lands have been brought under the plough and that population and production have increased in proportion, but it seems very questionable whether an acre of land in the present day yields larger returns than were reaped many centuries ago."

The consequences of this culpable neglect combined with ever-increasing revenue demands were soon to be seen in the disastrous famine of 1876-78. The productive power of the people did not improve, but the revenue per head went on increasing, so that it rose from 3½ millions sterling in 1858-59 to 4½ millions in 1876. "There are not wanting those' wrote the *Englishman* of Culcutta, 'who affirm that this increased taxation had much to do with the late calamity. The husbandmen were less able, according to this view, to bear the strain of bad seasons, *in consequence of the enormous increase in the revenue taken from them.*"

ESTIMATED LOSS BY THE FAMINE.

The figures, as shown below, give an estimated loss in 1881 of 3,777,657 or 10·17 %, on the population of 1881 *as it would have been but for the famine*:—

Corrected population in		1871	... 32,446,451
Estimated	,, ...	1881	... 34,912,632
Censused	,, ...	1881	... 31,134,975
Difference			3,777,657

Thus 3½ millions of people were missing in 1881. The figures as they stand are terrible enough. They point how deaths from sheer starvation or from starvation-induced diseases, by lost fertility, or by enforced migration terribly reduced the population of the presidency.

But the famine of that decade was not limited to Madras, but N. W. Provinces, Oudh and Bombay Presidency also heavily suffered from the effects of severe famines. 'The total loss in the four Famine-effected provinces during the decade, so far as it is shown in the bare census figures, was 3½ millions, and this loss merely represents the decrease on the population as counted at the previous census; the increment of the interval, which was also lost, is not included'. (P. 31) But allowing for the *natural growth of the populations of the famine stricken provinces, the estimate cannot be less than 6½ millions of persons.*

Such was the enormous loss of human capital in one famine alone, but India has become liable to recurrent famines and Madras can well be called the Land of Famines. Very severe famines decimated the people of the presidency five times in 1888-89, 1891-92, 1897, 1900, and 1907-08. Can there be, then, any doubt that the inhabitants of the affected areas must have been plunged into severe distress, misery and suffering? Madras can never escape from the clutches of famines, so long as she remains exclusively dependent on primitive agriculture alone. The only way out of this ever-recurring liability to famines lies in the development and diversification of her home and mill industries.

Another serious malady to which the Presidency is becoming more and more a prey is the outflow of the life blood of its land in the form of manures.

The following table shows the average weight and value of the exports of oil-seeds during the last ten years, also the number of gallons and value of the vegetable oils similarly exported :—

		Oils Rs. Value	Seed Rs. Value
Gingelly	...	5,42,189	25,73,457
Groundnut	...	30,36,554	1,27,58,776
Castor	...	6,98,633	22,58,205
Cocoanut	...	91,77,651	52,07,622
Other sorts	...	96,379	...
Cotton	...	...	4,26,460

The writer of the Census Report assigns the following reasons for the fact that oil-seeds are exported, and not the oils :—

1. Oil-seeds can be packed in bags, or carried in bulk, whereas oil must of necessity be carried in expensive casks.

2. There is a much better market for oil-cake in Europe than in India, and the freight on oil-seeds is less than the freight on oil-cake.

3. Protective tariffs encourage the importation of seed to the exclusion of oil, thereby securing to the importing country the business of extracting the oil.

Thus while other countries are sedulously encouraging all kinds of industries, by means of an active state-aid and protective tariffs we are constantly losing even the little we possess on account of the fatal free trade policy and the masterly inactivity and stoic indifference of the state to protect, preserve and encourage the home industries.

At the same time the following table shows that the foreign export trade is growing, and that the Presidency is parting with large quantities of valuable manures, which could, with very much greater profit, be employed in increasing the productivity of the soil :—

Years.	Animal bones	Fish-manure.	Oil cake.	Other kinds.	Total.
	Thou.Rs.	Thou.Rs.	Thou.Rs.	Thou.Rs.	Thou.Rs.
1901-02	110	...	...	29	140
1909-10	610	327	1376	262	2576
1910-11	427	630	1507	262	2827

It is obvious that in these ten years alone the export trade in manures of all kinds has increased 20-fold. We have the lowest yield of crops throughout the civilized world, our land is slowly deteriorating, it has, indeed, already reached the maximum limit of impoverishment, hence we need all the manuresand fertilizers for these lands. But the mass of our cultivating classes being ignorant and too poor to spend money on fertilizers, are constantly parting with them in ever-increasing quantities to the permanent loss of their own lands. This export trade is fraught with the most disastrous consequences to our economic progress and prosperity. But taken with the exportation of oil seeds, cotton and other food grains the evil of parting with manures adopts the most horrible form. A gradual murder of our lands in Madras as in the whole of India is being permitted by the export of all the food and commercial crops. In fact this is one of those fatal diseases which are eating into the very vitals of the economic life of the Presidency.

THE MAIN EMPLOYMENTS OF THE PEOPLE IN 1871.

The occupation tables in 1871 were framed so as to refer only to the male population, of an age to follow some calling, that is, males above twelve years of age, although in some instances younger male children were also included. The proportion of major groups to the total male population was as below:—

Cultivators	31· 1	Professional	2·
GeneralLabourers	13· 1	Personal service	3·
Industrial	7.72	Miscellaneous	2· 2
Commercial	3· 7		

Nearly one half of the whole number of persons were cultivators, while more than three-fourths of the labourers probably found employment in connection with the land. 'The cultivation of the land therefore gives employment to about two-thirds of the entire population. All other occupations fade into insignificance in comparison with that of the culture of the soil.' P. 178.

DISLOCATION DURING 1871-1881.

During the next decade Madras terribly suffered from a very severe famine. The industries of the presidency were appallingly dislocated. The labouring and the poorest agricultural classes were more than any other classes victims to the dire effects of famine. By reason of the most severe famine mortality these classes showed a relative decrease in the coming census.

The proportions in the several classes of male workers to the total male population in 1881 were 2·72 in professions, 0·71 in personal service, 2·30 in commerce, 44·37 in agriculture, 12·82 in industry and 3·45 in general labour. Comparing these returns with those of 1871 we find that the agriculturists increased 34·36 per cent. and the labourers decreased by 75⅓ per cent. If we combine the two classes of cultivators and labourers in one group and make some other amendments, then the percentage of workers on the total male population will be as follows :—

	1871	* 1881
Professional	2·04	2·72
Domestic	0·23	0·71
Commercial	3·16	2·30
Agriculture and Labour ...	48·77	47·82
Industrial	9·19	12·82

OCCUPATIONAL STRENGTH IN 1881.

Again the percentage of the general distribution of the working male population in Madras (1881) and in England and Wales (1871) was as below:—

	Madras	England
Professional	4	4
Domestic	1	3
Commercial	3	11
Agricultural	**67**	**20**
Industrial	**19**	**49**
Labourers and indefinite ...	6	10

From this table it appears that in Madras 67 per cent. of the total working population were making out their living from agriculture and 22 per cent. were engaged in commerce and industries, while in England and Wales the corresponding figures were 20 and 60 per cent.

---

* (Madras C. R. 1881, p. 176.)

Census Report of Madras 1881. Vol. I. p. 139.

Mulhull's Dictionary p. 424.

COMPARISON WITH OTHER PROVINCES.

Yet the position of Madras was one of peculiar advantage in India as is evidenced by the following comparison of the proportions engaged in agriculture to the total *working* population in the several Indian Provinces and in England and Wales.

Provinces		**% of Agricultural Population to Total Working Population in 1881.**
Assam	... ...	89·04
Berar	... ...	74·80
Central P.	... ...	68·66
N. W. P.	... ...	66·88
Bombay	... ...	66·65
Madras	... ...	**65·21**
B. Burma	... ...	63·02
Coorg	... ...	68·98
Bengal	... ...	56·24
India	... ...	64·09 Average
* **England and Wales**	...	**11·5**

In the above comparison Madras occupies the sixth position as regards the strength of her male working agricultural population. It is beaten by British Burmah and Bengal alone. However the proportion in Madras is slightly over the average for India. But at the same time a contrast with the English proportion in this class makes one of the essential differences between the occupations

Madras Census Report, Vol, I. p. 149. *Mulhull's Dictionary. P. 424.

of the English and the Indian population. About two-thirds of the Madras workers are workers on the land, and are producing food for themselves, for the other third, for the non-workers and for foreign manufacturers. In England about one-ninth of the workers are agricultural.

A comparison of the returns of the Provincial occupations for 1881 with those for 1891 is not practicable, because they by no means represent identical bases of classification and tabulation. 'In 1881, only those persons were shown who were returned as actually exercising an occupation, but, as the results obtained by this method were not found to be satisfactory, it was resolved, on the present occasion, to show under each occupation not only those who were actively engaged in it, but all those who subsist by it.'*

But with regard to the vocational distribution of the people in 1891, the Madras Census Report for 1891, Part I, P. 326 gives their percentages as follows :—

VOCATIONAL DISTRIBUTION IN 1891.

I.	Agriculture and Pasture ...	61·39
II.	Government	2·56
III.	Personal Services	2·99
IV.	Preparation and supply of material substances	18·64
V.	Commerce, transport and storage	2·47
VI.	Professions	2·3
VII.	Indefinite & Independent occupations	9·92

Madras Census, 1891, Vol. I, P. 325.

Taking the province as a whole 6,139 persons in every 10,000 or rather more than three-fifths of the population were supported by pasture and agriculture and 1,864 or nearly one-fifth by the preparation and supply of material substances. Indefinite occupations, the most important of which was general labour, formed the means of subsistence of 9·92 per cent. About three per cent. depended for their livelihood on personal services, while Government employment supported 2·56 per cent. Commerce, transport and storage follow with 2·47 per cent. and the professions come last with slightly over ·2 per cent.*

CORRECTION IN AGRICULTURAL PROPORTION.

General labourers numbering 2,609,224 consist acording to Mr. Stuart, the writer of the said Census Report, mostly of agricultural labourers, hence 2 million persons should be relegated to the agricultural class. Thus the real strength of that community by the addition of this large number would come up to 67 per cent. of the total population. In other words, agriculture and pasture claimed 67 per cent. people, while the indefinite and independent occupations could claim 9·92—5·6 = 4·32 per cent. of the total population.

It should, therefore, be remembered that although the figures for 1891 showed an apparently large decline in ruralization, yet this is not a fact as is attested by Mr. H. H. Stuart.

*Census or India, 1891, Vol. XIII. Page 348.

"As, however, it is desirable to see whether the agricultural character of the population is undergoing any marked change, I have perforce adopted the age distribution for urban male workers and applied this to all agricultural male workers. On this basis the proportion of male agricultural workers of 15 and upwards to the total population of both sexes was 19·52 per cent. in 1881. In 1891 the population of males of 15 and over, who depend on agriculture, was 19·62 per cent. The slight difference is fully accounted for by the fact that the figure for 1891 includes a number of youths and old men who only depend on agriculture and are not actual workers. On the whole we may conclude that agriculture holds practically the same place among the occupations of the people as it did in 1881." P. 325.

Notwithstanding the apparent incomparability of the two census returns it has been definitely pointed out by the official statistician that the predominently rural character of the presidency has suffered no decline. Let us now proceed to analyse the strength of the occupations of the next decade.

DISTRIBUTION OR CHIEF OCCUPATIONS IN 1901.

Agriculture and pasture ...	70·67
Government	1·66
Personal Services	2·84
Preparation and Supply of Material Substances ...	17·52
Professions	2·13
Commerce and transport ...	1·68
Indefinite and independent ...	3·50

A comparison with the preceding table shows that the strength of the agricultural community has increased apparently by 9 per cent., but really by about 4 per cent. The remarkable growth of the agricultural population can only be realized when we compare it with the increase of the provincial population. During the decade 1891—1901 the former increased by 25·78 per cent. against 7·2 per cent. of the latter, that is to say, the former grew at 3½- fold rate when compared with the growth of the population of the presidency as a whole. There is a very large decrease amounting to two million persons under the head of General Labour. It is therefore obvious that the agricultural conditions were more attractive than those of the non-agricultural occupations. General labour migrated from the depressed urban industries to the comparatively more remunerative agrestic pursuits. In short, while the increase in provincial population was 2,566 thousand persons the growth in the numbers of the people engaged in agriculture amounted to 4,296 thousand souls. Such an exodus to rural areas could not but cause an urban decline and decrease in urban professions. Each and every non-agricultural, highly paid and socially better occupation from the Government to the independent vocations shows a decrease. The total loss in their strength during that decade amounts to 9·28 per cent. ! Such are the mighty dislocations and disturbing readjustments in our industrial world ! Contrary to all the tendencies of the present day civilized world, in India we have been witnessing a continuous and progressive depression in our indigenous industries, arts, and professions. Such are the fatal economic maladies of Madras.

The following table will best serve to illustrate the state of the declining and prospering industries of the Presidency during the last decade of the nineteenth century :—

Declining Industries.	*Prospering occuptions.*
Sugar manufacture	Provision of animal and vegetable food.
Rice pounding	Petroleum.
Oil-pressing	Brick and tile making.
Thatching and building	Railway and tramway.
Cart-building	Ships and boats.
Musical Instruments	Watches, toys and scientific instruments.
Wool, fur, harness industries.	Furniture.
Cotton manufactures	Silk, jute, hemp and flax.
Metal working	Iron and steel.
Earthen and stoneware	Glass and chinaware.
Pictorial art and sculptor	Sale of hides & tanning
	Banking & Insurance.
	Law, medicine and engineering.
	Education.

The increase of industries which provide for comfort and luxury is no doubt for the prosperity of the country, but in India these do not absorb all those persons who are being thrown out by the declining occupations. The latter have therefore to migrate to land and become landless labourers.

Mr. J. C. Molony's Apprehension.

The next decade offers no interesting points in occupational distribution. Agriculture alone supported 68·18 persons per cent. in 1911 against 68·31 in 1901, but 'it is questionable,' says the writer of the census Report (P. 188), 'whether the very slight movement indicated by these figures is sufficient to justify the drawing of any conclusion as to a decrease in the popularity or possibilities of agriculture.' What an ignorance of the world forces operating in modern times is revealed in the last line of this official writer? He has forgotten that an extension of cultivation or an excessive growth in the output of agricultural products is taking place *pari passu* with a progressive decline in the number of persons engaged in agriculture in all the civilized countries. If agricultural improvements, mechanical inventions, scientific researches were applied in India and the economic efficiency of workers was developed by means of a rise in their standard of living, education and sanitation, then our agricultural produce could be doubled and trebled, and yet a smaller number will be required to work on the land as is occurring in all other progressive countries. Then why should the writer dread an unpopularity of agriculture in this country where four-fifths of the people are directly or indirectly supported by one precarious and primitive occupation? Is it because he shares with many of the bureaucrats the view that a diversion from agriculture in India and a direction to manufactures would be prejudicial to the interests of England?

URBAN DECLINE OR DEVELOPMENT?

DISTRIBUTION OF THE POPULATION BETWEEN TOWNS AND VILLAGES.

	No. per cent. residing in			
	1911	1901	1891	1881
Towns ...	11·7	11	9·56	10
Villages ...	88·3	89	90·44	90

It is obvious from this statement that during 30 years from 1881 to 1911, there has occurred a variation of 1·7 per cent. in the relative strength of the urban and rural populations. This does not however point to any industrial revival, because this urban increase is rather apparent than real. While in the European countries the application of machinery to agriculture is constantly reducing the demand for agricultural labourers and is on the other hand leading to an increased exodus to towns which are progressively becoming centres of manufacturing industries, while the tendencies of present day civilization being against rural life are facilitating concentration and congestion in developing industrial centres, while flocking into towns is the most striking phenomenon of the day, while the new as well as the old countries are becoming studded with large and rapidly growing cities, Madras like all other provinces

Madras Census Report 1911, p. 18
" " 1901, p. 21
" " 1881, p. 18

in India is in a moribund state. The real situation has been sketched by the writer of the Census Report in these words :—

'The movement is not apparently due to any increase in the industrial occupations open to the people, the percentages of the population subsisting by such callings having remained almost constant during the decade.'

But this explanation does not satisfy Mr. J. C. Molony, the Superintendent of 1911 Census who seeks the cause of this drift towards the towns in the contrast between the agricultural possibilities of the two decades. Favourable agricultural conditions arrested the townward quest of work during the *last* decade 1901-1911 is the dictum of the writer. It is, therefore, now abundantly proved that even the slightly greater urbanization has not brought with itself any improvement in the industries of the presidency.

But a shadow of doubt hangs upon the preceding figures when we compare and contrast them with the following comparative statement of the growths of the urban and provincial populations.

Madras Census Report, 1901, Vol. I, pp. 13-14.

		Percentage Decennal increase in Urban * population.	Total population.
1911	...	14·5	8·3
1901	...	24·8	7·2
1891	...	13·7	15·7
1881	...	—35·3	—1·24
From 1871 to 1911	...	+ 5·1	+ 33

Column 2 represents percentages on the total variation in urban population between decade to decade. There have been mighty oscillations in these percentage increases. The urban population rose since 1901 by only 15 per cent. againts 25 per cent. in the decade ending 1901, but the preceding decade of 1881 to 1891, had only 14 per cent. increase against its succeeding decade. However, the most depressing effects of the terrible famine of 1877 were felt by the urban population that declined by 35 per cent. against 1·24 % decrease in the total population. The net result of these oscillations is an insignificant increase of 5 per cent. during the forty years from 1871 to 1911, but as has already been shown, the net increase in the total population during the same period was 33 per cent. It is therefore clear as sunlight that the urban growth has fallen far behind the growth of the population as a whole.

Madras Census Report, 1911, P. 18, Table V.

FORTY YEARS' REVIEW OF THE COTTON INDUSTRY IN MADRAS.

Cotton Weaving in Madras, 1870.

In 1870, the Madras Board of Revenue published a valuable report on hand-loom weaving, from which the following figures are taken. The total number of looms at work in that presidency, with its population of 31 millions, was returned at 279,220, of which 220,015 were in villages and 52,205 in towns, showing a considerable increase upon the corresponding number in 1861, when the Mohartartarfa, or assessed tax upon looms, was abolished. The total estimated consumption of twist was 31,422,712 lbs., being at the rate of 112 lbs. per loom. The total value of the cotton goods woven was returned at 3½ millions sterling, or £12, 10 s. per loom; but this was believed to be much under the truth. The export of country-made cloth in the same year was about £ 220,000.

Exnccellence of Indian Fabrics. Manchester Beating them out.

The writer of the Madras census Report of 1871 has frankly admitted that free trade has caused and is still causing the deline of the most ancient weaving industry of India.

The produce of the Indian looms is not exported now to any great extent. In former days the chintzes of Masulipatom enjoyed a great celebrity abroad. They were celebrated for the freshness and permanency of their dyes, the colour being brighter after washing than before. There is still small demand for these articles in Burmah, the Straits, and Persian gulf; *but Manchestsr has nearly beaten the Indian exporter out of the field*. The home-made cloths, however, still hold their own in competition with British goods." P. 185.

Hunter's Indian Empire, P. 471.

Once again the writer has emphasized the point that foreign goods are crippling the once-prosperous weaving industry :—

The weaving business has, for many years past, been in a decaying state. Manchester floods the country with cheap piece-goods, loaded with China clay; and, if the fabrics imported would only wear, the weaving trade in India would decay faster than it is now doing, but the Lancashire manufacturers have not yet attained the secret of producing machine-made cloth, equal in strength and price to the products of the hand-looms of India, and consequently there is still a demad for hand-woven cloth, and occupation for a large number of hand-loom weavers." P. 155.

THE WEAVING INDUSTRY STRUGGLING AGAINST ODDS.

The Superintendent of the next census even more frankly enlarges upon the extreme depression and slow decadence visible in the weaving industry.

Including, as it does, the remains of the old weaving industry, it is of great importance. It is numerically strong, and contains nearly as many females as males. Its total strength is 1,452, 161, or 41 per cent. of the total of this Class. But it is probable that the numbers are lower now than they have been for many years, and that unless factory labour increases greatly, and gives life in a new form to the weaving industry, the numbers under this Order will be yet fewer at the next Census. The hand looms can no longer compete with imported machine-made cloths, and already the weaving industry has to struggle against odds.

DECLINE CONTINUES.

We have heard the laments of the writers of the preceding census. Mr. Stuart, in his 1891 Census Report, after an elaborate calculation which can satisfy none but himself,

Madras C. R., 1881, P. 154.

thus sums up his opinion. "There has thus been an increase of a little over 2 per-cent. (after the lapse of ten years). The assumptions that have necessarily been made involve some risk of error, but it is not probable that this seriously affects the comparison, and we may confidently conclude that the weaving industry shows no signs of declining *even though it is not advancing at the same rate as the population.*"

It will be remembered that the increase of population was at the rate of 15·58 per cent,. but 2 per cent. was the increase in weaving and yet, according to Mr. Stuart, the weaving industry has not declined! Can there be a more fallacious reasoning than this? His inference is wholly illegitimate and contrary to facts. Let us now examine the status of this important industry in the succeeding decennium.

140,803 weavers less in 1901 than in 1891.

We cannot to better than quote the remarks of Mr. W. Francis, the writer of the Madras Census Report of 1901 on the progressive decline of the weaving industry :—

"Putting it another way, the people now supported by weaving are 140, 803 fewer than they would have been, if the weaving population of 1891 had continued to multiply during the decade at the normal rate for the Presidency."

The figures for the actual weavers themselves nevertheless require further examination for they have only increased at the rate of 2·1 per cent. against the normal rate of the presidency of 7·2 per cent., or, in other words, they are nearly 57,000 less persons supported by cotton and silk weaving than under normal conditions, there would have been. The figures can, it is believed, be trusted."

72 WEAVERS IN 1911 INSTEAD OF 100 IN 1901.

This same tendency is visible in the next decade. While in 1901, 623,783 persons were employed in cotton spinning, sizing and weaving, the year 1911 saw 580,321 hands getting employment in these three occupations. There was, moreover, a marked decrease of 28·3 per cent. in the dyeing, bleaching, printing and sponging of textiles. In 1900 there were 167,806 hand looms in the Presidency, but no attempt was again made to estimate their number, hence real variations cannot be adequately determined, but the following statement gives interesting details of the progress made since 1881 in the mill industry of the Presidency. It shows that though this industry is not highly developed, nor has it made great strides onward, yet it is sufficient to throw hand-workers out of work :—

No. of	1881	1891	1901	1909-10
Mills ...	3	8	11	12
Looms ...	...	555	1,735	2,023
Spindles ...	48,000	173,000	288,000	339,500
Hands employed daily ...	1,400	5,900	12,600	18,860

SUFFERINGS OF THE HAND WEAVER.

But Mr. A. Chatterton has tried to institute comparisons between 1911 and 1871.

"I think," he says, "we may safely accept the following conclusion :—That in the last forty years the number of hand loom weavers has remained practically stationary but that owing to stress of competition, they now turn out a large amount of finished goods than was formerly the case; that is to say, *the majority of them have to work harder to make a bare living.*"

Census 1911, P. 208.

THE PRESEET SITUATION.

The decline in the cotton industry is no exception. A chilly cold air of decay has paralyzed all other industries, so that Madras with a population of 41,505 thousand souls greater than that of France is economically the poorest province. Rao Bahadur P. T. Chetty, president of the Southern India Chamber of Commerce, Madras in his written evidence before the Indian Industrial Commission summed up the industrial situation in these words:—

'This Presidency is industrially very backward. We have no manufactures to compare with the cotton manufactures of Bombay or the jute manufactures of Çalcutta. Agriculture is almost the exclusive occupation of the people, and the planting industry on the West Coast and over the Ghauts, is, perhaps, the only industry so far organised and scientifically developed; but this industry is mostly owned by Europeans who are raising coffee, tea, cardamums, pepper, rubber, etc. We have two weaving mills in the Presidency. If we exclude the Government factories and the Railway workshops, all that we could show by way of factory organisation is a number of rice mills, besides cotton-gins and presses.'

What a remarkable progress this !

CHAPTER XII.

BENIGHTED BOMBAY.

A study of the economic conditions of the Bombay Presidency reminds us of the immemorial adage that

All is not gold that glitters.

With its exceedingly varied climates from the almost rainless deserts of Sind to the damp and tropical giant forests of Kanara, with the rich and well-watered plains of unbroken cultivation in Gujerat, with the black clay soils of cotton-producing Khandesh, with the large tracts of rocky and uncultivable land of the scantily-watered lands of the Deccan plateau which 'is ever haunted by the spectre of famine' in striking contrast to the rich rice fields of beautiful Kokan watered by a never-failing supply from the storm-clouds of the south-west monsoon—the Bombay Presidency presents a great variety of picturesque scenery. On the whole, the presidency proper is one of the fairest, physically richest and most attractive of the Indian Empire. During the one-hundred years since the British Raj was established in the Mahratha territory, Bombay which with its long sea coast rich in excellent harbours, with its temperate climate and moisture-laden atmosphere and vast cotton-producing tracts was particularly well-fitted to be the Lancashire of India, has made some advance in the cotton weaving and spinning industry. But during the forty years from 1871 to 1911 for which reliable statistics are available, the Presidency has also witnessed the crippling and strangling of many indigenous industries, greater ruralization, lesser urbanization and comparatively small growth of its population. For these reasons, it cannot be called Progressive and Prosperous Bombay, but the epithet of 'Benighted' which was often given to Madras, ought to be transferred to it.

GROWTH OF POPULATION IN BOMBAY PRESIDENCY AS COMPARED WITH ENGLAND AND WALES :

Census year.	Bombay.	Decennial Increase per cent.	England and Wales.	Decennial Increase per cent.
1871	23,099,332	...	22,712,266	...
1881	23,397,763		25,974,439	14·36
1891	26,916,342	15	29,002,525	11·65
1901	25,424,185	−5·7	32,527,843	12·17
1911	27,084,317	6·4	36,075,269	10·90
1871 to 1911	*3,984,985*	*16·8*	*13,363,003*	*58·8*

It will have been seen that in Bombay the record of the movement of the population has not been one of rapid and un-interrupted growth like that of England and Wales. There was but a nominal increase of 1·44 per cent. against 14 $\frac{1}{3}$ % in England during the first decade, because a severe famine in the Deccan and Karnatak had carried away hundreds of thousands of men and women.

During the next decade there was a large recovery and recuperation and the population showed the highest increase on record but, unfortunately this progress was extremely short-lived. In 1896 came the plague and two years later began the disastrous famine. Mr. Euthoven, the writer of the 1901 Census Report computed that the loss of life from these two causes alone had been 3 million persons. Hence followed the discouraging decline of nearly 6 per cent. in population. The next decade again showed a very high mortality rate reaching 34·6 per cent. Consequently the rate of the increase of population was but 6·4 per cent. Looking over the period of forty years *we find that the net increase in population during this whole period has been only 16·8 in Bombay as compared with that of 58·8 in England and Wales.* This growth falls short of even the Indian average of the real growth of population which was calculated as 19 per cent. (P. 64 *supra*). No arts of sophistry can therefore in the face of these figures prove that the economic conditions of the presidency have much improved. What a marked difference is to be seen between Bombay and England that in 1871 Bombay being ahead of

England by 387,066 persons was in 1911 left behind her by as many as 9 million inhabitants! Can there be any doubt that the so-called prosperous Bombay is *par excellence* the benighted presidency? The next section will still more dispel the false ideas that might have been entertained regarding the *apparently* rapid progress and prosperity of this presidency.

VARIATION IN URBAN POPULATION 1871—1891.

We have next to examine in detail the changes that have occurred in the movement of urban population. In *1871* there were 179 towns with a population of five thousand inhabitants or more. Their aggregate population amounted to 2,778,822 persons. Ten years after, the number of towns declined to 165, but their total population was shown to be greater than before, reaching 2,925,190 inhabitants. *The town population thus showed an increase of 5·3 per cent. against 1·44 per cent. increase in the total population.* But this increase was only apparent, because famine always tends to drive villagers to centres of trade in search of employment or charity from their comparatively richer neighbours. However, this relatively greater urban growth was more than kept up in the next decade 1881—1891, when the number of towns was 232 and their aggregate population amounted to 3,502,678. There was thus a marked increase on the previons census as well as on the census of 1871. *The urban population grew by a little less than 20 per cent. during the decade against 15 per cent. increase in the total population.* Comparing the strength of the urban population in 1871 with that of 1891 we find that *there was an increase of 26 per cent. against 16·5 per cent. increase of the total population during these* twenty years. There was thus an unmistakeable tendency of a growing urbanization, but it was so slight that the Government in the Moral and Material Progress Report of 1891 (P. 473) remarked that, in Bombay 'the urban community has grown *more slowly* than the rural.'

GROWTH OF VILLAGES DURING 1881—1891.

It may be remarked in passing that there was to be seen a tendency of the growth of large villages and the decay of the smallest ones during 1881—91. For instance the proportion of villages having less than five hundred inhabitants was 6·33 per cent. in 1881, but it fell to 59 per cent. in 1891. The proportion of the next class of villages inhabited by persons above 500 but below 1000, was about 12·4 and 24 per cent. respectively in 1881 and 1891. Then the proportion of villages next above the former class, with a population raging from one thousand to two thousand, was 10 and 12·7 per cent. at the two census enumerations. Other classes of villages also showed a similar tendency.

The following table exhibiting the relative proportions of villages of the different sizes in

1881 and 1891, for the presidency would visualize the whole movements.

	Including Sindh and Bombay.				
	1—499	500—999	1000—1999	2000—2999	3000 and over.
1881	63·36	22·39	10·09	2·23	1·43
1891	59·05	23·92	11·77	2·71	2·55

JUSTICE RANADE ON URBANIZATION.

Unfortunately the pious wish expressed by the late illustrious Ranade that 'the increase in the population of towns, and the higher rate of increase in the population of towns, as also the slight increase in the relative proportion of urban and rural populations, show clearly that the tendency towards resuscitation has been checked, and that gradually but surely, the first signs of the new civic Life were manifesting themselves'.*
has not been realized. That tendency was abruptly arrested, and had such a countervailing effect that the net result of a forty years' growth is a slight decline in urbanization.

*Essays on Indian Economics, Natesan, P. 122.

PERCENTAGE OF URBAN POPULATION, 1901—1911.

In 1911 only a little over 18 per cent. of the people resided in towns of 5,000 and over and just 13 per cent. in towns with a larger population than 10,000; at the 1901 Census the figures were 19 and nearly 14 respectively, thus both the classes of towns mentioned here *show a positive decline of 1 per cent. each during one decade.* The remarks of the 1911 Census Superintendent on urbanization are summarized in these words:

'The figures throughout show that there has been very little variation, either in the number of towns or in their population taken as a whole, which shows an increase, for the decade of 117,000 or 3·4 per cent. It has already been shown that the total population of the whole presidency increased by 6·4 and of the British Territory by 6 per cent. alone. *Consequently it is obvious that urbanization has fallen short of the growth of population by 3 per cent.*'

Such is the growing prosperity of the industrially advanced Bombay!

URBAN GROWTH DURING 1891—1901.

Let us now compare this position with that of the preceding census. The total *urban* population of the British Districts was 3,502,678 against 15,398,445 *rural* in 1891. In other words, the proportions of urban to rural population were 18·6 and 81·4. Then towns of 10,000 and over contained 14 per cent. of the total population. That is, there was a little rise of ·4 per cent. in the total urban population during the period of 1891—1901, while places from 10,000 and over were perfectly stationary. The remarks of the Imperial Gazetteer of India, Vol. VIII, 1908, deserve special attention :—

'The percentage of urban population has increased from 17 (?) to 19 in the ten years since 1891 ; but in the face of the opposing in influences of plague and famine, it is difficult to assign any definite significance to this increase.' P. 297.

The net result of the last three census enumerations from 1891 to 1911 is

(1) A decrease of ·6 per cent. in urbanization.

(2) A decrease of 1 per cent. in the population of towns of 10,000 and over.

This is the one remarkable feature of our so-called prosperous and industrially supreme presidency. But another marvellous characteristic of urbanization comes out in contrasting it with the urban growth in England.

URBANIZATION IN BOMBAY AND ENGLAND.

A comparison with the number and size of towns in England and Wales is interesting especially when taken in connection with the total population.

VARIATION IN URBANIZATION SINCE 1891.

Country.		Total Population	Towns of 10,000 and over	Urban Population	Average per town Total	Urban per cent. to Pop.
Bombay Presidency British Territory	1891	18,857,044	78	2,672,254	34,269	14
	1911	19,672,642	102	2,557,443	25,073	13
England and Wales	1891	2,9001,018	358	17,826.347	49,794	61·5
	1911	3,6075,269	476	25,133,393	52,801	69·6

It is remarkable that in *Bombay*

(1) the towns in question grew in number from 78 to 102, an increase of 20·5%, but

(2) their aggregate population after twenty years was about one hundred thousand persons *less* as compared with 1891 showing

(3) *a decrease* of 9,196 persons *per town* on the average. However, another marvellous feature of these twenty years, so far as urbanization is concerned, is

(4) a *decline* of one per cent. in the urban population.

On the other hand, things are not so in that great country upon which this ancient and civilized India is dependent for progress and prosperity. England and Wales *show an increase of*

(1) 33 per cent. in the number of towns,

(2) more than seven millions (7,307,046) in their aggregate population and of

(3) 3,007 persons in the average population of each town and lastly what is the surest index of the industrial growth and economic prosperity of that country, there has been

(4) a remarkable rise of about 8 per cent. in the aggregate urban population as compared with the total.

Such are the tremendous differences in the economic conditions of Bombay and England, what can we then expect in the industrially backward provinces?

Let us now look at this important question of *urban depopulation* from another standpoint. The succeeding table gives in a summary way the percentage growths of the urban and total populations in parallel columns from 1872 to 1911.

In comparing the *urban* population, according to the writer of the Bombay Census Report, 1911, at the various censuses in this table the figures have been 'smoothed,' towns which have dropped out altogether have had their present population as villages added in and the new towns have been ignored.

	1871 to 1881	1881 to 1891	1891 to 1901	1901 to 1911
* Increase per cent in the pop. of towns as classed at previous censuses	—8	+12	+3	+3
Increase per cent. in total population of the whole presidency	+1·44	+15	—5·7	6·4

* Bombay Census Report, 1911, p. 21.

It is therefore clear that there have occurred marked differences in the relative growths of the two populations. All decades except the one from 1891 to 1901 show a persistent tendency for many places to drop out of the category of towns. But the full force of variation of these 40 years can only be realized by the succeeding statement wherein it *has been shown that there has been a rise of 12 per cent. as against 17 per cent. in the total population, if we take the towns of 1871 as a basis for comparison, but there has occurred a very marked decline of 10 per cent.* when we take the towns of 1911 as a base for a backword comparison.

INCREASE PER CENT. IN URBAN POPULATION OF EACH CLASS FROM 1871 to 1911.

In towns as classed in 1871	..	**+12**
In the total of each class in 1911 as compared with the corresponding total in 1871	...	**−10**
Increase of population	...	**+17**

VARIATIONS IN OCCUPATIONS FROM 1872 TO 1881.

The total population of the presidency increased at the insignificant rate of *1 per cent. at the maximum, but the increase in the agricultural classes was at the rate of 4·13 per cent. males and about 14·8 per cent. females during* the nine years from 1872 to 1881. Such is the discouraging result of one intercensual period of nine years. The Superintendent of the Census took all possible pains in getting the figures of the two censuses re-arranged, he brought them to an identical basis, thus eliminating all possible sources of error, yet the solid and stern fact of a great and greater ruralization stares us in the face, even in this presidency.

The following table gives the distribution of the two years and the differences between the respective classes on the two occasions:—

	Males.			Females.		
	Distribution by classes.		In 1881 more or less %.	Distribution by classes.		In 1881 more or less %.
	1872	1881		1872	1881	
Professional	3·68	3·04	—17·64	·08	·10	+38·56
Domestic	1·74	1·71	—1·93	·38	·47	+26·72
Commercial	4·24	2·29	—46·20	·36	·08	—315·27
Agricultural	38·32	40·01	+4·13	9·82	24·08	+147·71
Industrial	10·92	11·22	+1·03	8·03	7·68	—3·53
Indefinite and unoccupied	41·10	41·73	—1·56	81·33	67·59	—16·06

The professional, domestic, commercial, indefinite and unoccupied classes show marked decreases ranging from 1·56 to 17·64 per cent. in the males;

industries claim 1 per cent. more men at the end of the period, while agriculture occupies 4 per cent. more males than before.

The case with females differs, because among them women engaged in professions, domestic service and agriculture increased from about 27 to 148 per cent., but vast decreases have occurred in the numbers engaged in commercial, industrial and the indefinite occupations. *The one tact of greater ruralization comes out undisguised and prominently before all.* It is highly fortunate that persons engaged in industries show no decline, men have increased by 1 per cent., but females decreased by 3·5 per cent. The main result is apparent and deserves no comment from us.

SITUATION DURING 1881-1891.

This disheartening drift to the land was no more checked even during the next ten years, which were marked by no famine, nor even by a particularly bad harvest, nor by any specially severe epidemic like the previous decade, *yet the rate of ruralization was probably more than it had ever been before.* The following statement best illustrates this process of rustication :—

Bombay Census Report Pp. 418—19.

	Percentage of the total population.		Percentage of the rural population.	
Pasture and agriculture.	60	80	86	69
Preparation and supply.	21			13
Indefinite and independent.	6·48		6·83	
Commerce, transport and storage.	4·66		3·58	
Government service.	3·86		3·16	
Domestic service	2·70		2·39	
Professions ...	2·32		2·09	
	100		100	

In Class B persons subsisting partly on land whether as owners, tenants or labourers and partly on another occupation are not counted.

If we compare this statement with the preceding one we find that a most direful change has swept over the land. Assuming that there were inaccuracies in the preceding census, even then, such tremendous variations occurring in

Bombay Census Report, 1891, P. 176.

one decade alone can be expected from the removal of cotton duties in 1879, the large importatins of foreign manufactures to crush down the rising cotton-mill industry and the greater exodus to the land.

In 1881, the proportion of actual workers engaged in agriculture was 40 per cent. males and 24 per cent. females, but ten years after persons wholly and directly *supported* by agricultural pursuits were 60 per cent. of the total population.

THE DISMAL DECADE.

The last decade of the nineteenth century was full of dismal events in the whole of India, but specially for the Presidency of Bombay. While the writer of the Census Report **for 1891 had predicted on the basis of the rate of increase from 1872 to 1891 that the British Territory would contain 21,050,178 persons in 1901, the population instead of increasing, actually declined by 318,821 persons, that is, at the rate of 1·7 per cent. during the decade.**

Hence the net loss to the Presidency does not amount to what is apparent from the Census figures, it really comes up to this :—

Population in 1891 ...	**18,857,044**
Population what would have been according to the Census Superintendent in 1901 ...	**21,050,178**
Actual population in 1901 ...	**18,515,676**
Actual decrease during ten years ...	**2,534,502**

RURALIZATION.

These figures are the most eloquent testimonies of the ravages of plague and famine which carried away 2·5 million persons from one presidency alone. But what about our eternal exodus to the land ?

In spite of an actual decline of 318,821 persons in the total population, the pastoral and agricultural classes, instead of at least proportionally decreasing, increased by 82,982 persons, that is, the pastoral people multiplied at the tremendous rate of 24 per cent. and those supported by agriculture, at the rate of 2 per cent.

Thus it is clear as sunlight that even in such an industrially supreme province as Bombay, the exodus to the land was not stopped, even after the close of the 19th century.

There is, indeed, some improvement in certain industries and professions, but they are almost all *connected with providing comforts and luxuries*, the most lamentable appendaegs of the modern European civilization. For instance, persons engaged in personal, household and sanitary services in buildings, vehicles, and vessels, metal, glass, earthen and stone ware, earthwork and general labor and even in indefinite and disreputable occupations, show greater returns to-day than ten years before.

But on the other hand, the long established and indigenous industries have much suffered during the same period.

The following list would serve to illustrate the main dying industries of the province :—

Occupations.	Population supported in 1901.	Population supported in 1891.	Percentage of *Decrease*
Cotton weavers ...	227,303	294,509	— 23
Cotton cleaners pressers and ginners.	14,394	44,596	— 68
Silk carders, spinners and weavers, makers of silk braid and thread.	46,779	48,386	— 3
Oil pressers	52,156	98,422	— 47
Paper makers ...	2,570	3,555	— 28
Toy, kite, and cage makers ...	1,292	33,811	— 97
Cotton dyers	26,129	38,024	— 31
Silk dyers	882	1,353	— 35
Rosary, bead and necklace makers.	455	1,812	— 75
Tanners, curriers and hide sellers.	16,260	47,690	— 66
Chemists and druggists ...	1,395	2,722	— 49
Perfume and essence preparers.	2,015	4,905	— 59
Lac collectors ...	59	177	— 50
Knife and tool makers ...	191	3,653	— 95

The succeeding summarized statement containing comparisons of 1901 and 1891 in vocational distribution is highly illustrative of the dismal changes to which this land has long been subjected on account of the accursed policy of Free-Trade adopted by our rulers.

VOCATIONAL VARIATION DURING 1891-1901.

		1891	1901
A.	Administration ...	3·52	2·99
B.	Pasture and agriculture.	59.62	61·16
C.	Personal service ...	2·56	3·18
D.	Preparation and supply of material substances.	21·29	18·39
E.	Commerce, transport and storage.	4·13	3·38
F.	Professions. ...	2·21	1·79
G.	Unskilled Labour ...	6·67	9·11

Bombay Census Report, 1901, (P. 227)

There have been really disgraceful decreases in professions, commerce, industry and government service, but the percentages of unskilled non-agricultural labourers and domestic servants have risen from 6·67 and 2·56 to 9·11 and 3·18. Then inspite of a virtual decrease of population, agriculture shows an increase of 1·54 per cent.

Is any other evidence needed of the multiplication of the hewers of wood and drawers of water ?

Mr. Austen Chamberlain nobly cautioned his countrymen that India ought not to remain content to be a hewer of wood and a drawer of water for the rest of the Empire, but how can she be uplifted from this stinking slough of degradation, when year by year her various industries are being wrested from her palsied hands ? Just think of the magnitude of changes in the light of the following statistics relating to two important industries of the province.

Silk and cotton industries.

		1891	1901
British Territory	...	633,000	635,000
Native States	...	336,000	177,000

PARTICULARS OF THE COTTON INDUSTRY.

Throughout the Bombay Presidency—British Territory.—Cotton ginning cleaning and pressing employed in 1901

In Factories	...	28,064	persons
As Hand workers	...	14,394	„

But in cotton spinning and weaving were engaged.

In Factories	...	168,043	„
As Hand workers	...	300,609	„

Persons working in Silk Industry in thousands.

		1881	1901
British Territory	...	493	355
Native States	...	209	90

The Census Superintendent himself remarks:—

The decrease in Native States is formidable. The factory industry in the textiles shows only a few hundred workers in the Feudatories. They have thus had to submit to the competition of the machine-made goods, in the same way as British Territory, without the compensating advantage of a rising mill industry to occupy some of the workers displaced by the introduction of machine-made goods, and the result seems nearly to have led to the annihilation of the hand industries. (Bombay C. R., P. 222).

VARIATIONS OF 1901-1911.

It has been fully recognized by the writers of the Bombay Census Report of 1911 that statistics relating to occupations are of the greatest economic interest. Yet their report is extremely poor in comparative statements and in throwing any peculiar light on the character and strength of the economic changes that might have occurred during the first decade of the 20th century in this industrially important presidency.

Coming direct to the strength of the various occupations in the British Territory excluding Aden, we find that as a whole 68½ per cent. were dependent on agriculture, pasture, fishing and hunting, 12½ per cent. on industry, ·16 per cent. on extractive industries, 6 per cent. on trade, and 3 per cent. on transport. Public administration, army, navy, police, religion, law, medicine, instruction, letters, arts, sciences, occupations of independent means—all of these supported 4¾ per cent. of the population. The remaining 5 per cent. comprised those engaged in domestic service as well as in unproductive and insufficiently described occupations.

These bare figures can give little definite idea, Another table has consequently been drawn up to show similar details for the two censual enumerations. Even a cursory glance is sufficient to indicate that in this decade the 'benighted' presidency has come to enjoy some special advantages as compared with other provinces. Leaving aside the occupations included in one category—the exploitation of the surface of the earth—we see that men engaged in *industries* concerned with the working of textiles, wood, metals, ceramics, furniture, building and transport, in trades like those of textiles, metals, chemicals, and fuel and lastly in the diverse professions and liberal arts have increased more than the total population. In some of the above prodigious progress is fortunately to be seen. But while the sub-class of Industry shows an increase of 8 per cent., trade indicates a decline of 13 per cent. Thus there is no improvement even on the surface. But behind all this seeming progress and prosperity is to be seen the gloomy picture of a growing primitive agriculture.

The figures show an advance of nearly two millions under this head, which is rather greater than the total increase of population. In other words, there has been an increase of 16 per cent. in agriculture as against 6 per cent. in the total population Is it not a most dismal decline for this so-called industrially supreme presidency ?

The writers of the Census Report have cautioned their readers by writing that it must not, however, be supposed that this means that there has been a wholesale rush back to the land. In 1901, 1,232,000 persons were insufficiently described and had to be consigned to sub-class XI under the head of 'labourers and workmen otherwise unspecified.' On the present occasion this sub-class only contains 383,000. Hence for a comparison with the figures of 1901 sub-classes I and XI ought to be taken together. The result stands thus :—

PERSONS RETURNED AS AGRICULTURISTS AND UNSPECIFIED WORKMEN IN

1901	1911
12,710,518	13,656,387

The decennial increase therefore amounts to 945,869 or 7·1 per cent. that is, while, the rate of the increase of total population was 6 per cent. in the British Territory, that of the agriculturists amounted to 7 per cent. Here then is a strong proof of the continual ruralization of the Province, although the evil is not so intensive as appeared on the surface. The evil is really not so light as would appear from the above comparison. As remarked on page general labourers and unspecified workmen form a large class of floating population, they go where the demand and wages for them are higher. In 1911, most of them had migrated from non-agricultural occupations to agrestic pursuits hence there can be no doubt of the vast exodus to land or of a greater attractiveness of agriculculture as compared with urban professions.

We are now in a position to summarize the results of our enquiry concerning ruralization in Bombay. It has been seen from figures already given that the agricultural population at the last three Census enumerations was in

1891 ... 59·62 per cent. of the total population
1901 ... 61·16 „
1911 ... 68·40 „

It is therefore evident that there has been approximately 9 per cent. increase during the relatively short period of 20 years. The same indisputable fact is borne out by the relative growths of the agricultural and total populations of the presidency:—

DECENNIAL PERCENTAGE INCREASE IN

Decade.	Agricultural population.	Total population.
1872—1881	4 Male workers 15 Female workers.	+1
1891—1901	·2	—5·7
1901—1911	16 Maximum Corrected 7 Minimum	+6·4

DECAYING INDUSTRIES.

By this time it has been made abundantly clear that the growth of ruralization and the decline of urban population go handin hand in India. With the exception of textiles, wood, metal, furniture and building industries, all the other important ones showed sure signs of decay during the last intercensual period.

Occupations relating to tanning, dressing and dyeing leather, working in bone, ivory, horn and shell, manufacturing of plough and agricultural implements, construction of the means of transport, making of bangles did *severely suffer*. Persons engaged in public administration as well as in many trades showed an unfortunate decline. There are many coincidences in the decline and growth of the industries of this presidency with those of the other provinces. Comparative figures of the five censuses show a strong, steady and gradual decline of indigenous industries and point out how the principal part of the trade of the country is being concentrated in fewer hands. There is yet another dispiriting fact that there was during the decade a slight decrease of 3 per cent. in the number of persons who lived independently on their own incomes.

MR. HARDY'S VIEWS ON THE CAUSES OF INDUSTRIAL DECLINE.

The causes of the industrial decline of India have often been discussed in the previous chapters, but cumulative evidence is required to impress upon the reader the most vital, potent and overpowering cause of that decay. The remarks of the official writer of the Bombay Census Report, 1901 illuminate the subject so well in detail that no apology is required for reproducing them here in full.

Influences affecting the development of industries.

Apart from the effects of famine and plague, which are it may be hoped, of a temporary nature, there are two main influences at work on the economical distribution of industrial occupations in India. *In the first place, there is the well recognized depression in certain industries, such as weaving, paper making, glass-blowing, and the like, that can be traced to the competition of factories in Europe and America, manifesting itself in the imoprt of large quantities of piece-goods, glassware, &c.*

There is, in the second place, an industrial contet commencing within the Indian Empire, owing to the steady increase, in means of cheap and rapid communications. This development has led to competition between manufacturers in India, including many power industries for the command of markets in the country, formerly only open to the local producer. A successful tannery in Cawnpur, for instance, might injuriously affect the tanning industry of the province of Gujerat, and it is hardly necessary to point to the disappearence of the hand manufacture of paper before the competition of the paper mills of Bengal as an illustration of another result of such influences. The development of indutsries in centres where they enjoy natural advantages that are lacking elsewhere is of course, a legitimate and desirable feature of the industrial progress of the country, though it may result in the gradual local extinction of several indusries which formerly controlled local markets.

To form an estimate of the changes that are attributable to causes of this description, in reviewing the statistics of occupation for a Province or Presidency, it is necessary to take into consideraton the facts regarding industrial progress in all parts of India. The subject is, therefore, one which can only be adequately dealt with in the Census Report for all India. So for, the special province of Bombay in securing a share of the Indian market for goods produced in Bombay would appear to be in the textiles. The Presidency possesses 83 per cent. of the weaving mills of India. Bombay City has peculiar advantages, which it is needless to specify, for the development of the industry, and it has been seen that the recent decade has added to the numbers of those employed in the silk and cotton textiles in the face of obstacles of a formidable nature.

Foreign competition.

Apart from the contest between different centres of industry in India for the lion's share of the markets of the country, the conflict of interest which has been already referred to, between the industrial population of India—working with primitive implements, in an unscientific manner, without co-operation, and curiously heedless of the prospect of improvements in method,—and the manufacturer of foreign countries, who flood the ports with cheap goods produced by the very latest machinery, and by economical and highly scientific processes, tends to oust the products of the local hand-workers from the market. It is further a notable fact that, not unoccasionally, these imported goods may be manufactured from raw material previously exported from India.

Occupation.

Here lies the danger to the industrial future of the country. It is hardly necessary to quote again the case of the textiles, in which India once supplied Europe, until the rise of the power loom turned the tables on her. Cheap cutlery, cheap toys, glass and chinaware, hardware of all kinds, matches, lamps, are more recent instances of foreign products tending to displace the local hand-workers of India.

It may be that even the marvellous manual dexterity of the Indian worker, combined with the power to live on a wage which is only a fraction of the cost of labour in Europe, may not suffice to save the industries of India.

from extinction in contest with more enterprising rivals. But the country should at least make an effort to fit itself for the final struggle, and should not sit calmly awaiting defeat. There is evidence of the possibilities lying in Indian industries to be found in the rapid progress of factories for the manufacture of textiles, leather, metal work, soap, tiles, furniture, biscuits, etc., during the last few years. But, for a long time to come, the hand industries must be numerically superior in importance to these. It is open to question whether a cautious foresight would leave them without assistance. In a certain presidency in India enterprise of a farseeing order has protected metal workers from being subjected to the competition of cheap import of aluminium goods, by introducing the manufacture of this material into India. It should surely repay expense, time and trouble to investigate the possiblity of supplying the hand-workers in textiles, glass, pottery, metal etc., with improved implements, more skilled processes, and, if necessary, the incentive to co-operation, in order to establish the fact that the hand industries cannot endure, even with state assistance of this nature, before they are allowed to become extinct.

The industrial progress of the country, if it is to be of real value, must obviously be in the direction of industries which hold out prospects of employment *to large numbers of the working population. Pending the discovery or introduction of new industries, progress must, therefore, tend either to substitute indigenous manufactures for imports of considerable value, or to provide means for manufacturing in the country raw material now exported in large quantities to be worked up into finished articles elsewhere.*

THE CONDITION OF AGRICULTURISTS.

The condition of the agricultural classes of this presidency is not so deplorable as in other provinces, yet it is sufficiently low. The accounts quoted in pages 89-92,160-69 *supra* are applicable in their case with equal truth. The following evidence will serve to confirm what has been written before and hence will explode all the fatuous theories concerning the hoarded wealth, prosperity and the resisting power of the Indian peasantry against famines.

The condition of these classes could not, moreover, have improved since 1881, because the cultivated area per inhabitant has been decreasing at each decade.

CULTIVATED ACRES PER HEAD IN BOMBAY.

1881	1891	1901	1911-12
1·7	1·6	1-41	1·3

Then the density per square mile has, during the 39 years from 1871 to 1911, increased by 28 persons, in Karnatak by 6, in the Deccan by 31 and in Kokan by 36, but it shows a decrease of one person in the comparatively most thickly populated Division of Gujerat. The growth of density, however small, and the relatively smaller productive area per man combined with the decadence of native handicrafts and the destruction of the supplementary cottage industries, convincingly prove that the lot of the great mass of the community must have grown worse than formerly. There is a large apparent wealth. The export trade of the country passess through Bombay and the cotton mill industry is steadily developing, hence persons engaged in transport by water, rail or road, those employed in post office, telegraph and telephone services or occupied in textile trade, in banking, insurance, export and import agencies are growing in numbers and wealth, but all else have to struggle harder now to procure their scanty subsistence. In fact, the pall of deeper poverty settles over them all and presents gloomy and saddening outlook to those who will like to go behind appearances.

In 1893 the Hon. Mr. A. Rogers, of the Indian Civil Service and ex-Member of the Bombay Council, writing to the Under-Secretary of State for India stated :—*

"In the eleven years from 1880 to 1890 there were sold by auction for the collection of land revenue the occupancy rights of 1,963,364 acres of land held by 840,713 defaulters, in addition to *personal* property to the value of Rs. 2,965,081. Of the 1,963,364 acres, 1,174,143 had to be bought in on the part of the Government for want of bidders that is to say, very nearly 60 per cent. of the land supposed to be fairly and equitably assessed could not find purchasers, and only the balance of 779,142 acres was sold. The evils of the farming system in Bombay have been pointed out in my 'History of the Bombay Land Revenue,' but I doubt if that system at its worst could have shown such a spectacle as that of nearly 850,000 ryots (heads of families) in the course of eleven years sold out of about 1,990,000 acres of land."

Roundly, one-eighth part of the entire agricultural population of the Bombay Provinces was sold out of house and land in little more than a decade.

*The Causes of Present Discontents in India by C. J. O'Donnell, M. P., P. 109.

Not only were their farms brought to auction, but their poor personal belongings, their furniture and their cooking utensils, their beds and every thing but their scanty clothes were sold to provide money for the 'Imperial' expenditure."

*The above iniquitous treatment drew a strong protest from an American paper that wrote "Step by step, almost insensibly, the people of India are sinking deeper and deeper into poverty. Lord George Hamilton recently, in presenting the Indian budget to the British Parliament, described the prosperity of that great dependency, and based his arguments on the fact that there was a surplus in the revenue. He failed, however, to say how it was created and at what cost to the people of India. He did not describe the seizures from famine and plague stricken people for long arrears of rent, and how, to meet the inexorable demands of their alien rulers, the unfortunate *ryots* had to part with their brass cooking utensils which found their way to the brass foundries of Bombay by cart loads from the interior; and women had to sell their silver ornaments, which were in many cases cherished heirlooms and represented the poor savings of years and generations.

* British Rule in India by G. S. Iyer.

CHAPTER XIII.

AN ECONOMIC SURVEY OF THE STATES.

The economic history of the Native States since 1871 is in no way intrinsically different from that of the British Provinces. The picture is as sad and cheerless, as full of want, poverty and misery as in British India. The economic revolution is rather comparatively more disastrous, because more rapid. The tendencies of the continuous, de-urbainzation, ruralization, or of the decadence of home industries by reason of the ever-growing import of cheaper foreign goods, are evident in some of the states in a more intensified form.

The old industries have severely suffered either on account of keen foreign competition or of the court indifference to them. Many of our rulers have shown a stronger inclination to decorate their persons, and palaces, courts, and forts with foreign machine-made goods than to protect, encourage and stimulate the drooping, decaying and dying industries of their states. Nor has much been done by them in introducing and establishing modern mill industries. Gwalior, Baroda and Mysore have put forth great efforts in both reviving the decaying and decadant hand industries and in establishing modern factories, But this state aid alone has not sufficed either to save the former or to implant the latter. The unending stream of foreign imports has to be dammed and dammed effectively by very strong protective walls. No country in the world has succeeded up to this time to build up its diverse industries by state-aid alone. Every country—including Britain—had to adopt such protective and prohibitive measures to save its dying industries and start new ones. This history of the states is significantly instructive because it boldly points out that even the policy of an active state-aid adopted by the Government of India after the war would fail to achieve the end in view. It has been admirably tried in the states but has miserably failed. Hence both state-aid and protective tariff are the *sine qua non* of our industrial development.

INDUSTRIAL DECLINE IN RAJPUTANA.

The years from 1881 to 1911 have all along gloomily witnessed a heavy economic depression-a depression that is unparalleled in the Royal history of Rajputana. It is a thousand pities that an advancing civilization, a developing commercialism and a growing industrialism should have brought about such a disastrous result. The great cities which were once busy centres of commerce and manufactures have with few exceptions, ceased to be the important nuclei of wholesome prosperity and urban activity. That Pax Britannica should have ruined these centres is nothing but a puzzle to the man in the street. The real extent of the evil can be gauged from the great change that has come over the land with regard to urbanization. The following table gives the variation in urban, rural and total populations since the first census of 1881. The figures in *plain type* represent the rural and urban populations exactly as they stood in each year, according to the Imperial Table I of each census, without any appreciable attempt at adjustment, but the figures in *Italics* are the adjusted ones after classifying all places as towns or villages in 1881, 1891 and 1901 according to their classification as such in 1911.

	Percentage of Variation		
	Rural.	Urban.	Total.
1881—1891	22 *21·6*	11·6 *13·7*	+20·6
1891—1901	—22·4 *—22·3*	—7·1 *—8·8*	—20·5
1901—1911	9·1 *9·2*	—6·2 *—6·6*	+6·9
1881—1911	3·4 *3·3*	—3·6 *—3·2*	+2·4

The table is self-explanatory and requires but little comments. It will, however, be interesting to note a few points. Taking into consideration the adjusted figures in italics, we find that the total population of Rajputana increased 201 per

(Rajputana Census R, P. 1911, Pp. 36, 37, 44.)

cent. during 1881—1891 and 7 per cent. during 1901-1911, but it experienced a terrible set back of 201 per cent. during the disastrous decade of 1891-1901 as a result mainly of the severe famine, and even more terrible fever epidemics. As one would expect, these proved far more disastrous to the rural than the urban areas, for while the latter declined by only 8·8 per cent., the village population fell by as much as 22·3 per cent. *The net result of the growth of the Provincial* population is that in 1911, after thirty years there were only 102·4 persons for every hundred in 1881. How insignificant this growth is can be realized when it is compared with the growths of the inhabitants of other Indian provinces.

But a lamentable disparity will be observed in the growth of the urban and rural populations. In the first decade from 1881 to 1891 the urban grew by 13·7 per cent. against 21·7 rural and 201 total but in the third decade the movements of the two populations were in quite opposite directions. The Rural population *grew* by 9·2 per cent. against 7 per cent. total but the urban population *decreased* by about 6½ per cent Compared with 1891 the gross decrease was 14·8. These are the surest proofs of a sharp urban decline in the Land of Perpetual Famine, but the figures of the second intercensal decade present matter for no less serious consideration. The urban areas experienced a *decrease* of 9 per cent. against 20½ per cent. total and 22 per cent. rural, in other words, the urban decline was not as fast as that of the two populations. But it did in no case exhibit any permanent tendency to migration from country to town ; it was solely due to the fact that the starved and starving inhabitants of rural areas flocked to towns for getting charity or work from their comparatively richer neighbours. It is known to all that the failure of rains and the consequent shortage or failure of crops and the stalking abroad of the monster of fatal famine affects the rural population first and foremost. The famine-stricken people, to obtain an escape from distress, disease and death, temporarily migrating to the towns swelled the ranks of the urban classes and hence there was this comparatively little decline.

Looking over a period of thirty years, we are unfortunately confronted by the lamentable *decrease* of 3·2 per cent. in the urban population against 2·4 per cent. increase in the total, hence we are confronted by the natural result of a rural increase of 3·3 per cent. which is about 1 per cent. more than the rise in the provincial population.

This one fact alone makes it clear that there is a marked tendency among the Rajputs to migrate from manufacturing or commercial centres either to rural areas, to other provinces of India or to foreign lands.

The writer of the Rajputana Census Report of 1911 thus sums up the situation :—

"Compared with 1881, only three cities (out of nine) appear to be growing ones. Of these Ajmer has the most marked increase of 76·9, Bikaner's being 68·4 and Jodhpur's 25·9. All the rest show a decrease, Bharatpur's diminution of population amounting to as much as 87·7 (P.27).

Only four (out of the thirteen capital towns) have increased since 1881." (P.28).

VOCATIONAL DISTRIBUTION.

The occupational statistics of Rajputana offer many interesting and instructive points when they are compared and contrasted with those of the other Indian Provinces. It would be a matter of surprise to many that agriculture and pasture in Rajputana even now after the long decline, occupy the lowest perce..tage of the population except the Punjab and Ajmere-Merwara. It also takes the palm of all other Indian provinces in industries and commerce. Mr. E. H. Kealy has truly remarked:—

'It is some what surprising to find such a backwater as Rajputana standing so high on the list of Provinces in 'industries,' 'trades,' and 'professions' and 'liberal arts.' Excluding Ajmere-Merwara, the Province stands first in "professions and liberal arts," (the figures for which, it must be remembered, exclude those for the Native States' administration services and public forcs), and second both in 'industries' and 'trades.' The real explanation of this position lies probably, not in the more advanced and civilized condition of Rajputana, but in the low percentage of agriculture which is the necessary concomitant of the unfavourable rainfall and barren soil which are such distinctive features of the Province. It will be gathered from paragraph 13 *infra* that most of its industries are hand industries.' (P. 125).

Yes, these hand industries have declined, but no new industries have taken their place. Hence ruralization and rustication, famine and famine-produced diseases have come to hold sway over this Land of Provinces. Such a mighty economic change has swept over this land that within twenty years alone the strength of the agricultural community has risen from 54 to 64. per cent. It is yet time to save the situation. Still the tide of urban and industrial immigrants to a land which is already groaning under the unbearable pressure of its starving cultivators, can be stemmed. Let the people and their princes be Swadeshi in spirit, let them adopt all the means to establish the modern industries best suited to their states, and let them agitate hard to obtain fiscal autonomy for the Indian Government.

TRANSITION IN BARODA.

The economic history of Baroda during the forty years from 1871 to 1911 presents an unbroken record of gloomy and disheartening events in spite of the noble, patriotic and gigantic attemts of its enlightened ruler to uplift it economically, educationally and socially to a higher level. It shows a practically stationary population over the period of forty years; urban growth has all along lagged far behind the increase of the state population; sharp decreases have happened in several important industries; agricultural classes exhibit a large increase, and the sufferings of the poor classes have become unbearable during the last two intercensal periods. A few facts would illustrate these assertions.

DECENNIAL PRECENTAGE VARIATION OF

	1881	1891	1901	1911	1872-1911
General Pop.	9·24	10·7	—19·15	4·1	1·76
Urban Pop.		+7·5	—7·1	—8	—10·2(1) —4·9(2)

VARIATION IN AGRICULTURAL AND NON-AGRICULTURAL POPULATIONS.

The following statement shows the actual numbers and the percentages of the growth of the several sections of the general population during 1881—1891.

	1881	1891	Percentages of Increase.
Population ...	2,185,005	2,415,396	10·69
Agricultural ...	1,284,812	1,435,453	11·72
Non-agricultural	900,193	980,008	8.87
Rural ...	4,735,428	1,931,881	11·3
Urban ...	449,577	483,515	7·55

It is now more than obvious that the increase in the agricultural population during 1881—1891 was the greatest, it was even slightly higher than that of the rural population.

(1) In towns classed in 1871 (2) In the total of 1911 as compared with the corresponding total of 1871.

(Baroda Census Rep—,1891 P. 114)—

Then, in order comes the percentage of increase r the non-agricultural population; and more than one percent, lower than this, last of all, is the percentage of increase in the urban population.

During the next decade, there is to be seen a fall 27 per cent, in agriculture against 19 per cent, in the total population.

The terrible famine of 1898-1900 decimated and thinned down the rural population which fell easy victims to the monsters of Hunger and Starvation.

The strength of each sub-order of agriculture on the two census enumerations has undergone terrible alterations that are eloquent testimonie of the working of an Indian famine.

	1901	1891	Variation.
Landholders and tenants ...	634,688	11,96,580	.46·5
Agricultural labourers ...	372,964	190,896	95·4
Growers of special products	5,027	3,963	26·8
Agricultural training ...	2,248	11	223·3
Agriculture ...	1,014,927	1,391,450	— 27

Agriculture claims 376,523 less after 10 years, but the decline in the most important agricultural class of landholders and tenants amounts to 561,892 persons, or 46½% against 27% decrease in agricultural population. Other orders show large increases, for instance the labourers have nearly doubled. This means that the first class was reduced to such straits by reason of the terrible famine as to leave off land and adopt manual labour for earning their livelihood. Similarly the sub-orders of Earthwork and General Labour show an increase of 99,882 persons. These abnormal increases in the fold of labour are due exclusively to the helplessness caused by the terrible famine of 1898—1900. A large number of the cultivating classes being reduced to extreme poverty, utter misery and starvation found their way to the relief works or flocked into the the towns for getting some charity.

The next decade is full of no less mighty dislocations in the Baroda industrial world. In no other ten years' period was there a readjustment of such a disastrous nature as in the ten years from 1901 to 1911.

With an increase of only 4 per cent. in the total population, there has been an unusual increase of 25½ per cent. in agricultural occupations. The proportion of persons maintained by agriculture in 1911 was 634 per mille compared with only 519 in 1901. This large increase of 115 per mille shows a return to agriculture on the part of those who abandoned it ten years previously. The decline of 36 per mille of landless labourers points to the same conclusion. The increase in cultivated area of 4·5 per cent. or 249,226 bighas is another proof in the same direction (C. R., 1911, p. 347-58).

The actual percentage strength of the agricultural classes for the last four censuses would go a long way to sum up the preceding enquiry :—

1881...58	1901...51·9
1891...60	1911...63·3

Thus a lapse of 30 years has seen a rise of more than 5% in the percentage of the agricultural community.

The following figures would summarize the sharp decline of the textile fabric and dress industries in the state.

Year.		Textiles.	Cotton.
1891	...	124,111	90,751
1901	...	68,213	43,332
1911	...	91,869	44,437

" The last intercensual decade shows a slight improvement, mainly due to impetus given to the dying hand-loom industry and the rising power-loom weaving. However the ancient weaving industry which used to export fine cloths to Europe has practically died out. It was really dead in the early part of the 19th century, until there has come some resuscitation in the first decade of the 20th century. The enlightened ruler has stimulated mill industries by various means, so that from one

Census Report 1901, p. 646.

Census Report 1911, p. 355-6.

cotton spinning mill and 44 ginning factories and presses in 1901, there were 4 spinning and weaving mills and 55 ginning factories and presses besides 27 factories of many other industries. The writer of the Census Report has truly revealed that there is yet a great scope for further development, and with the continuance of the present liberal policy of its Government there is every scope that Baroda will in the near future take its legitimate place as a centre of manufacture in W estern India."

ECONOMIC CHANES IN HYDRABAD.

The Hydrabad State exhibits the same tendencies of progressive ruralization, urban decline, industrial decadence, growing dependence upon primitive agriculture, threateningly overwhelming rise of a landless class and hence a greater liability to famine and impoverishment. The net results of the ten years' progress from 1891 to 1901 were 3·431 *decrease* in the general population, and an *increase* of 45,427 persons in agriculture ; a decline from 724,338 to 527,630 persons in textiles, from 93,981, to 89,293 in glass, earthenware and stoneware and a shortage of more than 12 thousand persons engaged in the industries of food, drink and stimulants.

The next decade, however, showed a revival in the drooping textile industry because it claimed 11 per cent. more persons in 1911. But the process of ruralization was unparalleled in the economic history of every country. The growth of general population was 2,233,534 persons, but the agricultural increase was 2,844,848 souls. Speaking in percentages these growths come to be 20 and 25 % of their respective populations. The reader would hardly believe that in 1891 agriculture claimed 45 % of the total population against 46 % in 1901 and 62 in 1911.

While this overwhelming increase in itself is full of most serious dangers for the well-being of the people, the changes in the ownership of land have intensified the evil in a degree that calls for a most careful handling by the state.

'The extraordinary increase of 1748·8 per cent. in the number of rent receivers, if it at all represents an actual tendency means that the land is going out of the hands of the cultivators into those of rent takers. The relatively small increase (namely 17 per cent.) in the number of the latter, and the large increase of 172 per cent. in that of farm servants and field labourers, also point to the same result. The ranks of the latter are swollen not only by peasant proprietors who are ousted from their holdings but also by accessions from the more primitive occupations of the hunting and pastoral stages, as also from that of indigenous artisans thrown out of employ by their handiwork being superseded in popular favour by *cheaper imported* articles. The decrease in the number of agents and managers probably indicates that land is passing out of the hands not only of cultivators but also out of those of the hereditary landed proprietors who managed their estates through agents and managers. The two great lessons which these statistics convey are, first, that the pressure on the land is increasing from various causes. and, secondly that the ownership and the profits thereof are being increasingly appropriated by mere rent-receivers" p. 145.

RURALIZATION IN COORG.

The small state of Coorg enjoys no immunity from the general tendency of ruralization. In 1891 pasture and agriculture supported 72·72 per cent. of the people (Coorg C. R. 1891 , P. 40), ten years after the strength rose to be 82·1 (C. R. 1901, Pp. 29-30), while in 1911, it was 82·6 (C. R. 1911, p. 38). Thus Coorg was ruralized to the exten of 10 per cent. during 20 years alone.

Again, with an increase of 6,664 persons in the general population Coorg experienced a decline of 2,968 persons in its urban population during the thirty years from 1881 to 1911 (C. R. 1911, p. 28.)

DETERIORATION IN MYSORE.

The same rapid economic deterioration is visible in Mysore as in most of the other native states or British Provinces. Its population grew by 14·9 per cent. against 19 per cent. of India during 1871—1911. Its urban population was 11·3 in 1911 against 13 per cent. in 1901, while its agricultural classes grew by 11 and 15 per cent. in 1901 and

1911 against 12 and 5 per cent. increase in the state population. Then during 1891—1901 the total population increased by 12 per cent. but commerce, cotton, hardware, wool and fur industries, exhibited very large decreases amounting to 33 per cent. in the last two cases. The results of the last three censuses regarding the strength of the agricultrual community are :

1891	1901	1911
68·4	68·5	73·1

Thus the ranks of the agricultural classes were strengthened by about 5 per cent. during 20 years alone, and during 1901—11 at a rate thrice as great as that of the general population.

"Persons supported by the preparation and Supply of Material substances, Public Admininistration and Liberal Arts and Miscellaneous occupations show large decreases of 11·44 and 26·6 per cent. compared with 1901, Going into a little detail we find that there has been a decrease of 9·5 per cent. under the head of industries partly due to the new method of classification of occupations and partly to the displacement of manual labour by the labour-saving machinery particularly in occupations such as ginning, sizing, carding, spinning, and weaving of cotton, wool and silk, brick and tile making, sawing and carpentry and such like industries which largely employed manual labour in the previous decennium but which now employ machinery." (P. 196).

The insignificance of the mill industries may be seen from the fact that the total number of persons employed in factories, mills, works, etc., including gold and manganese mines and coffee, cardamom and rubber plantations was 58,613 of whom 3·7 per cent. were employed in direction, supervision and clerical work: 17·1 per cent. were skilled workers and 79·2 per cent. were unskilled labourers.

The small extent of industry and the growing ruralization of the state can be confirmed by the declining urbanization. In 1911, 11·3 per cent. of the population resided in towns, 88·7 in villages, while the corresponding percentages were 13 and 87 respectively in 1901.

The state has no doubt been making Herculean efforts to stimulate the indigenous industries by the establishment of Industrial and Weaving schools and state factories, and by the starting of Research institutions, Co-perative societies, Rural Banks and the Mysore Economic Conference. But all these have proved futile so far, because the country is being constantly flooded by ever-cheapening foreign goods. Home industries are being carried away by that flood, while the new mill industries are very slow to grow before the same onrush. Both state-aid and protective embankments to keep out the rising imports are consequently required to save the situation. Let us see how the greatest of her statesmen, Sir M. Visveshwarayya, K. C. I. E., the Dewan of Mysore has given expression to the foregoing opinions in his address to the sixth sessions of the Mysore Economic Conference:—

"A few weeks ago, we all read a Reuter's telegram which stated that the Commonwealth of Australia possessed property valued at 1,000 millions or Rs. 1,500 crores. Rough calculations indicate that the total value of property in Mysore, including the gold mines amount to about Rs. 124 crores. This dispatrity will seem particularly striking when it is remembered that the population of Australia is only 5 millions against our 6 millions in Mysore. The value of farm produce calculated per head of population in Australia is estimated at Rs. 138 and including dairying, pastoral produce etc. at Rs. 351. In Mysore the corresponding figure is Rs. 24. In industries and manufacture Australia produces articles valued at Rs. 171 per head and Mysore only Rs. 7 per head. The value of the total production of Australia comes to Rs. 621 per head as against Rs. 31 or about twenty times that of Mysore. In Australia, again, there are 3 acres of cultivated land per head of population against 1 acre per head in Mysore. Notwithstanding this, the Australians are not content with agriculture but are devoting special attention to the expansion of industries. The estimated total trade of Mysore amounts to Rs. 26 per head and that of Australia to Rs. 495 per head. Formerly, Mysore was fairly self contained in regard to the small necessities of the people, such as clothing, building materials, etc, but owing to the increase of communication and keen foreign competition, we get most of our supplies from outside at lower rates than we can manufacture locally with our crude hand labour.

A large number of our people have in consequence lost their former occupation, and have been driven to agriculture"

THE ATROPHY OF ARYA VARTA.

Thou art the garden of the world, the home
Of all Art yields, and nature can decree;
Even in thy desert, what is like to thee ?
Thy very weeds are beautiful, thy waste
More rich than other climes, fertility

India with its fascinating variety of climate and soil, of fauna and flora, of mineral and animal, agricultural and industrial resources is a veritable mine of wealth. But even amidst this lavish profusion of Nature "India is in poverty ! Midas starving amid heaps of gold does not afford a greater paradox ; yet here, we have India, Midas-like starving in the midst of untold wealth." Why, because all the resources of this richly endowed country are lying dormant and the children of the land have not the skill, the energy, the intelligence to control and utilize them. It is highly painful to see that the nations of yesterday that were wandering in the woods when Aryavartta was on the pinnacle of her glory and culture should have made such a wonderful progress within a century, while the inhabitants of this ancient and once civilized land are being reduced to be hewers of wood and drawers of water. India kept up her ancient glory and reputation, her beautiful arts and crafts even as late as the XVIII century, and the treasures of the West and the East long continued flowing in a copious stream in this Wealthy Aryavarta.

Who does not know that India from the remotest classical antiquity has ever been inviting foreign nations to her busy ports, that from age to age, enterprising merchants have visited her envied shores to engross her lucrative commerce, that her freedom, opulence, and civilization, the elegance of her arts and crafts, the excellence of her institutions have been the themes of many poets, philosophers historians and travellers. From times immemorial even to the 16th century, no other, at least none equally distant, was so anxiously explored or so industrially frequented by the celebrated nations of the world. From before the days of Solomon and Hiram to our own times, the command of this celebrated mart has been eagerly seized with jealousy by the Chaldeans, the Phœnicians, the Egyptians the Persians, the Greeks, the Romans, the Turks, the Venitians, the Portuguese, the Dutch, and the English in succession. But with the political supremacy of the English, the economic independence of Aryavarta began to vanish. Indian arts and industries began to fade, wither, decline and die. For full seventy years this dispiriting process of deliberate murder of indigenous industries continued. Only a few survived the universal wreck, or some sorry remnants of the once-flourishing arts could be seen here and there hidden in nooks and corners were the hand of the foreigner had not reached. These relics where counted in 1871 the year whence our enquiry begins. But we have seen how, as years passed on, these relics too were shouldered into the abyss of oblivion, so that the self-contained, self-sufficient and civilized Aryavarta of the 18th century has been transformed into an impotent, dependent, and industrially brutalized India. While on one side England became a workshop of the world, India on the other, became a good dumping ground for the world.

The British policy in India has all along been characterized by invertibrate drift, masterly inactivity, inhuman indifference, vacillation, suspicion and callousness to Indian interests on the one hand and sensitiveness to Lancashire demands on the other. It has constantly been in conflict with the true interests of India. The fatal consequences of this two-fold policy of inactivity and Free Trade are too numerous to mention. But suffice it to say that, while in the west the industrial stream has become a sea and a sea an ocean, in India the ocean of indigenous industry has contracted into a small lagoon and even there foreign ships are plying unopposed by the ships of the country.

We have seen that throughout the length and breadth of the country depression prevails in the industrial world, that the depression is being deepened, that paralysis extends to all the limbs of industry, that the body economic has been whitened to death by the bleeding of its life blood, that the sons of the soil are now impotently looking on the foreigner for the supply of even the articles of every day need. In short, we have witnessed the spectable of a nation gradually deurbanized and hence ruralized, pauperized and brutalized.

WHAT FREE TRADE HAS COST INDIA ?

The preceding chapters with their comprehensive figures, 'the dry eloquence of which reveals a lamentable state of things', might have often tired out the patience of an ordinary reader. Statistics are proverbially dry and insipid, but we are sure the importance of the subject must have many a time made these dry bones live for many readers.

Our survey has brought to light an enormous mass of degradation, decline and decay in the economic world of India, because

(i) This land of sturdy Aryas and lusty Muslams has become more and more agricultural under the British policy of Free Trade.

(ii) The indigenous industries have been constantly killed by the stress of unrestricted foreign competition.

(iii) Low paid workers and tribes of menials have increased by hundreds and thousands.

(iv) We have become a nation of petty shopkeepers in the sense of distributers of foreign articles alone.

But quite opposite are the tendencies of civilization in western countries.

AGRICULTURAL POPULATION DECLINING IN ENGLAND.

Between 1811 and 1831 the proportion of families employed in agriculture in Great Britain fell from 35 to 28 per cent. of the whole, and in 1821-31 the decline was absolute. From 1851 onwards the census was more uniform and tells a plain tale. The number of males over ten years of age employed in agriculture in England and Wales fell from 1,544,807 in 1851 to 1,153,185 in 1901 and from 23·5 to 9·5 per cent. of the occupied males, the females declined more rapidly from 1,68,652 (2·4) to 38,982 (or 0·3 per cent.) The place of agriculture has been taken by industry and commerce. P. 307.

The number of labourers, farmers, etc. (Males) engaged in agriculture in England and Wales has been constantly, not only relatively but positively, decreasing at each census in spite of the enormous increase of national population from 22,712,266 in 1851 to 36 millions in 1911.

1851	...	...	1,904,678
1861	...	...	1,803,049
1871	...	...	1.423,854
1881	...	...	1,199,827
1891	...	...	1,099,572
1901	...	...	988,340
1911	...	...	971,708

(Village Industries, p. 14)

These figures furnish strong evidence of the fact that Industrial conditions and tendencies are *toto coelo* different in England and India. 72 per cent. of the population is directly dependent on agriculture in India, as compared with less than 7 per cent. in England. Then Rural and Agricultural populations have continuously been on the increase in the one, but rapidly on the decline in the other.

Now a comparative table of the Functional Distribution of the Population of the three most progressive countries of the West would definitely but remarkably reveal the Economic Retrogression of India as well as of all its provinces. *The Agricultural produce of every kind has been fast increasing in those countries and yet men occupied in Agriculture have been constantly diminishing in numbers.* But such a good luck is not reserved for this unlucky country. Its peoples are more and more migrating to lands which, be it remembered, are always subject to the law of diminishing returns.

The proportions of the total population of the United Kingdom, Germany, and the United States engaged in the main classes of industry in those countries at three successive censuses were as follows:—

	Proportion *occupied* per 10,000 of Total Population.								
	United Kingdom.			Germany.			United State.		
	1881	1891	1901	1875	1882	1895	1880	1890	1900
Agriculture ...	711	601	495	1,783	1,783	1,554	1,517	1,338	1,348
Building ...	239	222	273	209	209	262	133	187	164
Mining ...	158	187	202	66	71	83	50	62	77
Principal textile industries ...	313	297	243	178	141	134	62	67	72
Iron and steel, and manufactures thereof (including ship building) ...	239	257	301	171	179	215	91	127	152
Leather, paper, glass, pottery, and chemical trades. ...	160	163	166	178	204	213	79	93	96
Total population in thousands ...	34,885	37,7,33	41,459	42,727	45,222	51,770	50,156	62,622	75,569

Webb's Dictionary of Statistics, P. 429.

Thus it is clear that all the three countries show a marked decline in the population engaged in agriculture.

PROPORTIONAL DECLINE OF AGRICULTURAL CLASSES IN GERMANY.

The comparative percentages of persons engaged in the chief occupations in *Germany* are still more remarkable : whereas in 1872 and 1882, 47·5 and 43·4 per cent. of the total number of *occupied persons* in Germany were engaged in agriculture, forestry, and fishing, the proportion in 1900 and 1908 had fallen to 35·6 and 32·7 per cent. The total number of persons dependent on agriculture for a living had fallen from 42·5 per cent. of the total population in 1882 to 28·7 per cent. in 1907.

The following summary table would best clear up this point :—

	1870	1900
Agriculture ...	47·5	35·6
Minerals and Manufacture ...	21·4	24·3
Trade and transport ...	9·9	16·3

Thus the relative strength of the agricultural population has fallen by 12 per cent. in Germany. But unfortunately, in India this healthy process has been reversed, for while in 1881, 64½ per cent. of the people were engaged in agriculture, the proportion in 1911 had risen to 71½ per cent.

(Nelson's Encyclopaedia of Industrialism, P. 308.)

We cannot compare ourselves even with such countries as Belgium and Austria.

Regarding Belgium Mr. Webb Writes.

The agricultural part of the community fell from 25 per cent. of the whole in 1846 to 22 per cent. in 1880, and to 19 per cent. in 1895.

What a striking difference in the economic structures of Belgium and India! The former had only 19 per cent. of the population supported by agriculture, against 64 per cent. in India! But the worst of it is that the agrarian life has been becoming even more and more predominant here.

(Dictionary of Statistics, P. 438.)

COMPARATIVE AGRICULTURAL STRENGTH.

The following table will be extremely helpful in visualizing the actual strength of the Agricultural community in each of the following thirteen countries.

Country.	No. of persons occupied in Agriculture.	% of total occupied population.
England and Wales...	1,061,836	15·3
Ireland ...	871,989	44·7
Austria ...	8,205,574	60·9 (2)
Belgium ...	697,372	22·7
Bulgaria ...	1,739,187	82·6
Denmark ...	530,689	48·2 (1)
France ...	8,843,761	42·7 (4)
Germany ...	9,833,257	35·2 (5)
Holland ...	592,774	30·7
Hungary ...	6,055,390	69·7 (2)
Italy ...	9,666 467	59·4 (1)
Russia ...	8,245,287	58·3 (3)
Switzerland ...	481,649	30·9 (2)

P. 15, Village Industries—J. L. Green.

INDUSTRIAL ADVANCEMENT OF THE U. S. A.

During the 19th century the striking phenomena of the U. S. A. are the decline in the rela-

(1) Figures for 1901 (4) Figures for 906
(2) „ for 1900 (5) „ 1907
(3) „ 1897

tive number of persons engaged in agricultural pursuits and the increase in the number of persons employed in trade and transportation; yet, owing to the opening up of old American Indian reservations for settlement, the constant alienation of the public domain, the breaking up of southern plantations and bonanza farms, the number of agriculturists ought to have immensely increased.

Reduction of Agricultural People in U. S. A.

		per cent.
1790	...	87·5
1840	...	77·5
1870	...	47·6
1880	...	44·3
1890	...	39·2
1900	...	35·7
1909	...	33·3

DISTRIBUTION OF POPULATION ACCORDING TO OCCUPATION IN THE U. S. A.

	1870	1880	1890	1900
Agricultural pursuits ...	47·6	44·3	39·2	35·7
Professional service ...	3·0	3·5	4·0	4·3
Domestic and personal service.	18·2	19·6	18·1	19·2
Trade and transportation	9·8	10·8	14·3	16·4
Manufacturing pursuits,	21·4	21·8	24·4	24·4
	100	100	100	100

At the last named census of 1900, 29 million persons were engaged in gainful occupations. Out of these, 10½ millions were engaged in agricultural pursuits; a little more than 7 millions in manufactures; 5½ millions in domestic and personal service; 4¾ millions in trade and transportation; and 1¼ millions in professional service. Thus the agricultural element was still the strongest, yet it had been constantly losing its proportional strength and giving place to manufacturing, industrial, commercial, financial and professional elements. Hence such an unbounded prosperity!

HAND *VERSUS* MACHINE.

How great this change has been in the United States in the thirty-year period from 1870 to 1900 will be apparent from a consideration of the figures showing the percentages of the total population engaged in gainful occupations in the several classes at the dates named. This decrease in the percentage of those engaged in agriculture from 47·6 per cent. to 35·7 per cent. was equivalent to a withdrawal of 3,459,819 persons from agriculture and their distribution among the other classes. For the United States as a whole, the percentage of increase or decrease in the several occupation classes during the period named was as follows:

Agriculture	**11·9**	**Trade and Transportation**	**6·6**
Professional service	**1·3**		
Domestic and Personal service	**1·0**	**Manufacturing pursuits**	**3·0**

The introduction of machine power increased the efficiency of the workers, increased the output of farm products, caused a fall in the price per unit, and hence a redistribution of the working force of the country.

Taking the United States as a whole, the efficiency of the average farm worker in the year 1900 appears to have been nearly 86 per cent. greater than in the year 1870. But more remarkable is this increase in efficiency when the relative productivity of American farm labour is compared in the years 1850 and 1900. It is found that it 1849 there was raised on American farms, of grain crops an aggregate of 80,672,000,000 pounds; while in 1899, the farmers produced 410,307,000,000 pounds. In other words, the agricultural production of 1899 was 5·1 times as great as of 1849. During this period national population increased only 3·3 times and the agricultural families and toilers increased only 2·44 times. It is obvious now that the productivity of farm labour must have increased very much. In fact the average male worker produced a total of 23,050 pounds of the crops named in 1850, but fifty years later he produced 48,000 pounds, or over twice as much. The efficiency of American farm labour increased most rapidly, so far so that no labourer in the world could compete with the American labour. The eminent statistician Mulhull in his Dictionary of Statistics gives figures of the relative productivity of farm labour in different countries. "In the United States 9,000,000 hands raised nearly half as much grain as 66,000,000 in Europe. Thus it appears that one farm labourer in the United States is worth more than three in Europe."

Thus the 30,000,000 people who, in 1900, resided on the farms of the United States therefore equalled in productive power an agricultural population of over 100,000,000 toiling under the conditions that prevail in Europe.

With these facts before us it will be hopeless to compare an Indian farm labourer with an American, whose efficiency has been slowly decreasing on account of his deepening poverty.

The following statement of the comparative produce by hand and machine methods will be highly interesting for the reader :—

Day's work necessary to produce by hand Methods.

	Crop of	Methods of	Day's work.	Day's work saved by machinery per cent.
Barley ...	1896	1829—30	14,771,515	95·7
Corn ...	1894	1855	117,487,098	60·9
Cotton ...	1895	1841	80,108,771	64·8
Hay ...	,,	1850	99,257,257	81·3
Oats ...	1893	1830	105,810,334	89·2
Potato ...	1895	1866	14,715,501	65·1
Rice ...	1896	1870	396,687	72·5
Rye ...	1895	1847—48	6,854,942	60·0
Wheat ...	1896	1829—30	130,621,927	94·5
Total ...	...	...	570,024,032	79·0

Cyclopedia of American Agriculture Vol. IV, P. 66.

The same can be expressed in another way thus:—

	By Hand	By Machine.
Sowing	1	$\frac{1}{5}$ to ¼
Harvesting	1	$\frac{1}{4}$
Threshing	1	$\frac{1}{15}$ to $\frac{1}{30}$

Then Qaintance states that the year's crop of barley, corn, cotton, hay, etc., about 1894—96 required for its production only 21 per cent. of the number of day's labour of one man which their product would have required by the methods of about sixty years before.

It is obvious now that within 60 years the Americans have been able to dispense with the services of 79 men out of every hundred for raising the same amount of agricultural produce as in 1836. But twenty years more have passed and during this period of progressive scientific research and prolific mechanical inventions much must have been achieved to save men's labour. These improvements are not, however, limited to the American continent. In every civilized country more extensive use of improved labour-saving machinery for cultivating and harvesting, mowing reaping, binding threshing and other operations is being daily made. But contrary to all these tendencies of modern civilization, the Indian peasant is using the same antidiluvian implements and following the same antiquated methods which his forefathers of the iron age might have done. The

(13th Annual Report of the U. S. Commissioner of Labour).

British Raj has done absolutely nothing to improve the condition of the Indian ryot up to the end of the nineteenth century. Hence there could be no possibility of saving human labour in Indian agriculture.

Then in the United Kingdom and elsewhere the phenomenon of the consolidation and absorption of small farms is to be seen necessitating fewer men in agriculture, but in India, the more minute sub-division of landed property is but a natural process.

UNIVERSAL CAUSES OF RURAL DECLINE.

In the west the following principal causes have tended to the decline of the agricultural population :—

(1) The greater demand in the mining districts with better wages and shorter hours of work on account of the ever-increasing development of mining, its subsidiary and supplementary industries.

(2) The ever-proving demand in other industries for young and capable country workers.

(3) The higher wages and superior attractions of the town industries draw men from the country.

(4) Higher wages and shorter hours of labour in urban than in rural districts.

(5) An increasing desire for independence on the part of the labourers, and a disinclination to follow the plough.

(6) Monotony of farm work which holds out little encouragement for thrift and hope of improvement even to an energetic man.

(7) The system of education causes dislike for agriculture and a desire for the excitements of town life. It fits the children rather for work as clerks, shop assistants, etc.

(8) The education of their children makes illiterate parents so proud of them that they put them to some trade or occupation other than farming.

(9) The educational advantages of the towns, the Saturday half holiday, absence of Sunday work and other enducements to leave the country.

(10) The decay of the village industries has also resulted in there being fewer chances for the agricultural labourer to find employment when his assistance on the farm is not required.

(11) Diminishing returns from the cultivation of land have discouraged many farmers who have been forced to go into the towns in search of employment.

(12) The taking of agricultural land for buildings, collieries and railways have contracted land available for cultivation.

(13) Swifter means of communication have made migration easy.

(14) There is a lack of suitable cottages and sanitary surroundings which should suit the taste of the better educated children of the labouring class. They cannot compare with the new houses and

seemingly healthy surroundings provided in industrial districts.

(15) The inducements offered for emigration to the colonies and foreign countries.

All or some of these causes have strongly conspired to transform rural countries like Germany, the United States and the British Colonies into the industrially supreme rivals of England. Within the forty years which cover our economic survey in India, the face of these countries has been thoroughly changed, rural decline has proceeded at a marvellous rate, the trend of industrial expansion has been inevitable and has grown to enormous proportions. In India of rich natural gifts and of vast potent resources the industrial evolution has proceeded on quite opposite lines. Here the trend of events was inevitably for going backwards and not forwards, for stagnation and degradation and not regeneration. Here the development of industrialism has been uniformally downward and not upward—deterioration and not evolution is the final result.

SURVIVAL OF THE FITTEST.

The reason of this abnormal and unparalleled event of the 19th century is not far to seek. Every country must have suffered the same terrible fate had a deliberate and effective policy of protecting and encouraging state industries been not adopted in every land. But in India contrary to what the world has done in the past and what it is doing in the present and what it will ever do in the future for self-defence, self-sufficiency, self-respect, self-culture and thorough independence. In India the policy of inviting every giant competitor to fight the weak and sick infant has been followed. Industrially infant India has been drawn into the vortex of keen, open, tooth and claw and free as air competition with industrial giants. There could be only one result and that we have been painfully witnessing throughout this book. In the animal as well as the vegetable kingdoms subject to man the infant life is thoroughly tended, protected and preserved from harmful influences. Every gardener protects his tender plants from the rigours of the climate and the invasions of birds and animals. Where the controlling hand of man is unable to extend its protection, nature works with it own laws of the survival of the fittest.

There the weaker must go to the wall; the weak must be eliminated and only the few strongest plants and animals can command the place for them from among the millions that come into being in this vast planet of ours. The policy of Free Trade works on the same lines in the industrial world as the law of the survival of the fittest does in the vegetable and animal worlds.

ACTION OF FREE TRADE.

A free commercial intercourse between equally strong nations will but tend to sharpen their best intellects, to revive their drooping energies, vigorously call up their resources, and in every other way will serve only to leaven the general mass. But a free intercourse between an industrially weak and an industrially most vigorous nation can but crush the former. Glasses and stones must be kept separate, otherwise their jostling and struggling will always be fatal to glasses. Following this fundamental principle, weak nations have by means of state-aid and protective traiffs, provided themslves with strong walls which their competitors can never climb up. Shutting themselves in their well-defended industrial forts and feeling themselves immune from external invasions, they have devoted their exclusive attention to develop their industries which in the case of Germany and America, have become a wonder of the world.

The politically dependent India was denied this right to build its industrial future on those first principles of fundamental importance, and hence the inevitable has come to pass. Her ancient and long-established industries, her excellent arts and crafts are on the verge of extinction and her new industries struggle as they must against odds—are extremely insignificant.

On the other hand, feudal, industrially backward, exclusively rural, despotically ruled Japan of 1870 has been changed within these same forty years into a free, democratic, educated and industrially forward Japan of to-day. Why? Let the answer be given by a Japanese historian.

SECRET OF JAPANESE SUCCESS.

'Many of the new industries dating from the advent of the new regime own their inception to encouragement and protection of the Government. Spinning industry, cotton and silk filature, ship-building, cement, glass factory, safety-matches, gas work, brick making, power loom weaving, and some others, are all traceable to the Government inception. As measures for extending protection to domestic industry there are a direct pecuniary help from the central authorities, the loan of machines, etc., that of loaning improved power looms to weavers and dyers being the most conspicuous instance in this connection. Provincial authorities are similarly helpful to various industries carried on in their own jurisdiction. Encouragement in the shape of training schools, experimental laboratories, ambulant lectures and inspectors, also co-operative organizations may also be mentioned.'

Had these methods been followed by the state in India, the evil day could never have been seen. But the Government being wedded to the polices of Free Trade and Laissez Faire ignored the industrial advancement of this country, nay, on the contrary invited the industrial giants of all lands to give us knock-down blows so that the brains were smashed out of the poor reeling heads of Indian astisans and handicraftsmen, who were sent wandering with bag and baggage to lands new and strange with no prospects of shelter and livelihood. The principle source of income from trade, commerce and industry the most envied by all the

The Japan Year book, 1912, P. 347.

nations, ancient and modern, has become 'a spring shut up, and a fountain sealed' to the inhabitants of this once magnificent Aryavarta—the 'Paradise on Earth' of the Parsis.

PLEA FOR INDIA.

In fact the country groans under the unbearable burden of the stupid, stolid, cumbersome, unambitious imperturbable mass of the 192 starving millions of uncultured cultivators. The tendency of a rapidly growing ruralization is written large in the occupation statistics of every province and every census report since 1871, but in reality this inexorable tendency had been operating in India long before the time since it is pictured in those figures and hence ever since the beginning of the XIX century has been, doing incalculable economic injury to the nation. India is being more and more subjected to the innumerable economic disadvantages that this growing dependence on one primitive and precarious occupation entails. India does not know the manifold advantages of the mutual influence of agriculture and manufacture. She does not feel the unimpeded circulation of the enlivening, enlightening and rejuvenating sap of culture, the free flow of the national energy, art, skill and intelligence. All the latter have long been cribbed, cabined and confined. All the outlets having been dammed up, national activity has been allowed to stagnate on the stagnant pool of withered and decadent industries and a backward agriculture, so that in turn it impeaded and arrested, nay choked up all Indian progress. When the energies of a nation are thus fettered down to one primitive industry, when all other channels of livelihood are shut up for them, then the glory of that nation cannot but soon pass away. Hence such a shakling of national enterprise and intelligence is incompatable with justice, humanity, culture, civilization. progress or national sufficiency. Such being the case it is inhuman to allow this monstrous and seemingly irresistible tendency to run its course.

Why such an inevitable movement which has loomed before us all threateningly for the past one hundred and fifty years, be not allowed to die its natural death? It is hardly credible that this ruinous and inhuman Monster of Ruralization which has been cruelly swallowing the long-establised, immemorial and world-known industries and glorious manufactures of India should have been fed and fattened with the life blood of the nation for a century and-a-half! But it is a fact, and the painful result is that the canker of Industrial decay has eaten into the very vitals of Indian society. But the world being deceived by appearances, have been labouring under a delusion that the whitening of the body of India was a sign of a new life in industry and manufacture. Alas! it was not early realized that ruralization has lain in the body of Indian society like a thorn that makes it fester and throws the entire system into a fever. It was altogether forgotten on this side of the globe by the industrially supreme Englishman that Ruralization is Rustication. Can it be denied that the Indian peasant's ignorance is colossal, his stupidity is profound, his poverty is abundant, his timidity is infinite and his forbearance incredible? It is on account of these that even in these days of hellish excitement he is living imperturbed in the waveless calm of an Elysium paradise!

No doubt, centuries of oppression, extortion, injustice have depressed his soul and tempered his nature to stolid forbearance, but does it follow that he should have continued to be the same loathsome mass of uncultured, ignorant and depressed humanity even under the civilized, humane, just, secure and liberal rule of a most democratic nation? Does not this economic, mental, moral and physical depression of the teeming millions of India seem monstrous in contrast to the high civilization of their masters?

The speaking portion of the English nation has been neglecting, nay looking, with envy and prejudice on the industrial development of India and the result is visible in this world-wide war. A poor, weak, uneducated industrially and commercially backward India must be a source of weakness and trouble to the rest of the Empire, but a rich, strong, educated and industrially supreme India will ever be a prolific and constant source of strength to that Empire. Let India, therefore, regain her lost position in the galaxy of free, rich and industrially supreme nations, let her regain her lost sacred self-sufficiency, let her utilize and develop her richest but dormant resources. These ends can only be achieved when the whole intellectual force of the ruled and the rulers is leagued together against the cursed policy of plantation, exploitation, ruralization or rustication, when India is granted full fiscal freedom, when the policy of active state-aid and protection come to replace the old baneful policies of state inactivity and Free Trade and when in a word, she enjoys the same economic freedom as do the self-governing Colonies of our British Empire. Then only dynamic India dealing justly with and exploiting freely and wisely her own vast and incredibly rich domain would transform not only itself, but the industry and civilization of the world.

To counteract the effects of the present economical disabilities, let the people themselves awaken to their sense of duty. It should be fully recognised that the silent industrial revolution, the distintegration of old institutions and the extinction of our handicrafts have necessitated an entire change in our economic and social life. We ought not to be wedded to our old systems of production. In the absence of state assistance, we should learn to stand upon our own legs. *Had a people with the ambition, enterprise, perseverance and freedom of the west possessed such a wealth of natural resources, as we do, they would certainly have made this land a veritable paradise.* It is we who are lacking the desirable qualities of self-sacrifice, activity, courage, enterprise, originality, industry, prudence, tenacity and perseverance, the study of economic, commercial and industrial questions. Let us therefore, educate ourselves in economic, technical and commercial matters and persuade the Government to co-operate with us in building magnificent and numerous technical academies, institutions, schools, stations for testing, well-stocked laboratories and in creating a technical literature, statistical bureaux and research institutes which should drive away the nightmare of harrowing sorrow from this sacred land. Then only shall we enter upon a higher form of life and fulfil our mission, then only industrial regeneration of India, the economic emancipation of the submerged millions and the pulling up of India out of the nauseating mire of dehumanizing poverty, will come within the range of possibility. Let us have a firm faith in the destiny of our Motherland, let all the uplifting influences be brought to bear upon to-day's India and let Education and Protection be our watch words, then alone we can check this unhealthy ruralization of the country, then alone our dreams of economic regeneration will soon be realized. Let us hope that the haphazard and wreckless policy of drift pursued by our Rulers in India will give place to one of effective control over our economic development, that India will be governed in the interest of India and not in the interest of Lancashire and Birmingham, that the British Democracy will soon rise above selfish motives and that this cradle of humanity will be raised in the scale of a civilization which is

"Sweet to the world and grateful to the skies."